A KOSHER CHRISTMAS

A KOSHER CHRISTMAS

'Tis the Season to Be Jewish

JOSHUA ELI PLAUT

FOREWORD BY JONATHAN D. SARNA

RUTGERS UNIVERSITY PRESS
NEW BRUNSWICK, NEW JERSEY, AND LONDON

Library of Congress Cataloging-in-Publication Data
Plaut, Joshua Eli.
 A Kosher Christmas : 'tis the season to be Jewish / Joshua Eli Plaut.
   p. cm.
 Includes bibliographical references and index.
 ISBN 978–0–8135–5379–5 (hardcover : alk. paper) — ISBN 978–0–8135–5380–1
(pbk. : alk. paper) — ISBN 978–0–8135–5381–8 (e-book)
  1. Christmas—United States.   2. Jews—United States—Social life and customs.
3. United States—Social life and customs.   I. Title.
 GT4986.A1P53   2012
 394.2663—dc23

                                                              2011046942

A British Cataloging-in-Publication record for this book is available from the British
Library.

Cover illustration: "Twas the Night Before Hanukkah" by Art Spiegelman, originally
published in *The New Yorker*. Copyright © 2000 by Art Spiegelman, used with
permission of The Wylie Agency LLC.

Visit our website: http://rutgerspress.rutgers.edu

Manufactured in the United States of America

To the love of my life, Lori, full partner in this book

To the light of my life, Jonas, may you be a man of letters

"*. . . if they were good Jews—firm, brave, constructive, progressive Jews—we would see no danger in all the [Christmas] celebrating around us. It might, on the contrary, give added importance to our [Jewish] religious life.*"

—Rabbi Judah Leon Magnes preaching in 1906 from
his pulpit at Temple Emanu-El, New York City

"*As Jews . . . we must, in a dignified, self-poised, thoughtful way, silently protest against beliefs which our conscience forbids us to accept . . . a Jew who brings into his home a Christmas tree and kindles lights upon it while he perhaps forgets our own chanucah lights, is, if thoughtless, making himself ridiculous, and if earnest, is weaning his children away from Judaism.*"

—Rabbi Samuel Schulman preaching in 1906 from
his pulpit at Temple Beth El, New York City

Both quoted in *New York Tribune*, December 24, 1906, 4.

CONTENTS

Foreword by Jonathan D. Sarna   xi
Acknowledgments   xiii

Introduction   Coping with Christmas: A Multitude of
Jewish Responses   1

1.   Coming to the New World: Can the American
Jew Keep Christmas?   10

2.   Hanukkah Comes of Age: The New Jewish
Christmas   41

3.   We Eat Chinese Food on Christmas   65

4.   "'Twas the Night Before Hanukkah": Remaking
Christmas through Parody and Popular Culture   87

5.   The Christmas Mitzvah: 'Tis the Season to
Be Giving   115

6.   Chrismukkah and Festivus: Holidays for the
Rest of Us   137

Conclusion   Menorahs Next to Madonnas: Shaping the Future of
Christmas in America   163

Notes   175
Index   201

FOREWORD

In his 1962 Christmas message to the nation, President John F. Kennedy declared that "Moslems, Hindus, Buddhists, as well as Christians, pause from their labors on the 25th day of December to celebrate the birthday of the Prince of Peace." He concluded that "there could be no more striking proof that Christmas is truly the universal holiday of all men."[1]

Kennedy, who was born in Brookline, Massachusetts, just blocks away from a large synagogue, should certainly have known better. Even in his day, as many as one in five Americans never celebrated Christmas as "the birthday of the Prince of Peace." December 25th is the only American national holiday rooted in a specific religious tradition that a significant minority of Americans fail to share.

Nevertheless, as Joshua Plaut demonstrates in this volume, Christmas has become a national holiday in the United States. Those who do not observe it religiously, like America's Jews, cannot ignore it and may even enjoy it. If, as a famous advertisement once declared, "You don't have to be Jewish to love Levy's Real Jewish Rye," then by analogy you don't have to be Christian to love Christmas. And even if you do not love Christmas (the more common Jewish attitude), there are still distinctive ways to mark the day. Filling in for non-Jews who have to work, celebrating culture at a Jewish museum, searching for love at a Jewish singles dance, laughing at Kung Pao Kosher Comedy, escaping to a movie and a Chinese restaurant— for Jews, these too are contemporary Christmas rituals.

Joshua Plaut explores these rituals and more in this extraordinary volume, the first to examine the subject of Jews and Christmas historically, ethnographically, and dispassionately. The fruits of many years of careful research, it teaches us more than we ever knew before about the multiple and varied responses of American Jews to the so-called "December dilemma."

Some readers will doubtless view this book as a cautionary tale, as evidence of how much American Jews have assimilated. But that reading is far too limited. In a world where so many faith communities have gone global—spreading north, south, east and west—the story of American Jews at Christmastime exemplifies whole classes of conflicts and contentions. It is, in microcosm, a story of "when religions collide."

Had President Kennedy lived to read this book, he would have learned the humbling truth that Christmas is not "the universal holiday of all men" and that Muslims, Hindus, Buddhists, and Jews do not, in countries where they are the dominant majority, pause to celebrate it. But he might also have discerned another humbling truth. In the words of Harvey Cox, "few faiths ever escape modification when they collide or interact with others. Most profit from such encounters."[2]

Jonathan D. Sarna
Joseph H. and Belle R. Braun Professor of American Jewish History
Brandeis University

ACKNOWLEDGMENTS

Each and every year, I anticipate with scholarly inquisitiveness the arrival of the December holidays. My research on Jews and Christmas in America began in 1994. The subject matter was a natural choice given my love of Jewish history, popular culture, and ethnographic fieldwork. My fascination with the subject has continued unabated until the present day. I am captivated by how Jews in America have fashioned a continually changing colorful rainbow of strategies to participate in and enjoy the December holiday season.

I appreciate the encouragement of my colleagues and teachers: Professors Jacob Marcus z"l, Jonathan Sarna (Brandeis University), Barbara Kirshenblatt-Gimblett (New York University), Hillel Levine (Boston University), and Lawrence Schiffman (formerly of New York University and currently of Yeshiva University). Above all other scholars, Professor Stephen Stern—rabbi, mentor, and friend—helped me in countless ways as I pursued a comprehensive examination of Jewish responses to Christmas during the December holiday season. Steve Stern's understanding of popular culture and folk religion provided historical perspective, depth, and analysis to the book. My gratitude and appreciation goes out to my friend of thirty years.

Thank you to Beth Kressel, my first editor, and also to Marlie Wasserman of Rutgers University Press for encouraging and managing my book in progress. I am most grateful to Marlie for her guidance in bringing my book project to fruition. My gratitude also extends to Lisa Boyajian for overseeing the permissions process. Lisa Nowak Jerry copyedited the text with great sensitivity. Thanks also to staff members Marilyn Campbell, Anne Hegeman, Liz Scarpelli, Lisa Fortunato, Jeanne Ambrosio, and Brice Hammack.

As this is the first book on Jews and Christmas in America, I was intent on using the best libraries and archives in the United States in my search for primary and secondary sources. As a Daniel Jeremy Silver Fellow at Harvard University, I spent a sabbatical semester in the Widener Library during one of my periods of concentrated research. As a Marcus Fellow at the American Jewish Archives (AJA) in Cincinnati, I immersed myself in the preeminent American Jewish history archival treasure trove, established by my esteemed teacher, Professor Jacob Marcus. Thank you to AJA executive director Rabbi Gary Zola, PhD, and to Kevin Proffitt and their diligent staff for assisting me in identifying and retrieving every single document pertaining to Jews and Christmas in America.

While I was the director of the Center for Jewish History, I became familiar with the best composite archival collections in Jewish history, among them the Leo Baeck Institute holdings, which I used through the gracious help of my friends, executive director Carol Strauss and research director Frank Mecklenburg. Thank you to the archivists at the Jimmy Carter, Ronald Reagan, and William J. Clinton presidential libraries for searching for the best photographic records of Hanukkah, to Francesco Spagnolo at the Magnes Collection of Jewish Art and Life at Bancroft Library, University of California at Berkeley, to Michal Friedlander and her staff at the Berlin Jewish Museum for sharing illustrations for the book, and to Peter Prokop at the Austrian National Library. Thank you to Art Spiegelman for graciously permitting the use of his wonderful cartoon image "'Twas the Night Before Hanukkah" on the book's cover—it perfectly captures the spirit of this volume. I am grateful to Mindy Strelitz and the staff at the Washington, D.C., Jewish Community Center, to Shraddha Borawake, to Angela Schillaci for arranging and preparing images to include in the book, and to Katie Zeitner, David Kudan, and Max Gershenoff. Thank you to Hal L. Singer and Georgane Berry-Singer for granting permission to quote from their album *I Saw Hanukkah Harry Beat Up Santa*, and to the Jewish Publication Society and Bloch Publishing for permission to use Hanukkah-related poems.

This book is about real-life experiences at Christmas and the real people who face Christmas in the dual capacity of being Jews and Americans, especially the unsung heroes who have created innovative and new Jewish traditions for Christmastime. Lisa Geduldig, creator and producer of the twenty-year-old Kung Pao Kosher Comedy event—Jewish comedy on Christmas in a Chinese restaurant in San Francisco—has created an event and a template that has inspired Jews throughout the United States to approach the Christmas season with confidence laced with a dose of comedic irreverence. Thank you to Lisa for all of her kindness over the many years of my attending the performances and especially for sharing her opinions and insights with me. Jan Luxenberg, a long-time patron of Kung Pao, was also a key informant who helped me to decipher and to understand the Kung Pao audience's appreciation of the event. Thank you to all the Kung Pao attendees and performers whom I met and interviewed over the years; I thank you for sharing with me unique and humorous perspectives of being Jewish at Christmastime in America.

While conducting ethnographic fieldwork during the Christmas season, I often divided my time between attending Kung Pao Kosher Comedy in San Francisco and then canvassing Boston and the rest of Massachusetts, where I observed and participated in Project Ezra, a Christmastime Jewish volunteer project. Project Ezra included 120 organizations, mostly synagogues, sending volunteers to work at shelters, senior citizen homes, and hospitals—helping the needy to celebrate Christmas with good cheer. Alan Teperow, executive director of Synagogue Council of Massachusetts, spearheaded Project Ezra, and I thank him in particular, as well as field coordinators Roz Garber and Toby Gutweil, for allowing me access to all of Project Ezra's archives, volunteers, and participating organizations. I am grateful for the considerable cooperation and insights offered by the Project Ezra volunteers who opened their hearts to me. I also appreciate the efforts of Jaymee Alpert and countless others who helped me with my fieldwork on Christmas by interviewing Jews at Chinese restaurants, movies, Israeli folk dance marathons, Matzo Ball singles dances, and volunteer venues. During my tenure as the Hillel Jewish chaplain at the Massachusetts Institute of Technology, many students helped to post my Christmas questionnaire online in 1994 during the early years of the Internet. I remain, to this day, grateful for that assistance.

Everyone has a favorite story or opinion about Christmas, and I have never grown tired of hearing and recording another personal holiday yarn or anecdote. During the past twenty years, so many Americans have shared with me their personal responses and strategies as Jews facing the Christmas season. I have heard an abundance of unique American tales about Jews shaping Christmas and magnifying Hanukkah. Thank you to those who have shared their precious American stories with me: Myrna Holzman describing her battle with the US Postal Service for a Hanukkah stamp; Nora Guthrie ruminating about her father Woody Guthrie's newly discovered trove of Hanukkah songs; Elaine Grossinger, Jack Landman, and Ben Kaplan recalling the December holidays at Grossinger's in the Catskills; John Rothmann reminiscing about how his family and relatives, the extended Haas family and their descendants, have hosted a lavish annual Christmas party for more than one hundred years at their landmark residence on Franklin Street in San Francisco; Michael and Sue Steinberg detailing the Christmas sweets once enjoyed by Jews in Germany, the nuances of exchanging holiday greeting cards in the world of department stores, and the Macy's Christmas tree in Union Square in San Francisco; Lisa Geduldig, Henny Youngman, Judith Sloan, Charlie Varon, Freddie Roman, and other comedians creating and performing a new genre of special Jewish holiday humor on Christmas at Kung Pao Kosher Comedy; Sean Altman and Rob Tannenbaum composing and singing sarcastic and ribald songs; Bruce Marcus and Lori Factor-Marcus writing the famous poem "*Erev* Christmas," the Jewish-style parody on Chinese food on Christmas Eve; the members of the Martha's Vineyard Hebrew Center,— participants in my oral history class, including Dorothy Brickman, Helen Issokson and Sarah Isenberg—sharing their personal life experiences at Christmas; Harvey Katz happily describing his dressing up to play Santa Claus every year at the local bank in Glastonbury, Connecticut; Ronnie and Janis Simon, joyously recounting their annual family tradition of exchanging Christmas gifts with their good friends, Frank and Carol Cannata, while receiving Hanukkah gifts in return; Herbert Anker recalling the gifts brought to him by "Hanukkah *Maennchen*"—Hanukkah men—during his childhood in Germany in 1938. Taken together these and other unique American tales of being Jewish at Christmas comprise a modern-day tapestry. I am grateful to these and other wonderful people who have shared their special stories with me.

From the beginning, my mother, Hadassah, urged me on with love and persistence. She wanted me to gain a doctorate, perhaps even imagining that a book might follow. I know that Imma and my late father, Walter, are now smiling together from heaven, for they taught me to take pride in my Jewish heritage and to share it with others. After my mother passed away, my friends Justin and Genevieve Wyner encouraged me, like devoted parents, and I approached the book with renewed verve.

My son, Jonas, has been a constant source of inspiration and amazement. His laughter became a welcome companion to writing. Jonas has grown up with this book, simultaneously learning in school how to become a good writer and to appreciate good writing, watching through example as his dad and mom spent early mornings huddled around the computer composing line and verse. I know that Jonas's proximity to the book project has resulted in our love of writing being transmitted to him. Perhaps, as a result, during the summer of 2011, our son proudly penned his first newspaper composition in the *Vineyard Gazette*, as a kid critic and columnist for Cinema Circus, the children's summer film festival on Martha's Vineyard.

Finally, my heart is full of gratitude to my wife, Lori, who has worked with me as a partner in writing this book. Her contributions have been infinite. Her ideas and intellectual vigor, the selfless time and her writing and editing skills, all were given with the utmost devotion and affection. Lori brought a lawyer's focus to this project, tempered by optimism and an underlying quality of tranquility, all of which translated to a can-do attitude that infused the research for and composition of this book. Lori's love and thoughtful analysis has touched upon every single page of this book. This volume is now finished because of Lori, my helpmate, my love and partner in all of life's journeys. To my sweetheart and to Jonas, I dedicate this book with an abundance of love and happiness.

A KOSHER CHRISTMAS

Figure I.1. Author Joshua Eli Plaut, age seven, on Santa's lap, Great Neck, New York, 1964. Plaut family collection.

COPING WITH CHRISTMAS

A MULTITUDE OF JEWISH RESPONSES

I have always been fascinated with Christmas. As a young boy growing up in Long Island, New York, in the early 1960s, my mother took me to sit on Santa's lap at Gertz Department Store. Inevitably, Santa asked me what I wanted for Christmas. I then felt compelled to explain that I celebrated Hanukkah. Santa still gave me a candy cane. Visiting Santa at the shopping center might not be unusual for most Americans, but it was out of place and strange for a Jewish child whose father was a well-respected rabbi and civil rights activist in Great Neck, New York. Years later, I asked my mother why she took me to sit on Santa's lap when we did not celebrate Christmas. She responded that she was simply doing what many American parents did for their children. She was never worried about any influence on me as a child because my family was secure in its Jewish identity.

I also remember that every year on Christmas Eve, we drove around our neighborhood to see the brightly lit Christmas trees adorning front yards and to admire our neighbors' Christmas decorations. We also went to Rockefeller Center in New York City to ice skate in the gently falling snow and to sip frothy hot cocoa with marshmallows, a magical moment that I have counted among my favorite childhood memories. While we always enjoyed the trappings of Christmas around us, at home we celebrated Hanukkah faithfully each night: reciting blessings over the candles, singing Hanukkah songs, playing dreidel, and giving and receiving presents for eight days. Indeed, Hanukkah gifts were stacked up high on the baby grand piano in our living room. These memories stand out in my recollection of my childhood as does one more December ritual: during our holiday break from public school in Great Neck, as was the wont of many American Jews, my brothers and I flew south to visit our grandparents in Florida.

I lived in America until the age of ten. In 1967, we immigrated to Israel, a land without December dilemmas and public displays of Christmas. With a myriad of other immigrants, many of whom were Russian Jews who had fled political and religious oppression in the Soviet Union, I attended a Youth Aliyah boarding school in Central Israel. I recall one particular December day in 1971 when I was in ninth grade. The school headmaster burst into a dormitory room to confiscate an evergreen tree that a Russian-born classmate had erected to celebrate the approaching secular New Year on January 1st. The student called the fir tree a Sylvester tree, a common and fully secular Russian icon of the New Year holiday. Even though the Russian-Jewish student had no intention of celebrating Christmas, our Israeli headmaster was steadfast, angrily proclaiming that a Christmas tree had no place in a Jewish school in Israel.

Later on in life, at the age of twenty-nine, I arrived as a newly ordained rabbi at my first pulpit in Glastonbury, Connecticut. I quickly learned that it was not completely uncommon for American Jews of seemingly diverse backgrounds to have Christmas trees in their homes. When my congregation invited the New York author Anne Roiphe to speak as a scholar in residence, I became familiar with Roiphe's biography and writings. Included in that body of work was the controversial op-ed article she had written in the *New York Times* in 1978 about growing up with a Christmas tree in Manhattan and deriving pleasure from its presence in her home. I read the many and varied responses to the article, including a letter to the editor of the *New York Times* by acclaimed author Cynthia Ozick, who asserted that Roiphe was a traitor to the Jewish people, a modern day Hellenist. I was surprised by the level of vitriol directed at Roiphe. In light of my own Christmastime experiences, both familial and professional, I was increasingly curious as to why Christmas evoked such strong reactions in Jews of all persuasions across the United States.

On a professional level, I was aware of congregants, many from interfaith marriages, who brought Christmas trees into their homes and decorated them, placing them in visible and large picture windows so that the colorful lights could be admired from outside. I also realized that some of my secular congregants, among them Harvard Law School professor Alan Dershowitz, were more interested in ensuring that no religious celebration, whether of Christmas or Hanukkah, appeared in civic places so as not to violate the Establishment Clause of the First Amendment to the U.S. Constitution.

Why does Christmas evoke strong feelings among Jews in the United States? Christmas is America's most popular national holiday. Of all the national holidays, only Christmas is founded on religious beliefs, with traditions and symbols associated with Christianity. Declared a U.S. federal holiday in 1870, all commerce ceases on Christmas Day, leaving the majority of Americans to celebrate the holiday with both religious and, progressively, more secular festivities. Christmas is celebrated privately in homes and in churches and publicly in town squares and shopping malls across the United States.

Whereas Jews in the United States can participate fully in Thanksgiving and New Year's Day celebrations, Christmas does not belong to all Americans. Atheists and secularists, as well as religious minorities such as Jews, Muslims, Hindus, and Buddhists, feel excluded. The problem is more acute because Christmas festivities and displays are not limited to Christmas Eve and Christmas Day. They span a season that extends from Thanksgiving until New Year's Day. Throughout this period, public squares, streets, and shops are festooned with Christmas trees, nativity scenes, wreathes, images of Santa Claus, snowmen, and reindeer. Music is piped into every shopping mall. Movies such as *The Polar Express, Elf, Miracle on 34th Street,* and *White Christmas* are shown on television and in cinemas. Holiday parties abound. Gifts are exchanged at home and in the workplace. And greeting cards are sent to relatives, friends, and coworkers. For both celebrant and noncelebrant alike, there is no hiding from Christmas.

If not celebrating Christmas, what then is a Jew to do on Christmas in America? How is a Jew to respond? These questions are at the heart of what the mass media and Jewish communal leaders in the United States commonly refer to as the December dilemma. The lure of Christmas entices some Jews to become involved in the nonreligious aspects of Christmas and other Jews to reject it as a stepping stone toward assimilation. This latter group promotes adopting the Jewish holiday of Hanukkah as the sole medium for display of Jewish seasonal joy, a holiday that, like Christmas, can be adapted to reflect American values and ideals. "Christmas or Hanukkah?" is a difficult choice forced each year on many Jewish parents, children, leaders, and educators.

These choices cause many Jews in the United States to feel displaced and marginalized. Rabbi Bertram Korn's remarks, delivered from his pulpit, at Congregation Keneseth Israel, in Philadelphia in 1950 about December dilemmas, still resonate today: "Every year at this time every thoughtful and serious Jew faces a problem which is intensified this season: how we as Jews deal with the popular aspects of the majority faith of our neighbors . . . how we adjust to the temptations of the tinsel and the holly—where we take our stand as Jews." Forty years later, Jonathan Sarna, a preeminent historian of American Jewry, argued that American Jews have a "Christmas problem." Although American civil religion calls upon all Americans to join in the Christmas spirit, on the actual holiday of Christmas the religious overtones of Christianity are apparent throughout American society, and, as Sarna concluded: "the fundamental dilemma produced by Christmas's unique status in the American national calendar remains unresolved."[1]

Jews in the United States have, in fact, made great progress in resolving December dilemmas. Such an ongoing resolution is evolving out of the creative efforts of American Jewry to coopt the Christmas season by reshaping it to reflect uniquely Jewish ideas, concerns, and practices and by developing a variety of strategies directed toward neutralizing Christmas in America. American Jewry's success in challenging Christmas's vaunted status rests upon forging an identity that is at once separate from the religious and historical dimensions of Christmas, yet convergent with its underlying spirit.

Jews in America, particularly during the late twentieth and early twenty-first centuries, employ a multitude of strategies to face the particular challenges of Christmas and to overcome feelings of exclusion and isolation. Jews have played a crucial role in popularizing Christmas. They have enhanced the national observance of Christmas by composing many of the Christmas songs beloved by all Americans. More secular than religious, these songs, among them Irving Berlin's "White Christmas," Walter Rollins and Steve Fletcher's "Frosty the Snowman," and, most recently, Paul Simon's "Getting Ready for Christmas Day," remind celebrants that Christmas belongs to all Americans who share in the spirit of patriotism, generosity, peace, and goodwill. It is ironic, however, that other Jews in the United States have developed strategies to downplay the significance of Christmas by composing poems and songs—in print, performance, and the media—that satirize and neutralize the religious nature of the holiday. Humorous songs and comedic performances offer outlets for the disenfranchised to vent disappointment over society's fixation with the crass commercialization of Christmas.

Jews have also developed strategies of inclusiveness to counteract feelings of exclusion and isolation during the holiday season. These strategies are implemented through organizing activities and attending events during the holiday season that concentrate on bringing family and friends together in temporary and public settings, thereby providing opportunities to identify positively as Jews and as Americans. On Christmas, Jews eat in Chinese restaurants, watch movies, and attend concerts and comedy performances. They also visit Jewish museums, attend singles' balls, and travel. These activities represent popular Christmastime traditions for contemporary American Jews.

Responding to the resurgence of Jewish identity in the United States, partially occasioned by support for the State of Israel, Jews in America have reinvented the celebration of Hanukkah as an alternative to Christmas. This strategy has made it easier for Jewish parents to influence their children to avoid Christmas in favor of celebrating Hanukkah. A different strategy, devoted to volunteerism on Christmas, provides a means for Jews to join their neighbors in dispensing charity, volunteering to spare fellow employees from having to work on Christmas Eve and Day, and even donning Santa Claus outfits as a way to bring holiday cheer to Americans who are celebrating Christmas.

As a result of the growing trend among Jews in the United States to intermarry with Christians, Jewish organizations and mainstream American businesses have responded by combining Christmas and Hanukkah symbols in what has come to be known as "Chrismukkah." To cater to these intermarried couples, greeting card companies issue lines of interfaith cards that tap into this new hybrid reality, making it appear as if Hanukkah and Christmas share a common set of values. These new hybrid traditions are not without controversy. Jewish religious groups often rally against the growing trend to secularize holiday symbols. Their spokespeople argue, as do adherents of American fundamentalist religious and conservative groups, that society needs more, not less, religious focus.

Following from this argument is the constitutional debate about religious symbols displayed in public settings. With a constitutional bravado emanating from a growing religious segment within the American Jewish community, the Hasidic Chabad-Lubavitch organization, for example, has waged war against strict separation of religion and state and has won from the courts the right to display menorahs in public venues. Members of the Chabad-Lubavitch group have been supported by Christian religious fundamentalists who want crèches allowed in these same municipally governed spaces. These religious groups, Jewish and Christian alike, have come up against the American Civil Liberties Union and Jewish organizations with a long history of winning court injunctions against any encroachment of religion on state.

Reacting to an overly commercialized holiday season, Jews have joined other like-minded Americans to create alternative secular activities drawn neither from Christmas nor from Hanukkah. Festivus, the secular December holiday credited to a scriptwriter of the 1990s television sitcom

Seinfeld, grew in popularity beyond its television roots as a secular societal celebration that allowed participants to express their feelings and frustrations with the holiday season. Across the United States, Festivus parties serve as magnets for younger generations of Americans, including many Jews. Celebrants of Festivus, who have stripped the holiday season of any religious meaning, instead rely upon irony and parody to carry the day.

Overall, the various contemporary responses to Christmas stem from different places, beliefs, and institutions. They reflect competing forces, changing ideals, and conflicting values that have left Americans, and Jews among them, with a rich repertoire of reactions to the Yuletide holiday. Differing attitudes arise from one generation to the next. Indeed, attitudes held by individuals may even evolve over the course of their own lives as they move from childhood to adulthood, marriage, and, particularly parenthood.

These changing responses reveal how Jews use this seasonal period to rethink, redefine, and negotiate what it means to be a Jew in America. Befitting their status as one of America's most successful constituent groups, Jews have reshaped Christmas and challenged society to broaden the December season to recognize festivities sponsored by secular and minority groups. Writing in 1990, Jonathan Sarna argued that Christmas is one barrier that Jews cannot overcome in their quest to be regarded of equal status with their American neighbors who celebrate Christmas.[2] By the end of the first decade of the twenty-first century, Sarna's words no longer ring true. Jews in the United States have, indeed, surmounted this barrier because they have not allowed Christmas to force them into silence and exclusion during December. Rather, Jews have created a parallel seasonal universe of Jewish praxis that allows them to coexist with other Americans in the United States, despite Christmas's status as a national holiday. At the same time, the story of how Jews approach Christmas demonstrates how American society is willing to bend to accommodate constituent groups that seek greater public recognition for their holiday's particular calendars and observances.

While Christmas and Hanukkah customs and activities are at once contemporary and historical, this book delineates the recent history of how Jews challenge Christmas. Using an ethnographic lens on the threshold of the twenty-first century, the book analyzes recent and current major phenomena in American Jewish popular culture during Christmastime. I consider certain defining events, based upon interpretation of my fieldwork and interviews with participants. Comedians, composers, charity organizers, media representatives, Hanukkah postal stamp activists, and inventors of new combined Christmas-Hanukkah formats have opportunities to tell their stories of how they stood up to Christmas and overcame its influence.

For more than twenty years, I have studied the wide range of annual December events, conducted extensive fieldwork, and used rich gleanings from popular culture to understand Jewish behavior and attitudes about the holiday season. This approach arises out of my scholarly background in Jewish folklore, religious studies, and modern Jewish history, academic disciplines that aim to understand and gain insight into Jewish life in America and how it impacts the evolution of holiday traditions, customs, and ceremonies. In studying Christmas, I had the added advantage of engaging directly with a large cross-section of American Jewry through my professional career in the congregational rabbinate and university chaplaincy.

I have used participant observation as an important research tool for understanding contemporary Jewish holiday behavior, particularly regarding the emergence of new forms of popular culture. While living in Boston, Massachusetts, during the 1990s, for example, I joined Jewish volunteers on Christmas to serve meals at soup kitchens and prepare food for distribution to the needy, activities that Jewish organizations duplicate in many parts of the United States. When I visited many Chinese restaurants throughout the United States on Christmas Eve and Christmas Day, I observed and analyzed why and how this penchant for Chinese food reached its apex at the holiday. For five years, I attended the wildly popular San Francisco event known as Kung Pao Kosher Comedy. More than twenty years after its inception, Kung Pao has proven to be a seminal event in modern comedic performance focused on Christmas. At these events, thousands of attendees have been exposed to Borsht Belt comedians such as Henny Youngman and Freddie Roman, as well as to young comedians joking about Christmas and Hanukkah in ways that would have made their immigrant ancestors blush. As a participant-observer, I interviewed the founder and creative director of Kung Pao Kosher Comedy and solicited opinions, both formally and informally, from attendees about the event.

Harboring an appreciation for music, I listened to many Hanukkah record albums and compact discs that introduced new songs to the public. This led to my discovering musical parodies of Christmas and Hanukkah that were recorded on specialty labels and eventually re-created on CDs, DVDs, and YouTube. Since the 1980s I have been amassing an extensive collection of holiday and interfaith greeting cards, a new medium that offers insight into Jewish contributions to the popular cultural expression of Christmas and Hanukkah.

Coupled with my observation of a wide variety of new rituals and customs emerging in response to both Christmas and Hanukkah, I have participated in many continuing debates surrounding critical issues that the holidays raise. As a Jewish parent, I can well understand the pressures facing Jewish parents in deciding whether their children should participate or absent themselves from public school Christmas pageants and concerts. Many variants of the same issue have presented themselves over time and place in different ways. Two distinct examples come to mind. First, my wife, who grew up in a small town in Connecticut with few Jewish residents, resolved this dilemma by participating in Christmas school concerts but fell silent during the singing, particularly at the mention of the names Christ or Jesus. Her silence exemplified the behavior of Jews in America during the 1950s and 1960s.

Second, by the end of the twentieth century, when Jews in towns and cities across the United States faced exclusion from the December holiday season, they no longer remained silent. They spoke out collectively by joining together with like-minded Americans to make the Christmas season inclusive. In the mid-1990s, public school advisory committees were formed throughout the nation to work with local school boards to review, create, and implement policies regarding the celebration of Christmas in public schools. In 1995, during my tenure as the rabbi of the Martha's Vineyard Hebrew Center, a local public school advisory committee, which included residents of the Jewish faith, advised the local public school board to eliminate the public celebration of Christmas in the Vineyard Haven public school. The committee suggested that no representation of Santa Claus be posted in the hallways or classrooms, a decision viewed by a fundamentalist Christian group on the island as a conspiracy to remove Christmas from the public schools. This fundamentalist group organized a strike with a picket line outside the school, intimidated children and teachers who crossed the line to enter the school and accused them of supporting the ban on Santa Claus. Placards carried by members of the picket line stated: "The Jews Killed Santa Claus." A year and a half after this community conflict, local school board deliberations resulted in guidelines that permitted education about the holiday but not its observance.

Times have certainly changed since my mother took me to sit on Santa's knee in the early 1960s. By the second decade of the new millennium, Jews have transformed a once-silent night into a holiday season characterized by a flurry of activity that recognizes the importance of the holiday season for all Americans. This book presents a recent history and contemporary ethnography of one of America's most outspoken constituent groups.

Perspectives from the past and present illustrate how Jews are shaping the character of both Christmas and Hanukkah in the United States in the late twentieth and early twenty-first centuries. By focusing on Jewish activities and responses during the December holiday season, we encounter in the following chapters a multitude of distinctive strategies that portray how Jews survive and thrive in American society and how they transform Christmastime into a holiday season belonging to all Americans.

CHAPTER 1

COMING TO THE
NEW WORLD

CAN THE AMERICAN JEW
KEEP CHRISTMAS?

Every Christmas Eve, Samuel and Joel Rothmann unlock the door of their great-great grandparents' house at 2007 Franklin Street in San Francisco and feel as though they are coming home. On Christmas Eve the direct fourth- and fifth-generation descendants of William and Bertha Haas gather for their annual family reunion. Even though the family donated the house to the San Francisco Architectural Heritage in 1974, they have retained the right to gather at the house every Christmas Eve, just as they have every year since 1886. Forty family members attended the Haas-Lilienthal gathering in 2010. John Rothmann, Samuel and Joel's father and a fourth-generation scion of the Haas-Lilienthal family, reflected: "None of the third generation is still living, so the torch has been passed to the fourth and the fifth generations to keep the tradition alive. . . . For the Haas family, Christmas Eve at the Haas-Lilienthal House evokes and creates wonderful memories and reaffirms the strength of our tradition from generation to generation."[1]

Alice (1885–1972) and her sister Florine (1881–1973), daughters of Bavarian-born William and Bertha Haas, hosted annual holiday parties for the elite Jewish families of San Francisco. The socialite sisters celebrated Easter and Christmas rather than Passover and Hanukkah. Though they had reserved seats and attended High Holy Day services at Temple Emanuel, Alice's niece Frances Bransten Rothmann recollects that her mother and aunt had little knowledge about Jewish rites: "The menorahs, the beautiful lights adorning their Franklin Street homes, were merely artifacts ornamenting their dining and living rooms."[2]

Each December the social world of Alice Haas revolved around Christmas. Alice hosted the annual family Christmas party at 2007 Franklin Street.[3] Preparations began months in advance. As Alice's daughters grew, they were enlisted: "For days on end, they would be closeted behind locked doors, deep in secret schemes. Aunt Alice seemed to be Mrs. Santa Claus personified; her daughters, elfin helpers." The focus of Alice's preparations centered on the choice of the Christmas tree, its ornaments, decorations, and the guests to be invited to her lavish home. "Every Christmas," related Frances Bransten Rothmann, "either in the windowed alcove of the second parlor fronting on Franklin Street or on the platform in the ballroom, a ceiling-high tree shone as it revolved slowly on a music stand and exuded the heady fragrance of fir." Through marriage, the San Francisco aristocratic Jewish families of Lilienthal, Gerstley, Brandenstein, and

Figure 1.1. The Haas family: (left to right) Alice, William, Charles, Florine, Bertha (née Greenbaum), and cousin Louis Green, circa 1889. Courtesy San Francisco Architectural Heritage.

Stern joined the Haas family's Christmas festivities: "When the Christmas gatherings grew to include between fifty and sixty cousins, sisters, uncles, and aunts, the party was transferred from the warmth of upstairs parlors and dining room to the bare and colder regions of the basement ballroom."

Every Christmas, Alice and her helpers decorated the basement ball-room in a different fantastical theme to allow guests to travel the globe—from Mexico, to the Alps, to the Orient, to the North Pole: "One Christmas, the guests were magically transplanted to Mexico, Santa Claus piñatas dangled from gas fixtures while colorful sombreros, Indian baskets, papier-mâché chickens and horses, and full-blown paper poppies deco-rated the long dining tables. In a scramble of merriment, children whacked noisily at the Santa piñatas and were showered with small gifts and can-dies." Alice invariably enlisted a family member or friend to don a Santa Claus costume stuffed with pillows and appear at the party while "bound-ing down the stairs with a rush of sleigh bells and roaring belly laughs." Centerpieces for the buffet table were also the subject of lavish attention. One year, reflecting the theme of winter in the Alps, a miniature ice-skating pond was constructed on a mirror, surrounded by tiny snow-laden bushes, a forest, and a gingerbread ski chalet. Another year, the centerpiece was a "plump suckling pig with a shining red apple protruding from its open snout. It was garlanded with holly and gloriously glazed." Hand-sewn giant Christmas stockings "that looked more like Santa-sacks than stockings" hung over the fireplace ready for the children when they awoke on the morning of Christmas Day.

Elizabeth Lilienthal Gerstley, Alice's daughter, wrote that German Jews celebrated Christmas, not as a religious celebration, but as a demonstration of how well integrated the Haas families were in the upper echelons of San Francisco society.[4] Author Frances Dinkelspiel, a Brandenstein-Bransten descendent, whose family arrived in California in the 1850s, confirms the thorough integration of Christmas in the lives of San Francisco's German Jews. "It turns out that Jews in California have been celebrating Christmas since the 1850s. But they did not consider it a holiday to celebrate the birth of Jesus. . . . My family is not rejecting Judaism. We are just celebrating it a uniquely American way. Or maybe a way that is just unique to the West Coast. But there are cultural reasons for our celebra-tion, not religious ones."[5]

The family reunions that now occur on Christmas Eve at the Haas-Lilienthal House differ from the parties hosted by Alice Haas. John Rothmann describes the change: "None of the trappings of Christmas remain. Santa Claus no longer makes his appearance. Christmas Eve in 2010 coincided with *Shabbat*. The candles were lit, the *kiddush* was chanted, and two loaves of challah were on the table. We welcomed the *Shabbat* as a family. The house, which is open to the public for tours and events, has a Christmas tree, but were it not present as part of the decor of the season by the house management there would be no tree. When Hanukkah falls on December 24, we will light the candles, have potato latkes, and spin the dreidel."[6]

CHRISTMAS EVOLVES INTO A NATIONAL AMERICAN HOLIDAY

At the same time that San Francisco's Jews began celebrating Christmas as a secular holiday for their families and the social elite, Christmas was evolving into what would become America's most popular holiday. Declared a national holiday in 1870, Christmas was a day when all commerce ceased and the majority of Americans came to celebrate the holiday with religious overtones but with increasingly secular festivities.

According to scholars of Christmas, American and British authors and illustrators of the first half of the nineteenth century are credited with forming the images, many drawn from ancient traditions and different nations, which have become universal at Christmastime. By the late nineteenth century, such disparate elements as the German Christmas tree, the Dutch Christmas cookie, the American Santa (borrowing from the Dutch Sinter Class), and the British tradition of Christmas cards were woven together into American Christmastime traditions.[7] An industrial process that created a strong commercial demand for Christmas displays and decorations fueled the popularization of Christmas in America, an ascension in importance that coincided with America's struggle to find its own identity and its need to bind the myriad of ethnicities and population groups that came to its shores.[8] Rather than the drunken revelry often associated with ancient celebrations of Christmas (and the reason such celebrations had been banned at one time in England and colonial Boston), writers, poets, and cartoonists in both America and England began to refashion the idea of Christmas. In the 1820s, American writer Washington Irving wrote short stories sentimentalizing the harmonious Christmas festivities he experienced while visiting in the English countryside. In 1822, Clement Clarke Moore composed the poem "A Visit from St. Nicholas," usually known by its first line "'Twas the Night Before Christmas." With this poem, Moore helped to popularize the image of a Santa Claus and the tradition of gift-giving. In 1843, in England, Charles Dickens reinforced the secular aspects of Christmas with the writing of *A Christmas Carol*, a book that became immensely popular in the United States. The central character, Ebenezer Scrooge, through a series of trials and tribulations, learns that charitable giving to the needy is central to redemption. *A Christmas Carol* emphasized the secular aspects of a family-centered festival, hallmarks of which are seasonal foods and drink, games, dancing, and generosity of spirit.[9] In 1863 Thomas Nast drew a classic version of Santa Claus for *Harper's Weekly*: a plump man sporting a long white beard. This magazine's illustration permanently fixed the depiction of Santa Claus in the popular media. In 1874, Louis Prang introduced the first Christmas card to America.[10] Through these customs, both new and adapted, Christmastime in America grew to symbolize family, community, generosity, and a child-centered time identified with conviviality, abundance, and goodwill.[11]

By 1870, for urban Americans Christmas in America had become the primary national holiday; its essential character, however, had been slowly metamorphosing from a religious to a secular celebration. The religious aspects of Christmas continued to decline into the twentieth century.[12] During the twentieth century, the religious and secular character of the holiday merged into the family setting as families created their own home traditions: purchasing a Christmas tree, decorating the tree, exchanging gifts, and attending church services. The commercialization of Christmas contributed further to the holiday's secularization. Industry and business exploited the custom of gift-giving, which almost singularly transformed Christmas into a secular and commercial time of year. The exchange of gifts reached all facets of society: school, office, home, and the business world.

Residents of towns and cities across the United States expanded Christmas celebrations from the home into public and civic areas by organizing public festivities. By 1912, citizens from New York supported a community Christmas tree, the first in the country's history. The year 1912 also marked the time when the cities of Boston and Hartford arranged open-air concerts during Christmas week. In the following year, 160 towns sponsored similar holiday-oriented musical events. Hallmarks of the public celebration were gifts to children, decorated Christmas trees, nativity scenes, and singing of Christmas carols. The city center, adorned with Christmas decorations and lights, allowed all who entered the physical boundaries of the city center to participate in the celebratory ambience. According to historian Penne L. Restad, the public celebration of Christmas caused many to feel and act differently.

CHRISTMAS TREES ENTER THE HOMES OF GERMAN JEWS

As Christmas evolved into a national holiday during the nineteenth century, an outside observer to Jewish life in America during the early 1800s would have had difficulty finding Jews who reacted unfavorably to Christmas. In fact, quite the opposite proved true. For German Jews in the United States, as evidenced by the Haas-Lilienthal family's elaborate recognition of the holiday, Christmas signaled a festive time in which they gladly participated as both a reflection of their status and a means to assimilate into American society.

German Jews became comfortable with Christmas in nineteenth-century Europe where they were well integrated socially into German society. Unlike their Eastern European brethren, emancipated German Jews did not live in ghettos and were not afraid to venture out in public during the Christmas season. Enjoying civic equality, urban bourgeois Jewish families in German-speaking European countries enjoyed, like their Christian counterparts, intimate family celebrations at home during Christmas. German Jews placed gifts under their trees and ate customary Christmas foods, particularly sweets like stollen, lebkuchen, and pfefferkuc (although they prepared the treats with butter instead of lard).[13]

The custom of having a Christmas tree at home, adapted by affluent German Jews, trickled down to the middle class. German period photographs from the years 1850 until 1933 portray large, affluent Jewish families photographed in front of decorated Christmas trees. The decorated tree served as the centerpiece of festivities, which included singing Christmas carols and exchanging gifts, reflecting the German cultural life of bourgeois German-Jewish families. Jews celebrated Christmas as a family festival devoid of religious meaning.

The introduction of Christmas into Jewish homes was not, however, without criticism. According to one son of a middle-class Jewish family from Berlin, his parents brought a tree into their home, but to their children they tried to justify their decision to decorate a Jewish home with a Christmas tree. His parents explained that the tree was for their Christian maid, an answer that the son realized was untruthful because his parents treated the tree like a "work of art."[14] When the Christmas tree entered German-Jewish homes, it was condemned by the *Juedisches Volksblatt* newspaper in 1859. In 1871, the Synod of Reform Rabbis in Germany tried to counter this trend by recommending that Jews celebrate Hanukkah.

The Christmas tree was, however, too ingrained in German-Jewish society, where many a prominent German Jew is on record as possessing

Figure 1.2. The Meschelsohn family and their governess with their electrically illuminated Christmas tree at home, Berlin, 1912. © Jewish Museum Berlin, donated by Hilda Mattei.

a Christmas tree. Cosmopolitan Fanny von Arnstein—a Berliner by birth (1757–1818), cofounder of the Music Society of Austria, and a member of Viennese high society—was among the first known European Jews to introduce the Christmas tree into a Jewish home.[15] Fanny's father, banker Daniel Itzig, was court-financier to King Frederick II of Prussia. He also was a leader of Berlin's Jewish community and, in 1791, acquired full civil rights. By 1812, Fanny von Arnstein and her married daughter Henriette (who later converted with her husband to Catholicism) introduced the new custom of a home Christmas tree to Vienna. This custom was already prevalent in Berlin. Arnstein also added a personal touch, attaching little poems to the presents. Fanny held court over her celebrated Viennese salon that attracted notable intellectual personalities who were comfortable viewing a Christmas tree in her home. Arnstein's practice of having a Christmas tree then became *de rigueur* in the homes of the Jewish intelligentsia and cognoscenti of Vienna. (It is interesting to note that Wolfgang Amadeus Mozart received early support in the salons of Fanny von Arnstein and her sister Cäcilie Eskeles. He lived at the Arnstein residence in Vienna for an extended period of time, and there he composed several of his most inspired works.)[16]

Perhaps most surprising is that Theodore Herzl (1860–1904), the founder of modern Zionism, also brought a Christmas tree into his Vienna home. Indeed, after Herzl completed his seminal book on Zionism, *Judenstaat* (*The Jewish State*) in 1895, Vienna's chief rabbi, Moritz Gudemann, visited Herzl to discuss the new book. This visit occurred on December 24, Christmas Eve. The chief rabbi was surprised to find that the Herzl household displayed a Christmas tree. In his diaries Herzl wrote, "I was just lighting the Christmas tree for my children when Gudemann arrived. He seemed upset by the 'Christian' custom. Well, I will not let myself be pressured! But I don't mind if they call it the Hanukah tree—or the winter solstice."[17]

Gershon Scholem (1897–1982), esteemed scholar of Jewish mysticism, remembers his parents creating a festive mood in their Berlin home on Christmas Eve. The atmosphere was enhanced considerably by the inclusion of a Christmas tree. Under the tree was, ironically, a photograph of Theodore Herzl in a black frame, given lovingly to Scholem by his parents who knew how much Gershon admired Herzl and Zionism. Scholem wrote that "since the days of my grandparents, Christmas was celebrated in our family with roast goose or hare, a decorated Christmas tree which my mother bought at the market by St. Peter's Church, and the big distribution of presents for servants, relatives, and friends." Scholem's parents told him

Figure 1.3. Fanny von Arnstein, portrait of a noble young lady, Vienna. Courtesy
Austrian National Library.

that Jews participated in Christmas because Christmas was a German national festival celebrated by all German citizens, including Jews. He remembered how his aunt played the piano and treated the household cook and servant girl to "Silent Night, Holy Night." Scholem, as a child, was dazzled by Christmas until 1911 when he begun to study Hebrew and realized that his Jewish identity was not consistent with the presence of any form of home-oriented Christmas celebration.[18]

German Jews felt that they could celebrate the cultural aspects of a Christmas celebration without making any religious commitment. Jewish acceptance of the Christmas tree was not tantamount to adopting Christianity. The Christmas tree, in fact, had already been recognized as a secular artifact originating in early eighteenth-century Germany as a popular custom that spread elsewhere, to Denmark and Norway in 1830, to England and France in the 1840s, and to Sweden in 1863.[19] In 1892, folklorist Alexander Tille observed that in Germany "the Christmas-tree has long since broken through the barrier of different creeds, and many Jewish families have adopted it to celebrate Yuletide."[20]

The celebration of Christmas by Jews in Germany and other German-speaking European societies, however, was not universal. Not all German Jewish families condoned bringing Christmas trees into the home. Many sought ways of using the celebratory mood of Christmas and Hanukkah to organize gatherings that could substitute for the joyful celebrations accompanying Christmas activities. Gershon Scholem mentioned that his generation in Berlin sought alternatives to mark Christmas Eve and Christmas Day in the form of festive parties and balls to which Jewish friends were invited. Scholem referred to a Maccabean Ball: "Christmas was not celebrated at my uncle's home. Instead he celebrated Chanukah, the Jewish feast of lights from which the Church derived Christmas. . . . The Zionist movement really played up the occasion [Chanukah]. On Christmas Eve, mostly for the benefit of the many unmarried young men and girls who did not wish to participate in their parents' Christmas celebrations, the so-called Maccabean Ball was held—a peculiar invention."[21] Jews organized such balls after the pattern popular among non-Jews in Germany to which Jews were not invited.

Many German Jews recognized that Christmas was not a holiday of Jewish provenance. Using symbols drawn from Hanukkah, they called Christmas Eve "Weihnukkah"—"Holy Hanukkah"—lampooning the German Protestant name for Christmas, WeihNahkhten, or "holy night" and merging it with the word Hanukkah. A 1904 cartoon of Weihnukkah, on display in the permanent exhibition of the Berlin Jewish Museum and entitled "Darwinistisches," shows a Hanukkah menorah metamorphosing into a Christmas tree.[22] The *Weihnukkah* tree presages the label "Hanukkah bush," a designation given by American Jews to the tree put up in their homes in the United States. While many families refused to adopt German Christmas-time customs, the influence of a Santa figure was carried over to Hanukkah in Germany. German-Jewish children received gifts on Hanukkah. Gershon Scholem mentioned that the giver of the gifts was well known: "When I visited my uncle at Chanukah in one of the war years and asked his daughters who had given them all those beautiful presents, they replied, 'Our Good Father Chanukah brought them to us.'" And, foreshadowing the future Hanukkah Harry who arose in America in the late 1980s, a German-Jewish child who was eight years old in 1938 remembers a tale in Germany: the gifts were brought by "Hanukkah *Maennchen*" (Hanukkah men) who were assigned that distribution but who were not adorned in any special Santa Claus garb.

German Jews Face Christmas in America

German Jews brought the custom of displaying a Christmas tree in their homes from Europe to America. In the 1800s, upon emigrating to America, German Jews recreated European Christmastime activities to share in the celebration of the December holiday season. They found comfort among other Jews who were searching for secularized alternatives to either Christmas or Hanukkah festivities. By sharing a Jewish identity within the framework of a seasonal celebration, these newly settled Jewish immigrants and their offspring took the opportunity to express their civic pride as well

Figure 1.4. "Darwinistisches." Zionist cartoon on assimilation, from the journal *Schlemiel*, 1904, Germany. © Jewish Museum Berlin, photo: Jens Ziehe.

as their American patriotism. According to Frances Bransten Rothmann, her mother, Florine Haas, and her aunt, Alice Haas, lived in a "tranquil, protected segment of time ... when Jews who sought freedom from persecution and the right to further their fortunes emigrated from Germany

Figure 1.5. Cartoon of a Jewish boy, a member of the Blue-White Zionist youth (scout) movement in Germany, being presented with a menorah as a gift from the Christmas man (Santa Claus). Cartoon by Franz Julian Levi in *Schlemiel*, December 1919. © Jewish Museum Berlin, photo: Jens Ziehe.

to America. . . . The sisters never knew the rigors of immigration, never felt the flames of extermination, and were never lashed by hate, vituperation, or intolerance. . . . They grew up in a culturally integrated world; their parents and grandparents assimilated the customs and rituals of Christian Americans. There was no discernable anti-Jewish prejudice during the early years in San Francisco."[23]

The celebration of Christmas was part of a wider trend toward incorporating the celebration of American secular customs into German-Jewish homes. At the same time that Christmas was being introduced into Jewish homes in America, historical records indicate that from 1850, German Jews celebrated Thanksgiving upon their arrival in the United States. Effectively combining Jewish and American rituals, in 1873, Congregation Berith Kodesh of Rochester, New York, participated in the first Jewish Thanksgiving interfaith congregational service in the United States.[24] In 1888, Thanksgiving and Hanukkah were coincident, and comparisons were made to the themes of freedom that underlay the two holidays. Newspaper reports at the time recorded conjoint celebration of the two holidays.[25]

The custom of celebrating a secularized Christmas is documented among Jewish families of the late 1800s in New York, San Francisco, Cincinnati, Boston, Hot Springs, Baltimore, New Orleans, and Toledo. In perhaps the earliest written mention in an American Jewish periodical, Rabbi Julius Eckman, of the classical Reform Temple Emanuel of San Francisco, described the 1867 celebration: "It so happens that Hannucah falls about Christmas time, and that in many Jewish families in which their own festival is scarce noticed, Christmas is celebrated with presents to their children and illuminations in their parlors."[26] Also, in San Francisco, thirty years later, a Jewish newspaper correspondent wrote about the abundance of Christmas trees in the city's Jewish community.[27] In Hot Springs, Arkansas, the local correspondent to the *American Israelite* wrote: "Christmas here was observed by almost everybody, more from custom, no doubt, like everywhere else, than to do homage to the anniversary of Jesus Christ. The day was one like you might read about; spring-like and charming in its loveliness. The stores and business places generally were closed after 12 o'clock and the battle against the martyred turkey was commenced soon after."[28]

Incorporating both Christmas and Hanukkah symbols, regardless of whether Hanukkah fell earlier or later on the calendar, German-Jewish families in America decorated Christmas trees, exchanged gifts, and hung wreaths on the doors of their homes and stockings on the fireplaces. Certain of these events were recorded in the society pages of local newspapers.[29] Mr. and Mrs. Charles Rosenthal of Las Vegas, New Mexico, for example, announced their Christmas plans in the local newspaper. In 1888, the Rosenthals hosted their friends for a Christmas dinner, as did Mr. and Mrs. Louis Marcus in Trinidad, Colorado. In 1889, the Schlessengers of Newton spent Christmas with Mr. and Mrs. Burgauer in Winfield, Kansas, while Mrs. Hexter and her daughter Minna spent Hanukkah and Christmas with the elder Hexter's sister, Mrs. Halff. Predating the Christmas charity activities of today's Jews, one St. Louis couple, a Mr. and Mrs. Julius Weil, held a Christmas event that included the raffle of a doll donated to the Cleveland Orphan Asylum Manual Training School Fund.

There is even the occasional reference to a Christmas tree displayed at a Reform Temple in America. An article published in the December 27, 1878, issue of the *Jewish Advance* in Chicago mentioned that Sinai Congregation of Chicago displayed a Christmas tree in celebration of Hanukkah around which were gathered "grown people and children" who "commenced with the singing of the first stanza of the Chanukah hymn by the Sabbath-school children." And, in 1891, in Toledo, Ohio, a correspondent to the *American Israelite* wrote that lacking a rabbi, the temple was closed, and there would not be a Hanukkah festival that year; however, "lots of Christmas presents and Christmas trees" awaited the children of congregants.

Although seasonal holiday decorations provided a means whereby German Jews could partake of the Christmas tenor without directly participating in the Christmas holidays, this practice was not without controversy. A letter written by the Baltimore correspondent "Sulamith" (a nom de plume for Henrietta Szold) to the *Jewish Messenger* dated January 10, 1879, decried this custom: "Why need we adopt the Christmas tree, ridiculously baptized a Chanukah bush?" she asked. "Have we not the Menorah, connected so closely with the visions of the prophets and the allegories of the Bible?"[30] The *Sabbath Visitor* published an editorial on November 12, 1880, that echoed the above sentiment. The writer pleaded with her readers to reject Christmas trees when Hanukkah rolls around. "No Christmas trees in Jewish houses," she declared. She asked that instead the Jewish home use Hanukkah lights and provide Hanukkah presents.[31]

SOCIAL BALLS ON CHRISTMAS AND HANUKKAH

The very first Jewish social balls on Christmas Eve in the United States took place in the 1880s. American Jews of German-Jewish descent hosted social balls and dances for their friends on Christmas Eve, although the purpose—to celebrate either Christmas or Hanukkah—remains unclear.[32]

These balls often featured dinner, dancing, and a concert. Opulent celebrations were staged in cities across the country, variously referred to as Christmas or Hanukkah parties. The Christmas parties included the grand masquerade ball in 1876 at Bellevue House in Cincinnati, the Christmas Eve party (on the Jewish Sabbath) in 1881 at the Progress Club of New York, the opening ball on Christmas Day in 1883 at the Apollo Club of Minneapolis, the Christmas Hop at Martin's Hall on Christmas Day in 1885 at the West Chicago Club, and the Christmas Soiree of 1888 at the Concordia Club in Pittsburgh.

Other socialites preferred to stage Hanukkah balls that would be held in similar style any time during the eight days of Hanukkah, as well as on Christmas Eve. Hanukkah balls in the late nineteenth century were celebrated all over the United States.[33] In 1885 the Jewish community of San Antonio, Texas, hosted a Hanukkah ball, and the Progress Club of Kansas City, Missouri, hosted a Matinee Ball in celebration of Hanukkah for all the children of its religious school, including those whose parents were not members of the club; the ball followed the rabbi's home reception for all the children of the religious school. Also, during that same season, the Young Men's Hebrew Association (YMHA) of St. Louis hosted a promenade, hop, and concert with supper for Hanukkah.

While costume, food, and dance were selected based on popular custom and taste, seasonal holiday decorations were also present. Christmas trees were ubiquitous at the Christmas balls. Hanukkah pageants, even in the absence of Christmas trees, were typically festooned with garlands of holly, wreaths, and evergreen boughs. The ladies of Congregation Beth El Emeth in Philadelphia decorated the room with silk banners reading "Maccabee" and "Chanukah 5639" during a Hanukkah festival, but they also decorated their refreshment tables with arches of evergreens.[34]

A variety of historical accounts illustrates that seasonal decorations often resulted in confusion about their intent and purpose. This confusion caused by the allure of the celebration of Christmas dated to the 1840s when Christmas holiday festivities had already become part of the national consciousness. Jonathan D. Sarna in his book *Jacksonian Jew* comments that "trees, lights, gifts, glitter, and Christmas stockings created a merry holiday, one which held enormous allure for Jewish children. Hanukkah possessed no similar magic. An unimportant Jewish holiday, it was then unconnected with gifts and merriment."[35] Mordecai Noah, the subject of Sarna's book, in a time before Hanukkah became disproportionately magnified, faced this problem with vigor. He reinterpreted Christmas into a celebration of the birthday of the religion that enabled monotheism's spread throughout the world. The Noah family's practice adhered to his newly espoused beliefs. Although Noah had certainly not converted to Christianity, "in his declining years, as in his earlier years, he sought to act as a good Jew, to be recognized as a 'good Christian,' and to identify as a good American—all at the same time."

Christmas trees and evergreens were occasionally used in Jewish settings to enhance the celebration of Hanukkah. Members of Temple Emanuel of New York City hosted a Hanukkah celebration for its religious school in 1879 that included evergreens. Several young children commented that the holiday symbols "looked just like Christmas."[36] This impression was countered by remarks of a Mr. Sanger, who told the children that "Christmas was not an event that should interest them." The use of evergreens as seasonal decorations was also encouraged by the media of the time. The *Sabbath Visitor*, a popular children's publication, encouraged the decorative use of evergreens. A story published in its January 9, 1880, issue described a family celebration of Hanukkah that included a menorah covered with flowers, and wreathes and evergreens hanging adjacent to pictures of Moses and George Washington.[37] A second story, entitled "Christmas at the Cedars," which appeared in the December 1888 issue of *Sabbath Visitor*, describes the excitement of Jewish children upon being permitted to host a masquerade ball on Christmas Eve. The event is announced by a child holding an armful of evergreens, later used to make garlands and wreaths to decorate the house.[38]

THE RABBIS' DEBATE:
CAN THE AMERICAN JEW KEEP CHRISTMAS?

In the early years of Jewish immigration to the United States, the *Philadelphia Times* reported in 1877: "the Hebrew brethren did not keep aloof" from Christmas. As expected, rabbis during the 1800s were outspoken against the use of Christmas decorations, although a few were sympathetic to the need for Jewish parents to please their children. A controversy arose in 1883 surrounding a Friday night lecture in St. Louis; Reform Rabbi Dr. Solomon Sonneschein of Temple Shaare Emeth proposed that it might be appropriate for Jews to celebrate Christmas.[39] "Can the American Jew keep Christmas?" he asked. He answered summarily, "I say he can, without in the least disgracing his religious convictions or interfering with the building up of a stronger and nobler Judaism."[40] He reasoned that Christmas was celebrated as a national holiday because its strong secular orientation did not conflict with Jewish beliefs. More shocking was his claim that Jews should celebrate Hanukkah on December 25 regardless of when Hanukkah fell on the calendar. The suggestion had a certain allure because on the Hebrew calendar, Hanukkah falls on the 25th day of the Jewish month of Kislev as does Christmas on the 25th day of December. In Sonneschein's opinion, Jews could better appreciate both Christmas and Hanukkah if they shared a mutual date on the calendar.

Across America, rabbis, responding harshly to Sonneschein's suggestion, were incensed that a colleague would encourage congregants to participate in Christmas and feared that Jewish children would choose to celebrate Christmas over Hanukkah. The rabbis supported their contention with statements about the many German-Jewish families bringing Christmas trees into their homes and recognizing Christmas as a day of joy and peace. In 1896, Dr. Emile G. Hirsch of Chicago's Zion Temple reportedly encouraged his congregants to observe Christmas as a great holiday and Jesus as a great Jew.[41]

At the beginning of the twentieth century, according to Penne L. Restad, the debate about whether a Jew should celebrate Christmas continued and expanded within the Jewish community, parallel to the growing influence of Christmas as a public holiday. Precisely at the beginning of the twentieth century, Christmas had so vastly changed in observance and scope that it posed a serious dilemma for American Jews. Previously, during the nineteenth century, the celebration of Christmas in America had been confined to the domestic and church domains. With the emergence of a more public form of Christmas in the early decades of the twentieth century, private ritual overflowed into the public domain, altering both the environment and the experience of public space. An expectation evolved: "in Christmas lay a key to social peace, a goal grown more important as immigration rates rose higher and higher in the late nineteenth and early decades of the twentieth century."[42] As early as 1903, a public debate about the issue of Jews celebrating Christmas laid bare two opposing, albeit prevalent, views. In 1906, Rabbi Judah Leon Magnes (at the time, the rabbi of Temple Emanu-El in Manhattan), proffered that Jews should neither fear nor reject Christmas. Magnes, aware of the social trends of the day, suggested that Christmas might even facilitate Jews in strengthening their own beliefs and noted that, although many Jews protested the celebration of Christmas, others "'silently brought trees and lights into their homes."[43]

A contemporary of Magnes, Rabbi Samuel Schulman of Temple Beth El in New York City, espoused the contra viewpoint. Schulman adamantly opposed Christmas entertainment in the public schools and its inherent Christology. Schulman's position was prophetic in that as early as 1905, a New York school principal, F. F. Harding, exhorted his mainly Jewish audience to be more "Christlike." The Jewish community responded dramatically and resolutely by persuading the Committee on Elementary Schools to censure Harding for sectarian teaching in the public schools. During the following year, Jews in synagogues throughout New York City convened meetings to discuss the impact of Christmas celebrations in the public schools on Jewish school children; as a result, Jewish parents and their school-aged children staged a boycott of the school's closing holiday ceremonies.

The public debate persisted until the onset of World War II. Christmas became increasingly ingrained in the American popular ethos at the same time as the first generations of American-born Jews (whose parents were part of the historic turn-of-the-century exodus from Eastern Europe) were struggling to make decisions regarding acculturation. In the December 6, 1939, issue of the *Christian Century*, Rabbi Louis Witt of Dayton, Ohio, published an article entitled "The Jew Celebrates Christmas." Rabbi Witt described his experiences as a rabbi in addressing the growing number of Jews who celebrated Christmas: "I pleaded and scolded, waxed wrathful and tearful, year in and year out—in vain! The Jew today observes Christmas more than ever."[44] Rabbi Witt argued that Christians had become more liberal in their teachings, which accentuated the "universal humanness" of Jesus' teaching rather than a specific religious doctrine: "If Christmas were only Christian, the Jew would be only Jewish. . . . A theological, ecclesiastical Christmas finds and leaves the Jew the same 'infidel' he has ever been." Witt further commented that his own children felt deprived of the joys inherent to the holiday and that the "friendliness and goodwill" of Christmas made it alluring to people of all credos, including Jews. For Rabbi Witt, celebrating Christmas did not proclaim that the Jew was "thereby drawn by even the breadth of a hair nearer to the worship of an ecclesiastical Christ and that he [was] meeting the Christian on common ground which is both nobly Christian and nobly Jewish." The celebration of Christmas by Jews meant that the Jew was creating what could be termed a common denominator with the Christian. Witt concluded, "I say then, as a rabbi, thank God for Christmas! May it, in the spirit of its Judeo-Christian founder, bring forth in ever fuller measure the love that is hidden away in the hearts of men. . . . Is it neither treason of Jew nor triumph of Christian but partnership of Jew and Christian in the making of a better world in which the Christ can have part only by energizing and perpetuating and hallowing the partnership." According to Witt, this strategy of self-protection protected the Jews from being shunned by a culture that had assisted them in their successful Americanization.

Interestingly, and not surprisingly, the Christian editor of the *Christian Century* sided with Witt's argument to "release the spirit of Jewry from bondage to a tradition which denies it the right to participate in a free and gladsome celebration of the birthday of Jesus."[45] Arguing that both Jewish and Christian Americans living in "a world of tolerance, of political liberalism, of democracy," should naturally acknowledge "Jesus' Jewishness" and share "this common historical ground. . . . [I]n the environment of American tolerance . . . it is not fair to democracy to cherish a religious faith which provides a sanction for racial and cultural or any other form of separatism." The exchange in the *Christian Century* did not go unnoticed. Rabbi Edward Israel of Har Sinai Reform congregation of Baltimore introduced his letter: "It ought to be stated at the very outset that practically one hundred percent of the spokesmen of contemporary Jewish religious life will differ from Rabbi Witt's conclusions."[46] Furthermore, Israel termed Witt's comments "an affront to my devout Christian friends." Rabbi Israel continued, "the truly devout Christian . . . has far more respect for the Jew who, conscientious in his own religious loyalties, does not observe Christmas, than for the Witt type of Jew who tries to crawl into Christmas observance, salving what remains of his Jewish conscience by endeavoring to water down and compromise with Christian doctrine. . . . The only one honest way for the Jew to celebrate Christmas . . . is as Christ's birthday." Penne L. Restad in *Christmas in America* concludes that Rabbi Israel had neither the history of Christmas nor American societal trends on his side. Christmas had increasingly emerged as a secular community-based holiday, fraught with public pageants, an extended and calculated shopping period, and alluring, imperceptibly Christian accoutrements of which everyone, even Jews, if they so desired, might participate.

The debate about Christmas within the Jewish community may have been stoked, in part, by fundamental differences in attitudes of the two prominent waves of Jewish immigrants. The relatively affluent community from Germany that arrived first had a more open attitude toward the Christmas holiday, and, over successive generations, their attitudes took root both at home and in the Reform temples that they established. Meanwhile, the much larger and impoverished wave of immigrants from Eastern Europe that followed later was more restrictive. The contrasting experiences of these two groups affected their adaptations to mainstream America and their attitudes, in particular, toward Christmas. I now will consider the Eastern European Jews immigrating to the United States nearly fifty years after the wave of German Jews became incorporated into mainstream America.

Eastern European Jews Reject Christmas

Between 1880 and 1924, a wave of two million Eastern European Jewish immigrants brought to America a much stronger antipathy to Christmas. By the time they arrived in the United States, Christmas had already been declared a national holiday, and most people celebrated the nonwork day both in church and at home. Eastern European Jews saw symbols of Christmas displayed in public spaces and greetings exchanged between family members and coworkers. Eastern European Jews were puzzled about this holiday, for their memories were often mired in anti-Semitic experiences in Eastern Europe.

In Poland, very few Jews had embraced Christmas customs. The small number of Eastern European Jews who celebrated Christmas did so in a fashion similar to that of the secularized German-speaking Jews; however, written accounts of such behavior among Polish immigrants are few. A rare exemplar of Jews who did embrace Christmas traditions was Rosa Luxemburg (1871–1919), the economist and intellectual Marxist revolutionary who helped establish the Social Democratic Party of Poland and Lithuania before emigrating to Germany in 1898. As a child, Luxemburg studied at a Polish Catholic school attended by few other Jews. As an adult she celebrated Christmas. Writing from Breslau prison in Germany in December 1917 to her friend, Sonya Liebkneckht, Luxemburg reflected on her second year in prison: "The Christmas tree this year is rather inferior to the one I had last year. I don't know where I'm going to put the eight candles I bought for it."[47] (Luxemburg was later murdered by German army officers in Berlin.)

Another example from Poland derives from an anonymous Jewish teenager's autobiographical statement, which refers to her youth in the 1920s and 1930s: "Both Mother and Father were brought up in extremely religious households. They felt liberated when they left their childhood homes, away from this pressure, and—as often happens in such cases—they became completely secular. In addition to their lack of religiosity, my parents developed a desire to assimilate. We children didn't really know who we were, because of the way we were raised. At Christmas we put up Christmas trees; we had Christmas Eve suppers, and we broke wafers. The main reason for this was that we lived on country estates. These celebrations were held for the servants, so we took part as well."[48] The breaking and sharing of wafers, part of a traditional Polish Christmas Eve dinner, signifies a close bond with family members.

In neighboring Russia and other countries where the Russian Orthodox Church prevailed, Christmas was celebrated on the eve of January 6, the feast of Epiphany, and the day of January 7. Because Jews lived in fear, they shuttered themselves in their homes on Christmas to protect themselves against assault. In Jewish hamlets (*shtetls*), small towns, and villages, the local Jews avoided all contact with their Christian neighbors during Christmas. In Russian and in White Russian towns, Jews, fearing that dogs would attack them, remained in their homes on Christmas and Easter.[49] Jews placed protective covers over holy books and vessels containing food and liquids because they worried about demons being unleashed on this most unholy of nights.[50]

Christmas and Easter were dangerous periods for Jews in Eastern Europe because local Christians were incited by their clergy's reiteration of the polemic that Jews were cursed for killing Jesus. One of the most violent waves of pogroms occurred in April 1881 in the south central Ukrainian city of Elisavetgrad. Month after month the violence spread from village to village and hamlet to hamlet until 265 Jewish communities in this area were affected. Ultimately, the violence spread outward to every region in Russia and Poland.[51] The last of this groundswell of pogroms during that year broke out in Warsaw on Christmas Day, December 25, 1881. A panic in a Warsaw church triggered this insidious event. Many inside the church suffocated. Provocateurs insinuated that Jews were responsible. Incited to frenzy, gangs of hooligans burst into Warsaw synagogues and Jewish homes and shops. Most Jews barricaded themselves in their houses. The Warsaw chief of police went on vacation on Christmas Eve and resumed work after the pogrom was over.

Violent attacks against Central and East European Jews on Christmas continued until the outbreak of World War II. Few Christmas-specific personal testimonies have been documented from the years leading up to World War II, but the following firsthand account attests to what were probably representative fears that Jews experienced during the Christmas season in Europe. Figee Heimfield recalls her husband's Christmas travails in Central Europe, in the 1930s in Czechoslovakia:

> My husband was stoned because they blamed him for killing their God, Jesus, and on Christmas night he didn't dare to go out because the gentiles used to go caroling from house to house and beating up the Jews who were outside so he stayed in our home, and my mother always prepared sour cabbage soup with potatoes and toast with garlic. Why this kind of food? It smelled right, I don't know what it symbolized. Christmas Day was a regular day, we were very sad because we saw them caroling and we saw them to be happy and we were very unhappy. We were always beaten up as children, [they] told us to go to Palestine

and we couldn't go there. This happened when I was a child in between the years 1930 and 1939.[52]

The history of violence incited against Jews at Christmastime in Christian Europe and the fear with which Jews reacted to Christmas date from the Middle Ages. This historical anxiety is reflected in the traditions surrounding the words and names invoked by European Jews to identify and describe Christmas. To insulate Jews in Europe from the potential harm of Jesus and the holiday commemorating his birth, Jews were admonished by their rabbis not to mention the names "Jesus" and "Christmas." As far back as the twelfth century, Rabbi Eliezer of Metz prohibited mentioning the name of Jesus.[53] Uttering the name "Jesus" was taboo. In this spirit, East European Jews referred to Jesus using folk names such as *Yoshke* and the holiday of Christmas as *Kratzmach. Yoshke* is a play on Jesus' Hebrew name *Yeshu,* coupled with *Kratzmach,* which sounds like Christmas, derives from the Yiddish *kratz,* meaning to scratch. Other Yiddish folk names for Jesus were *Yoyzl* (referring to the cross on which Jesus was hung), *Yosl Pondrik,* and *Taluy* (the Hebrew word for one who was crucified).

East European Jews' use of euphemisms to refer to Christmas transcends being merely descriptive and actually denote feelings of fear and dread. According to Jeffrey Shandler, these names varied by region.[54] In Galicia and the Ukraine, Christmas was referred to variously. *Moydredike Nahkht* (the fearful night) directly alludes to being fearful of persecution on Christmas Eve. The name *Blinde Nahkht* (blind night) denotes a night in which the light of Torah study is curtailed. *Finstere Nahkht* (the dark night) signifies the darkness maintained in Jewish homes during Christmas Eve. Each of these names, as well as *Beyz Geboyrenish* (evil birthing) and *Veynahkht* (woe-night), reflects the character of the Eastern European response to Christmas. The Jews in southern and central Europe used several terms to denote Christmas Eve: *Goyim Nahkht* (gentiles' night), *Tole Nahkht* (night of the crucified one), and *Yoyzls Nahkht* (Jesus' night); each of these verbally scoff at the very source of Jewish fear while simultaneously acknowledging its existence.

The most popular name given to Christmas Eve, gaining currency both in Europe and later in the United States, was *Nittel Nahkht.* The roots of this Judeo-German word can be traced to the Latin *natalis,* as in *Natalis Dies,* day of birth with direct reference to Jesus.[55] Some scholars derive the word *Nittel* from the Hebrew word *taluy,* the "hanged one." Yet others sought the origin of *Nittel* in the Hebrew word *Natal*, meaning "taken away," referring to Jesus having become an apostate from the Jewish religion or to the fact he was ultimately arrested.[56] Another explanation of *Nittel*, referring to Christmas Eve—a time when Jews customarily abstained from studying Torah—is the acronym that stands for the Yiddish "*Nit Iden-Tore-Lernen*" (Jews do not study Torah). Of all of the various names Jews used to refer to Christmas in Eastern Europe, *Nittel* was that most commonly transported to America by Ashkenazi Jews, in general, and Hasidic Jews, in particular.

The fear of Jesus and Christianity, as expressed by Jews on Christmas, actually has deeper roots and harkens back to a time in which Jews provided explanations for why Jesus was such a powerful figure among Christians and how his special status might be countered. Jesus' power, according to medieval Jewish sources, derives from magic that he acquired by stealing the mystical name of God (in Hebrew, *shem ha-meforash*), pronounced only by the High Priest one day of the year on Yom Kippur in the Jerusalem Temple. Jesus affixed this mysterious name of God to his foot; he was thus able to fly in the air and perform extraordinary feats. Because of this misuse of divine powers, God punished Jesus for his apostasy by causing him to fall to the ground.

This tale is found in *Ma'ase Talui* (Fables of the Crucifix) and *Toledot Yeshu* (Tales of Jesus), early Jewish compilations of stories about Jesus that discredit his divinity by using an unorthodox life history. These narratives portray Jesus as a demonic and evil spirit and reject him as a messiah or divinity. They appeared in Hebrew in the thirteenth century and were translated in different versions and languages, including Arabic, Yiddish, Judeo-Spanish (Ladino), and Judeo-Persian.[57] *Toledot Yeshu* describes Jesus as the illegitimate son of Mary, resulting from her relationship with the Roman soldier Panthrera. God punishes his use of black magic by decreeing that he crawl each year through the excrement and filth of latrines on Christmas Eve.[58]

Although, for obvious reasons, these tales were read and recounted in secret, particularly on Christmas, they became a matter of public record through Christian polemicists—some of whom were Jews who converted to Christianity and wished to discredit Judaism for blaspheming Jesus. The sixteenth-century apostate Johann Pfefferkorn writes: "They [the Jews] believe and maintain that the lord Jesus, punished by God because of his apostasy and false teaching, has to wander in all pits of excrement or latrines throughout the world that same night [Christmas Eve]."[59] According to Jeffrey Shandler, the "language, lore and custom" of these

tales were the means by which East European Jews negotiated their relationship to Jesus and Christmas, thereby helping them to deflect their own
sense of social vulnerability.[60]

PLAYING GAMES ON CHRISTMAS

In Eastern Europe, Jews stayed in the safety of their homes on Christmas
Eve. On *Nittel* night (Christmas Eve) many played a special game of cards,
called "21" (in Yiddish, *ein und tsvansig*). Why did Jews in Europe play
card games on Christmas? Orthodox Jews in Europe believed that Torah
study should occupy Jews day and night. Through Torah study, the world
has reason to exist; without Torah study, the world would simply cease to
exist. Regarding the practice on Christmas Eve and the commemoration of
the birth of Jesus, one of their brethren who had gone astray, Jews, however, did not wish to lend Jesus credence through study of holy texts.
Beginning in the sixteenth century, Jews in Europe, particularly in an array
of Hasidic sects, adopted the custom of not studying Torah on Christmas
Eve. Instead, they played cards, an activity that would have been
forbidden on any other night of the year because of its association with
gambling.[61]

Because Jews refrained from studying Torah, they filled their Christmas
Eve time with leisurely activities. Beginning in the fifteenth century, card-
playing was a popular pastime during Hanukkah. Despite having strong
associations with gambling, card-playing on Christmas Eve was a logical
extension as it often overlapped with Hanukkah. Abstention from Torah
study facilitated the rabbis' relaxation of stringent rules regarding card-
playing on *Nittel Nahkht*.[62] Israel Abrahams, in his book *Jewish Life in the
Middle Ages*, asserts that "sometimes, as was also the case with the Christian
students of the Cambridge University in England in the age of Milton
(1608–1674), card-playing was permitted by Jews at Christmas." While
there are no other early sources describing Jews playing cards on Christmas
Eve, Hanukkah nights were, however, occasions for playing cards and other
games of chance, especially soon after the candles are lit.[63] Chess, the game
of heads and tails, and a dice game called ticktack were also played on
Hanukkah.[64] It is interesting that evidence of game-playing as a Hanukkah
pastime among Jews endures through the medium of illustrated artwork.
An 1880 Moritz Oppenheim painting provides a glimpse into the living
room of a Jewish family in Germany. The painting depicts Hanukkah
candles flickering in the window while the Jewish family is absorbed in
chess, cards, children's games, and conversation.

Figure 1.6. Moritz Oppenheim, *The Kindling of the Hanukkah Lights*, 1880.
Oil on canvas, 80.4 × 57.2 cm. Gift of Sally Cramer, London, in memory of her
brother Herbert. The Israel Museum, Jerusalem. B51.01.0104. Photo © The Israel
Museum, Jerusalem, photographer: David Harris.

Among the Chabad-Lubavitch community, playing chess on Christmas
Eve was a popular activity in Europe. To corroborate the tradition of playing chess on *Nittel*, certain Lubavitcher Hasidim point to a famous photograph portraying Rabbi Yosef Yitzchak Schneersohn, sixth Lubavitch rabbi,
and his son-in-law and successor, Rabbi Menachem Mendel Schneerson,
playing chess in 1937 at a spa in Austria where Rabbi Yosef was resting from
an illness. (The historical validity of this photograph is now questioned by

the Chabad-Lubavitch community.) Whatever the activity, the purpose of chess and other games for Hasidic Jews, aside from their simple value as entertainment, is to engage in activities and tell stories that would lessen Jesus' powers and reduce the importance of Christmas.

This antipathy to Christmas coupled with the custom of playing cards and chess on Christmas Eve continued unabated in the United States by many Hasidic groups, who brought with them from Europe longstanding attitudes toward Christmas Eve. Anthropologist Jerome Mintz, interviewing the Hasidim of New York, quotes legends he collected that mention the dangers posed by Christmas. "There is always a war between light and darkness," between Jews and Christianity, said one Hasidic Jew. Jesus "was drawn to the other side of the fence. And so in effect he becomes an inverted magnet." A *tzaddik* (rabbinic master), he explains, pulls the sacredness of heaven toward him. In contrast, Jesus attempts to draw sacredness to him on Christmas. Ceasing to study Torah is an important way to thwart Jesus' power.[65] Based on the teachings of the late Lubavitcher Rabbi Yosef Yitzchak Schneersohn and his son-in-law and successor, Rabbi Menachem Mendel Schneerson, a Hasidic website implores Hasidim to use *Nittel* in a positive way to negate the power of Jesus, "to perform acts connected with wisdom, or connected with charity and kindness, or connected with the proper functioning of . . . home."[66] Today, Satmar Hasidim in New York communities call Christmas Eve *Bittel Nakhkht*, which means "wasted night," a wordplay of *Nittel Nakhkht*; the communities refer to the Hasidim's frustration about Christmas that is rooted in temporarily suspending their study of Torah.

CHRISTMAS ON HENRY STREET

Rejection of Christmas was one powerful response to a holiday that harbored negative associations for Jews hailing from Eastern Europe. Certain of these immigrants settling in the United States were not able to leave behind haunting memories of persecution against Jews on Christmas Eve. Once in America, they did not know what to expect when Christmastime arrived. Illustrative of this mindset were members of a secular Romanian-Jewish family living in the Bronx in New York who remembered the persecution they suffered on Christmas Eve in Romania, and, as a result, no one in the family was permitted out of the house on Christmas Eve in America.[67]

Many Eastern European Jewish immigrants simply could not fathom that Jewish families of German-Jewish descent brought Christmas trees, a symbol of Christianity, into their American homes. The historian Ruth Gay, the daughter of Russian-Jewish immigrants, wrote emotionally about her family's perception of Christmas in New York City in the 1920s and 1930s:

> For them [my parents], the associations with any Christian celebration were of potential danger. In the Old Country, holidays were periods of heightened tempers when an unlucky word, a misunderstood gesture, could have violent consequences. We who were born in America had no such fears and could enjoy the cheer, the music, the parties to which we were invited, and the seductive atmosphere. . . . The immigrant generation could never have been made to believe that there was any equation between Hanukkah and Christmas because fortuitously they fell together in the calendar. Nor did we think that Christmas was a secular holiday.[68]

Further, Gay wrote about her family's repulsion by the thought of having a Christmas tree: "It was no more possible for us to have asked our parents for a Christmas tree than to have asked for a suckling pig for dinner. There was no context for a Christmas tree in our lives."

And yet, the idea of avoiding or rejecting Christmas among the Eastern European Jewish population in New York City was not absolute. Historian Andrew R. Heinze noted that the impact of the Christmas tree on Jewish children was immeasurable. The appeal of the holiday trickled down from the highest echelons of society to the immigrant Jewish population. Acknowledging the sway of Christmas upon immigrant Jews, the January 11, 1899, Yiddish *Tageblatt* newspaper opined that it was unnecessary to venture uptown to behold the holiday's effect as "East Broadway and Henry Street showed quite a number of Christmas trees in Jewish houses."[69]

Feature stories in the *New York Tribune* and the Yiddish daily *Forward* profiled the extent to which the Jews had embraced Christmas gift-giving. On December 25, 1904, the *New York Tribune* reported: "Santa Claus visited the East Side last night, and hardly missed a tenement house." The report continued with a later remark: "In the homes of the poor Hebrews, as well as of the well to do, Christmas is being celebrated with never a thought that it is the birthday of Him whom their forbears crucified more than nineteen centuries ago." In confronting the tone of this article, Heinze contended, "despite the attitude of pretentious bigotry behind this report, its findings were substantiated by the Jewish press."

An article, bearing the headline "They Are Pious, But They Observe Christmas Too," appeared in the *Forward* on the same date as the *New York Tribune* article. The *Forward* article claimed that many Jewish families, running the gamut between freethinkers and the traditionally observant, bought Christmas presents to assuage the demands of their children. And yet, according to this same article, children were not the only beneficiaries of the Christmas gift-giving ritual. The *Forward* article stated that spouses and neighbors in tenement houses also exchanged gifts. Regardless of the reason for its adoption, the practice of gift-giving was not without its detractors. One social commentator derided devout Jews who would indulge the whims of their children by forsaking the dictates of their religion, by invoking: "the soul-commanding voice of Isaiah" who would "chide the people for this error—could he but speak today."

Interestingly, Andrew L. Heinze argued that the sudden popularity of gift-giving among Jewish immigrants reflected "not an inclination toward Christianity but an effort to embrace the American spirit." Heinze rested his argument on a *Forward* article that asked: "Who says that we are not Americanizing?" Buying Christmas gifts constituted "the first thing that demonstrates that one is not a green-horn," and Heinze thus concluded that the Jewish immigrants were attracted to America's seeming devotion to monetary generosity and not solely to material consumption. In fact, Heinze asserted that, despite the seeming pervasiveness of emblems of a Christian holiday in the tenements of the Lower East Side of Manhattan, "Jews had no intention of adopting Christmas. The festival had become secular in nature, its symbols posed a minimal threat to Judaism."

As for the ritual of decorating Christmas trees, which was firmly established in public schools and settlement houses, Heinze provided anecdotal evidence from Abraham Stern, a member of the New York City Board of Education in 1906. Stern was quoted in the *Tageblatt* as saying that most kindergartens in Jewish neighborhoods had trees and that "in many cases the Jewish mothers helped in trimming the trees."[70]

Jenna Weissman Joselit has demonstrated that the Yiddish press facilitated the cooption of Christmas. Yiddish newspapers familiarized readers with not only the smallest details of the national holiday but also the so-called Christmas spirit by drawing comparisons between Yom Kippur and Christmas that highlighted each holiday's underlying philosophy.[71] Throughout the early decades of the twentieth century, the *Forward* contained articles and editorials about Christmas presents and other holiday topics to enlighten readers about the American Christmas spirit as a season of giving and receiving gifts.

GOING TO THE NICKELODEONS ON CHRISTMAS

Even though most commercial establishments were closed on Christmas, immigrant Jews frequented entertainment venues that catered to

Americans who did not celebrate Christmas. Jews residing in New York City were fortunate in being surrounded by a world of entertainment consisting of Yiddish theater, movies, arcades, dance halls, cafes, and vaudeville houses to which, in fact, Jews contributed as store owners, actors, movie theater proprietors, and audiences. The fact that Jews lived in crowded conditions in the Lower East Side meant that entertainment centers catered to a built-in constituency that clamored for diversion from their long and difficult living and working conditions. Jews on the Lower East Side of Manhattan became avid purveyors and consumers of commercial leisure.[72] Eastern European Jews, who spoke Yiddish, enjoyed attending performances of the Yiddish theater, which stayed open on Christmas.[73] As early as 1917, theater advertisements for plays being performed on Christmas Day appeared in the Yiddish press; some plays actually opened on Christmas.

A film that generated significant controversy at that time was entitled *The Jew's Christmas*. The narrative involves a rabbi who sells his copy of the Torah to buy a Christmas tree for a poor little girl. It is ultimately revealed that this little girl is the rabbi's granddaughter, and the film ends happily with the family reunited around the Christmas tree. According to Jewish film scholar Judith Thissen, *Moving Picture World* documented that a large delegation of rabbis witnessed the projection of the film and was satisfied with the story and its treatment of Jewish ceremony and custom. The rabbis did look with disfavor on the title of the film. Thissen then asserts that the film was viewed with less tolerance by *Tageblatt* newspaper, which found the last scenes particularly offensive.[74]

On a broader scale, the Lower East Side saw the expansion of the nickelodeon, a moving picture of short-duration accompanied by illustrated songs. The price of admittance was a nickel. This medium was very popular among Jewish residents; nickelodeon shows ran in a continuous loop from morning until evening. People went from one theater to the next: "It is heaven and earth and moving pictures," reported the *Forward* in May 1908. There were more nickelodeons situated in the Lower East Side than anywhere else in New York City. Andrew Heinze notes that nineteen nickel theaters were scattered along the Second and Third Avenue streetcar lines of the East Side. By 1908, forty-two nickelodeons were located in or adjacent to the Lower East Side, and ten were in the uptown area branded as Jewish Harlem.[75] In 1904 Adolph Zukor, the first nickel theater entrepreneur in Manhattan, opened above his penny arcade a modest theater that was accessible through a glass staircase beneath which water cascaded over lights of changing hue.[76] On Jewish holidays, the nickelodeons and Yiddish theaters attracted big crowds.

The high attendance levels of Jewish audiences in movie theaters did not go unnoticed. Christian authorities apparently were distressed by the fact that Jews went to the movies on Christmas Eve in New York. In fact, Mayor George B. McClellan Jr., believing that the new medium degraded community morals, ordered the closing of all New York City nickelodeons on December 24, 1908.[77] The National Board of Review of Motion Pictures was founded in 1909 to protest the mayor's censorship. Its lobbying effort was successful in facilitating the reopening of nickelodeons on Christmas.

Jews living in the New York metropolitan area were fortunate in having vacation and travel venues where they could spend quality time during the Christmas break. The children and grandchildren of Jewish immigrants frequented the Catskills in upstate New York as a way to enjoy the country and the company of other Jews.[78] Prior to the Second World War, the Morningside Hotel was the only resort in upstate New York to remain open for Christmas. Most of the hotel patrons were Jewish. After the Second World War, people remember the crowds at the Catskills hotels at Christmastime to be particularly large, where the resorts attracted as many people as attended services on the High Holidays. From Christmas through New Year's Day, Grossinger's resort reached its full capacity of fifteen hundred guests, a pattern characteristic of Passover week and the Jewish high holidays.[79]

Jewish-owned hotels in the Catskills did not acknowledge the period between Christmas and New Year's Day in any special manner. Jack Landman, the activity director at Kutsher's hotel resort in the Catskills, remarked that Kutsher's was a Jewish resort with a Jewish clientele, and that no special holiday celebration was necessary. "In a sense, we were insulated from the Christmas observance," Landman commented.[80] The hotels staged nightly live entertainment showcasing a comedy or a variety show. Although not Christmas-specific, these comedy performances were the first on record to be held on Christmas. Comedians such as Danny Kaye, Jerry Lewis, Sid Caeser, Red Buttons, and Henny Youngman became Catskill headliners, beginning their careers as *toomlers* (from the Yiddish word *tumlen*, meaning to cause a commotion) that created constant entertainment for the guests.[81] Catskill comedians performed their regular routines emphasizing Jewish-themed jokes; however, there was an occasional mention of Christmas. In the 1950s, the following joke was widely circulated: "Mrs. Moscowitz tells her Orthodox rabbi, 'My grandchildren are driving me crazy. They want to have a Christmas tree. Could you maybe make some dispensation, a *broche* [Hebrew benediction] over such a tree?' 'Impossible,' says the rabbi. 'But tell me, what exactly is Christmas?'

She consults a more lenient rabbi, a Conservative. 'No,' he says. 'I'm sorry. But tell me, what exactly is a Christmas tree?' She turns to the young new Reform rabbi. 'I'll be glad to,' he assures her. 'Only tell me: what exactly is a *broche*?'" Kaplan deems this joke about Christmas to be rare and stereotypical, but the joke is telling in its notice of the differing Jewish denominations' responses to Christmas.[82] The Orthodox rabbi, in adapting a position of ignorance about Christmas, accords it no recognition. The Conservative rabbi, who represents a modernizing force within religious tradition, understands well the impact of Christmas but cannot fathom placing a Christmas tree in a Jewish home. The Reform movement, often the brunt of jokes for its relaxed views of Jewish ritual, is represented by a rabbi who is more familiar with Christmas than with Judaism. This kind of joking about Christmas, while not widespread at that time, can be viewed as the harbinger of modern Jewish comedic performances on Christmas half a century later.

The multitude of early Jewish responses in facing Christmas in America provides a firm foundation for understanding contemporary Jewish attitudes to Christmas. Whether hailing from Germany or Eastern Europe, Jews who emigrated to the United States in the nineteenth and early twentieth centuries discovered in Christmas an occasion for considering their relationship to the larger American society in which they lived. They faced a national holiday with a strong and growing public presence. Christmas was difficult to avoid or ignore. Depending on their religious outlook and family's European country of origin, American Jews who could not accept the religious or cultural elements of Christmas endured the holiday season as an American reality. By the middle of the twentieth century, however, the children and grandchildren of these immigrants developed new strategies to cope with Christmas. One of the many new strategies was to find a Jewish parallel to Christmas by magnifying Hanukkah and providing home celebrations and children's programs that would vie with the excitement that surrounded Christmas.

CHAPTER 2

HANUKKAH
COMES OF AGE

THE NEW JEWISH CHRISTMAS

Beginning in 2009 and during each year of his presidency, President Barack Obama and First Lady Michele Obama hosted Hanukkah parties at the White house for more than five hundred guests. For his first Hanukkah party at the White House, President Obama continued the approach of his predecessor, George W. Bush; he served kosher food at the presidential Hanukkah party. The White House kitchen was ritually cleansed and koshered (including ovens, appliances, dishes, and cutlery) by rabbis of the Chabad-Lubavitch movement. President Obama started a new presidential tradition, however, by becoming the first president to distribute two versions of a national Hanukkah message, one in English and another in Hebrew.

National religious celebration is not new to the White House and its occupants. Calvin Coolidge was the first president to preside over the first national Christmas tree-lighting ceremony in 1923 at President's Park.[1] A sitting president of the United States had not officially acknowledged Hanukkah until the latter half of the twentieth century when President Jimmy Carter first lit a menorah in 1979 in a formal ceremony at Lafayette Park, which is situated across the street from the White House and near the national Christmas tree. President Carter's official presidential daily diary for December 17, 1979, notes that the "President participated in a lighting ceremony for the National Menorah" from 6:53 to 7:05 P.M.[2] The first formal menorah lighting, organized in the White House's Oval Office in 1993 during the presidency of Bill Clinton, gave Hanukkah a level of increased formal presidential attention previously reserved for the Christmas tree. President George W. Bush expanded the Hanukkah celebration in 2001 when he organized a Hanukkah reception for leaders of the Jewish community.

With all of this national attention, it is difficult to imagine that there was a time when Jews in America considered Hanukkah to be a minor holiday. Depicting events that took place in the year 165 before the Common Era, Hanukkah was primarily a home-based observance, celebrated by lighting a menorah (originally filled with oil) and reciting appropriate blessings. During colonial times in America, for example, scant mention is made of congregational menorah lightings, such as by Jews settling in Georgia in 1733, in New York at Shearith Israel synagogue, and in Newport, Rhode Island, where the lamp was lit with "sweet oil, and the holiday was observed in a formal fashion."[3]

When German Jews arrived in the United States in the middle of the nineteenth century, they devoted scant time to Hanukkah and directed more attention to Christmas. The German Jews perceived this as a way to identify as Americans, to assimilate culturally, and to advance in American society. Beginning in the 1850s, the Jewish press repeatedly charged that many Jews did not celebrate Hanukkah and that some even lost sight of when it occurred during a given year.[4] This lack of focus and shift in level of observance was not overlooked by the rabbis and leaders of the Reform movement in the United States, the Jewish religious denomination of choice for these German Jews. These religious leaders bemoaned the decline of Hanukkah celebration in Jewish homes.

In February 1867, Rabbi Julius Eckman of Congregation Emanu-El in San Francisco rebuked congregants for abandoning their own festival (Hanukkah) in favor of Christmas.[5] Eckman, railing against the practice, stated that Jews guilty of "such a want of taste" came only rarely from "families of education and refinement." He exclaimed vehemently that only those "who know little of Judaism and less of Christianity" would "betray their littleness of mind and their misplacement by fortune, by playing such a ridiculous part as for a Jew to be aping Christians." Eckman reproached such Jews for playing "the pigmy while he ought to prove himself a giant," stating that "self-negation" of this type "must meet with the condemnation of the sincere Jew and the contempt of the intelligent Christian." Lastly, Eckman augured that these acts would render any such parent "contemptible in the eyes of his children, who, one day, will find out the imbecility of their parents and judge them accordingly." Dr. Eckman concluded with the following advice to his readers: "Drink water from thine own cistern (Proverbs 5:15) and do not ape the stranger."[6]

American Reform rabbis of the time looked at Hanukkah anew for the inspirational message it sent about the struggle for religious freedom, a principle that resonated with Americans of all persuasions. To help promote Hanukkah, Rabbi Isaac Mayer Wise in 1859 ran a serialized fictional account of the Maccabees in thirty-nine installments in the *American Israelite* newspaper.[7] Because of this renewed focus, the 1860s saw a mushrooming of synagogue Hanukkah celebrations involving students and faculty of Sunday Schools housed in Reform temples. The press first mentioned this wave of Hanukkah euphoria in 1870 when the *American Israelite* identified Sunday Schools across the country that were organizing Hanukkah pageants.[8] These Hanukkah celebrations made such an impact on the Jewish population in the United States that they were touted as an antidote to, and worthy competitor of, Christmas. Hanukkah was fast becoming the Jewish Christmas. The list of synagogues and rabbis promoting Hanukkah grew exponentially.

As Hanukkah observances moved to larger public venues, its promoters searched for new celebratory models. During the 1880s, experimental and eclectic temple celebrations included elements not solely identified with the story of Hanukkah. Most interesting, aspects of the popular holiday of Purim, which had made a large impact through the civic Purim Ball, found expression during Hanukkah programming. Queen Esther, the heroine of the Scroll of Esther that is traditionally read on Purim, was often found to make her grand entrance during Hanukkah.[9] Hanukkah celebrations in America were alluring to Jewish civic and fraternal youth organizations, such as B'nai B'rith and the Young Men's Hebrew Association (YMHA). These institutions were founded in the 1840s and 1850s in the United States by German Jews seeking fraternal support for social, recreational, and charitable activities. During the late 1870s and early 1880s, the YMHA sponsored a "Grand Revival of the Jewish National Holiday of Chanucka" that was held in New York at the Academy of Music. Organized by young professionals seeking to stem the tide of assimilation, a veritable cadre of Jewish philanthropists and business leaders, including many well-known German-Jewish bankers and businessman, supported these Hanukkah festivities. Investment banker Jesse Seligman (younger brother of Joseph), financier J. H. Schiff, bankers E. and M. Lehman of the Lehman Brothers firm, entrepreneur J. Rosenwald of Sears Roebuck, and clothier S. Bernheimer are just some of the notables in attendance who secured preferred seating.[10]

Elected government officials lent credence to this event by their presence, as noted not only in the Jewish press but also by the *New York Times*.

These papers gave the event considerable coverage, befitting its status as a premiere Jewish social event. This coverage also offered the non-Jewish public the opportunity to see the Jewish community in a positive light while celebrating victory over persecution. On December 17, 1879, the *New York Times* commented that the performance, consisting of "a series of tableaux, interspersed with Hebrew melodies ... were powerful in their conception, and in their execution artistic and brilliant."

In 1900, the very successful Manhattan-based Educational Alliance, another educational and social organization founded by German Jews for the benefit of new immigrants and the general Jewish community, hosted a performance of *Judas Maccabees*, based on Henry Wadsworth Longfellow's 1872 five-act play by that same name. Observing the emotional loss faced by immigrants who gave up traditions in order to assimilate (as represented in the play by the forces of ancient Hellenism), Wadsworth was keen to notice a confusion of identity, resulting in a person who was neither Greek nor Jewish. The play's message was not lost upon Jews at the precipice of a new century, many of whom were faced with deciding how much Jewish tradition was worth perpetuating.[11]

In contrast to their German-Jewish brethren, Eastern European Jews immigrating to America in the 1880s brought with them a history of commemorating Hanukkah at home. The more religious among them treated the holiday as an important part of the sacred calendar. These Eastern European Jews joined fraternal organizations established by their German forerunners and participated in public Hanukkah celebrations. By 1924, when Jewish immigration ceased, Hanukkah had become popular in Jewish homes, synagogues, and organizations.

Several forces, internal and external, converged in the United States during the period between 1880 and the close of immigration in 1924 to transform Hanukkah from a minor to a major holiday. As Jews immigrated and then prospered in America, they witnessed a surge of anti-Semitism at home and abroad. An era of "no Jews welcome" excluded Jews from hotels, medical colleges, and country clubs. In 1877, Joseph Seligman, a well-connected banker, and his family were suddenly denied entry into the Grand Union Hotel in Saratoga, New York, a vacation resort that he had frequented for many years. Exclusion from organizations and institutions of status forced German Jews to question how equal they were to their non-Jewish American counterparts. On the international scene, American Jews were shocked by false charges of treason made against the French officer Alfred Dreyfus who was found guilty in 1894 and incarcerated, despite worldwide protest.

Both German and Eastern European Jews began to rethink the benefit of assimilating and looked to Jewish traditions as bulwarks against anti-Semitism. Hanukkah's status in the United States was elevated to serve as a symbol of victory against tyranny, of the weak against the strong, of the need for strengthening Jewish identity and community. Younger, educated, college-aged Jews enrolled in greater numbers in major universities and relied on Jewish values to make their presence felt. The Menorah Society, a college organization formed at Harvard in 1906, adopted the Hanukkah menorah as a symbol of the light of Jewish knowledge that would support democracy and dispel world tyranny. Beginning in 1915 the society published the *Menorah Journal*, offering writers the opportunity to comment on how Judaism's values help promote a universal spirit of equality.[12] In their vision, Hanukkah would be elevated to a universal status on a par with Christmas, advocating both American idealism and civic responsibility.

Aware of the temptations presented by the celebration of Christmas, Anglo-Jewish and Yiddish presses exhorted Jews to "kindle the Chanukah lights a new, modern Israelite! Make the festival more than ever before radiant with the brightness and beauty of love and charity." Another leading press, the *Jewish Messenger*, suggested "trying the effect of the Hanukkah lights. If just for the experiment, try it."[13] The Festival of Lights had, in Andrew Heinze's words, "survived the impact of Christmas" and the "shocks of immigration." Heinze concluded that the increasing popularity of a secular Christmas, rather than debilitating Hanukkah, resulted in its revivification. Heinze supported this contention with a report in the *Jewish Daily News* on December 21, 1897, of passengers on the Second Avenue "E" train heading down First Street being awestruck by "rows of burning candles that illuminated the windows of tenement house after tenement house."[14]

HANUKKAH GIFT-GIVING

As Hanukkah grew in popularity, merchandisers produced a line of Hanukkah decorations and games to parallel the commercial wares and decorations offered for sale at Christmas. Less emphasis was placed on the religious aspects of Christmas and Hanukkah and more on secular components and expressions of popular culture, "modernized and co-modified," in the words of Jenna Joselit.[15] Religious rites commemorating Jesus' birth gave way to family celebrations, visits from Santa Claus, and holiday gift exchanges. These secular qualities easily spilled over into Hanukkah, which traditionally brought family members together to light the menorah, to offer gifts (such as Hannukah *gelt*, or money) to children, and to send greetings to Jewish and non-Jewish neighbors. As Heinze observed, "The increasing sophistication of retail displays, the growing mythology of Santa Claus as a grand dispenser of merchandise, the ornamentation of home and the tree, the development of card sending as social obligation, all of these qualities of the secular Christmas insured the superiority of the day in the hierarchy of festivals."[16]

Traditional Jews, who were less influenced by the popularity of Christmas, nevertheless saw the value in promoting gift-giving as means to entice children to celebrate Hanukkah. Despite castigating Jews for being overly involved in Christmas, the tradition-oriented *Yiddishes Tageblatt* newspaper sanctioned the popularity of gift-giving during the holiday season. The newspaper called "not for the abolition of gift-giving among Jews, but, instead, for the use of presents as a means of bolstering the enthusiasm surrounding Chanukah." And from the *Forward* newspaper in December 1910: "There's nothing sadder than a Jewish kid at Christmas. It's even more difficult in America, where the barriers between Jews and others are not as big. But there is a cure for what ails the Jewish child. It's Hanukkah! Does this holiday not fall around the same time as Christmas? And is this holiday not better than Christmas? When you get slapped, you turn the other cheek—that's Christmas. If you're willing to fight for it, you can win your freedom—that's Hanukkah."[17]

The Yiddish press in the United States was more than happy to accept advertisement dollars from retail establishments that promoted gifts for Jewish children and adults on Hanukkah. Yiddish newspapers advertised gifts "from automobiles to waffle irons."[18] A series of advertisements from the Colgate Company in 1925 suggested that "perfumes, shaving embroilments, and dental cream" would make ideal gifts.

Jewish gift-giving among immigrants soon expanded to recognizing non-Jewish neighbors in an act that made them feel less foreign and more typically American. Jews and those Americans who celebrated Christmas jointly participated and promoted the holiday spirit for the enjoyment of all. According to Jenna Weissman Joselit, the history of Hanukkah commercialization at this time demonstrates that the rise of gifts specifically tailored for Hanukkah ensured that Jewish children would not be jealous of the Christmas gifts being given by most American parents to their children.

Gifts for children included toys, books, decorations, and Hanukkah greeting cards filled with Hanukkah *gelt*. Children's books filled with

Hanukkah stories and rhymes often reinforced the benefits of gift-giving: "Aunt Mollie̊ came for Chanukah/Aunt Mollie is the bearer of gifts, specially selected for girls and boys." Popular children's books were also serialized, such as *The Adventures of K'tonton*, the Jewish Tom Thumb, beginning in 1935.[19] Joselit also mentions that toy manufacturers produced "boobas" (dolls) for girls and "kadurim" (balls) for boys, as well as games, records, papier-mâché decorations, and menorahs. Menorahs, the mainstay of Hanukkah celebrations, moved from simple homemade holders of candles or oil to elaborate designs fashioned from a variety of metals and in all kinds of shapes and sizes, including for the first time "electric menorahs, musical menorahs, and plastic menorahs."

The child's expectation of receiving plentiful and novel gifts, even if not through the hands of Santa, helped diminish attraction to Christmas. Gustav Gotheill, the rabbi of Temple Emanu-El in New York who played a significant role in tailoring Hanukkah to American culture, emphasized this point in 1889 when he said, "Family gatherings, merry making, presents, feasting, and giving the little ones a good time are things which the Jew takes as much pleasure as his Gentile neighbor."[20] Editorials thereafter reminded readers that Hanukkah has to become first and foremost a "true Children's Yontef (holiday)."[21] A 1925 *Morgen Journal* newspaper article made it clear that Hanukkah should become "an occasion for story-telling, gift-giving, and general festivity," including exchanging presents. Much creativity went into involving the children, including adapting games drawn from popular culture to Hanukkah, such as "a Hanukkah peanut hunt, a Jewish version of scrabble, and Hanukkah bowling." Rabbi Emil Hirsch of Temple Emanuel in Chicago wrote that Hanukkah provided as intense a manifestation of joy as Christmas. Both holidays shared a "vigorous story, dramatic incidents, strong personalities, fine home scenes, abundance of imagery, plenty of traditions, and home cheer."[22]

Rabbi Mordecai Kaplan, a professor at the Jewish Theological Seminary of America and later on a founder of the Reconstructionist movement in American Judaism, called for a pragmatic reformulation of the observance of both Purim and Hanukkah. Because Hanukkah falls on the calendar close to Christmas, Rabbi Kaplan deemed it necessary to shift the gift-giving tradition from Purim to Hanukkah, making gift-giving endemic to the Hanukkah celebration.[23] Kaplan observed that "Hanukkah . . . must be made as interesting and joyful for the Jewish child as Christmas is made for the Christian child."

By the 1940s, Zionism and the dream for a national Jewish homeland added a new dimension to Hanukkah and products were manufactured to reflect this theme. Chocolate candies, for example, were labeled with the slogan "Valor against Oppression," featuring the latter-day Maccabee Moshe Dayan, Israel's famous military chief of staff. Barton, the chocolate manufacturer, advertised "a map of Israel, miniature Israeli flags, menorahs," and equated the contemporary defense of Israel with the heroic story of the Maccabees.[24] The Zionist Organization of America provided a collection of Hanukkah materials for the purpose of fusing Zionism and Hanukkah.

New Music for Hanukkah

Beginning in the 1900s, distinctively Jewish Hanukkah music and lyrics as well as poems and plays were composed as the demand for greater expression of Hanukkah grew. New art forms were in demand to lure Jewish children away from Christmas, with its large body of Christmas music, carols, and plays. As early as the late 1880s, Rabbi Gustav Gottheil took creative license with the translation of the most popular Hanukkah song "Ma'oz Tzur." This song, originally with seven stanzas, intoned God as the "Rock of Salvation" who would protect the Jews from persecution at the hands of the Greeks and other anti-Semitic tyrants. Gottheil shortened the number of stanzas to three and offered a more modern translation to reflect the American experience. He was the first to realize the potential for the story of Hanukkah to stir the emotions of immigrants who, because of their new-found freedoms, realized how Jews had suffered in the rest of world. As Dianne Ashton points out in her seminal study of Hanukkah songs, Gottheil emphasized the universal spirit of Hanukkah rather than a specific historical event; his message lauded the values of heroism and patriotism.[25] Rather than await the messiah to take the Hebrews back to their homeland, as expressed in the traditional lyrics, Gottheil referred instead to a messianic age in which people of all religions, races, and creeds would be free to practice their religion. The "children of a martyred race" could as easily refer to Jewish victims of tyranny who suffered the loss of religious liberty. The song title "Rock of Ages" reflected a move away from religion to universal brotherhood. Now the theme of Hanukkah dovetailed with that of Christmas, which allowed Hanukkah to move closer in parity with Christmas.

   The composition of distinctively Hebrew and English songs devoted to the theme of Hanukkah added to this corpus of holiday expression. Looking for appropriate songs to use during Hanukkah Sunday school parties across America, Jewish educators and cantors began to compose songs that would then be notated and distributed though selected song-books. Ashton points out that, as early as 1918, a *Jewish Songster* was compiled for voice and piano. The book was so popular that "it went through three printings in its first year and was reissued and expanded into two volumes eleven years later."

Capturing the rise of Zionistic fervor in the 1920s, the 1927 edition of the *Jewish Songster* contained fifteen Hanukkah lyrics (sans music), most in Hebrew and English.[26] The inclusion of only two Yiddish selections showed Yiddish to be waning as an influence in synagogue Hebrew schools in favor of Hebrew and English. "Our Heroes," an anonymous poem included in the *Songster* and written in English, reflects the theme of Gottheil's "Rock of Ages" by focusing on the generic theme of victory as an expression of patriotism, without mention of the Maccabees, Israel, or Judaism.

The supplement to the 1928 edition of the *Jewish Songster* added a poem by Rabbi Isidore Myers, which is to be read before lighting the candles.[27] The poem, lacking reference to any miracle or to specific instances of persecution, describes the Jewish condition as one of despair for which Hanukkah supplies the light: "When all our race was as dark as the night/ Said the Guardian of Israel, 'Let there be light.'"

The parallelism between the democratic spirit and Zionist yearning was the theme of Emily Solis-Cohen's *Hanukkah: the Feast of Lights*, published in 1937.[28] The Supreme Court Justice Louis Brandeis set the tone for this work in a preface in which he equates the struggle for democracy by Jew and non-Jew with the challenges faced by the Maccabees: "It is the struggle for the Jews today . . . as well as of those two thousand years ago. It is the struggle in which all Americans, non-Jews as well as Jews, should be vitally interested because they are vitally affected." (It is interesting to note that Brandeis celebrated Christmas with his family.)

Solis-Cohen's book offers a compendium of articles, songs, and plays as a way of demonstrating how the creative Jewish spirit is called on year after year to fight Hellenism (i.e., the forces of assimilation) and to seek a Jewish renaissance in every age. The period of the late 1930s saw both the winds of anti-Semitism and the emergence of Zionism grow, the two being inexorably woven together in this Hanukkah anthology. According to Solis-Cohen's compendium, Hanukkah's resurgence originated in the late nineteenth century and is best exemplified by the American poet laureate of immigrant hopes, Emma Lazarus. Lazarus's several poems, published in 1899, are included as an ode to the reawakened spirit of the American Jew, paying homage to victories won by Jewish ancestors. This reawakening, in turn, inspired not only a future revival but also Lazarus's own Jewish awakening. Illustrating this theme is her composition "The Feast of Lights," which was put to song and named "Kindle the Taper," a title drawn from the poem's opening line. The final verse of this song draws the direct parallel to the past and future heroism of the Jewish people:

> Sound the brass trumpet and the harsh tongued horn,
> Chant hymns of victory till the heart takes fire,
> The Maccabean spirit leaps new aborn.

Similarly, the line from ancient to modern Israel is drawn in Elma Ehrlich Levinger's poem "Soldiers:"

> Halutzim [pioneers], you are Maccabees,
> You hold the battle line;
> Your ploughshares are the weapons
> That give us Palestine.

Born in 1887, Levinger, an accomplished novelist and playwright, wrote books for Jewish youth. The play *At This Season,* written by Samuel Pitlik, also draws a straight line from ancient to modern Israel, from the "Cave in Judea" to "In Palestine," as the "Young Israel casts off ancient Israel," taking with it the children clapping hands and dancing the *hora* while chanting the song "Am Yisrael Hai" [The people Israel live]. Ostensibly written as a resource for Jewish schools to be used in synagogue programming, the underlying messages of hope and resilience, using as trope "the light of freedom," reflect the moods of both Americans and Jews in Eastern Europe during the 1930s, peoples saddened by threats to Jewish survival.

Modern secular Zionism was based in reclaiming the land of Israel. Solis-Cohen included in the 1937 collection the Hanukkah song, "Who Can Retell?" (*Mi Yemalel* in Hebrew) and substituted the word *Israel* for the word *God* in the biblical Psalm 106:2 that originally asks, "Who can retell God's strength?" Composed by Russian Zionist Menashe Ravina (né Rabinowitz), who lived in Palestine in the early years of the twentieth century, the words capture the new Zionist aspiration: "Hark! In days of yore, in Israel's land, brave Maccabees led the faithful band. But now all Israel must as one arise, redeemed thru deed and sacrifice."[29] This dream, indeed, became a reality twenty years later, and this song became a staple of Hanukkah song festivals.

The birth of the State of Israel in 1948 fostered a flowering of new Jewish songs, including Hanukkah melodies by composers in the United States. Coincident with the founding of the State of Israel was the Conservative

movement's rapid expansion into the suburbs where magnificent synagogues were erected and Hebrew schools were filled to capacity. Harry
Coopersmith's 1950 anthology entitled *The Songs We Sing*, published by
the Conservative movement's United Synagogue of America, supplied the
songs to be used in these schools.[30] This anthology was a collaborative
effort among some of the country's best Jewish musicians and educators
who were looking to inject a creative spirit into the Hanukkah celebration.
Included were many new compositions in Hebrew and English, among
them seventeen Hanukkah selections. In addition to new music for
standard liturgical pieces, such as "Haneros Halolu" (These Candles),
Coopersmith included songs penned by J. K. Eisenstein, Rabbi Mordechai
Kaplan's daughter, L. Kipnis, the Russian Zionist who moved to Palestine,
and the noted author E. E. Levinger. The majority of the songs were geared
toward capturing children's attention, as reflected in such song titles as:
"Oh, Come, My Dreydle," "Y'hudah Hamakabi," "Hanukkah Pancakes,"
"My Candles," and "S'vivon." By including these songs in a 450-page
volume filled with songs for all occasions, Coopersmith captured the drive
and energy present in these schools, whose teachers sought greater and
more creative means to enrich the Hanukkah holiday.

As Jews moved to the American suburbs in the 1950s reflecting a rise
in their economic status, Hebrew schools demanded more sophisticated
Hanukkah pageants. Dianne Ashton records that Jewish educators met
for the first time in 1951 to employ music as a way to enrich the classroom
experience.[31] Similarly, in the public schools, the concentration of Jewish
students in these new suburbs meant that music directors would include
Hanukkah selections in their Christmas pageants, thereby encouraging the
further development of Jewish Hanukkah music. These songs, needed to
accompany the many plays performed by children, allowed the students to
act out Hanukkah themes by taking the role of candles or dreidels or latkes.

The Reform movement's entry into the songbook genre, the *Union
Songster: Songs and Prayers for Jewish Youth*, published in 1960, was meant
to accompany the *Union Prayer Book*, thereby filling a gap for age- and
grade-appropriate music.[32] Songs were integrated into plays that could be
used as ready-made services for Hanukkah school programs. The majority
of the Hanukkah songs were, as in Coopersmith, devoted toward the very
young in making Hanukkah activities fun and entertaining. Many songs
focused on the dreidel: "Stop! Stop! Hanukkah Top!" "Twinkle, Twinkle,
Little Light," "In the Windows," and "Dreidel Spin."

The most popular of these songs was "The Dreidel Song." Most commonly known as "I Have a Little Dreidel," it achieved nearly universal

recognition. So popular was "The Dreidel Song" that people thought it was an unattributed folk song. Its origin is with Eastern European Jewish entertainers who wrote many Hanukkah songs in Yiddish, which were then reissued in English to great success. The Yiddish and English versions were composed in 1930 by Mikhl Gelbart and Samuel Goldfarb (supervisor for the entertainment department at the New York Bureau of Education), and the lyrics for both are written by Samuel S. Grossman.[33] Grossman adapted the lyrics to English with very little change, except that the Yiddish version had the dreidel made out of lead (Yiddish *blay*, leading scholars to believe that the Yiddish lyrics preceded the English) while the English version describes it as being made out of clay:

> I have a little dreidel, I made it out of clay.
> When it's dry and ready, then dreidel I shall play.
> Oh dreidel, dreidel, dreidel, I made it out of clay.
> Oh dreidel, dreidel, dreidel, then dreidel I shall play.

Both the Yiddish and English versions made it plain that by the 1930s Hanukkah had become principally a child-centered holiday in America.

As popular as these songs were in the schools in which they were used, they did not reach wider audiences and enter the home en masse until Hanukkah records were introduced in the 1950s under a growing number of Jewish labels that employed new longer playing vinyl records. Perhaps the earliest of these was the *Chanukah Song Parade*, composed by Gladys Gewirtz and Eve Lippman.[34] Gewirtz, who attended the Julliard School and the Jewish Theological Seminary, graduated from Columbia University and became the music director for the first Jewish Theological Seminary's Camp Ramah. Her experience with youth led her to believe in the value of not only composing new songs but also teaching families how to introduce these songs into their homes. Thus, on her first album, she and narrator Eve Lippman devoted one side of the record to teaching families how to introduce Hanukkah songs, games, and quizzes. Songs and albums of this era also focused on children and introducing families to the joy of Hanukkah celebration, including the 1951 *Chanukah Music Box* and the 1955 *The Chanukah Party*.[35]

In addition to the growing corpus of Hanukkah songs and recordings, Hanukkah stories were being written and targeted to parents to read to their young children. Jane Bearman's 1943 *Happy Chanuko*, which was colorfully illustrated and printed in large typeface, captures the family's excitement at the onset of the holiday, including children's holiday preparations, from shopping to setting up the menorah.[36] "What night of

Chanuko can this be?" Bearman asks. "Count the candles and you'll see! One, Two, Three, Four, Five," she answered.

Sara G. Levy designed her 1945 *Mother Goose Rhymes for Jewish Children* to appeal to young children who are already familiar with this genre.[37] These rhymes, written for Jewish holidays and festivities, strategically intersperse Hebrew words with the English, reflecting the growing use of Hebrew in Jewish song. Included were seven Hanukkah poems beautifully illustrated with joyous images of toys, family gift-giving, game playing, and the pleasures of the winter season. One such poem, "Chanukah Toys," describes "Toys, toys, Chanukah toys, some for girls, and some for boys. The *Imma* [mother] doll can smile and dance. The *Soosim* [horses] here can step and prance. Our soldier dolls are Maccabees and the Dreidels spin around with ease."

A review of the *Union Songster* illustrates that Hanukkah had so infused the Jewish home and synagogue environment that one could find a variety of English spellings to transliterate the Hebrew word for this Jewish holiday. The editor writes: "It will give you an idea of the complications of transliterating if you would think for a moment of all the various forms of the word [to spell Hanukkah in Hebrew] you have seen in English letters: Chanukah, Hanukkah, Chanuka, Chanuko, Hanukka, and so on."[38] These alternatives, which inspired endless discussions among family, friends, and educators, came from different historical periods—the *ch* prefix for Yiddish speakers and the more modernized *h* prefix—neither providing an exact equivalent because there is no Hebrew *ch* sound in English. The fact that so many spellings for Hanukkah coexist indicates how pervasive Hanukkah had become in the liturgy and within the arts and how an accepted corpus of music, plays, and games evolved over time to provide children with rich content to rival Christmas celebrations.

HANUKKAH ACHIEVES PARITY WITH CHRISTMAS

By the 1950s, sociologists were proclaiming that Jews had achieved parity with all Americans. In his influential book *Protestant—Catholic—Jew: An Essay in American Religious Sociology*, Will Herberg considered Judaism to have reached mainstream status because it appeared as if America's Christians welcome Jews as equal citizens.[39] Hanukkah played a role in developing this parity and became recognized by Americans—Christian and Jew alike—as an American national holiday. Marshall Sklare, in his celebrated study of the population of a midwestern suburban town, a quarter of which was Jewish, concurred with this finding when he said that

Hanukkah had become the most popular Jewish holiday in America. "Hanukkah," in short, he said, "was becoming the Jewish Christmas."[40]

By the 1960s, Jakob J. Petuchowski, a leading theologian of the Reform movement in the United States, could speak with pride about how Hanukkah had been magnified to the status once accorded only to Passover and the High Holidays.[41] In 1965, Rabbis Solomon Bernardo and David Greenberg touted Hanukkah as a national holiday celebrated throughout the land, infusing the ancient festival with a renewed spirit as demonstrated in "parties, orations, songs, and hymns, pilgrimages and parades."[42]

The 1960s saw the emergence across the United States of a new ethnic pride, and Jews employed Hanukkah to reinforce that concept. The rising movement toward ethnic awareness, the presence of a baby boom generation cognizant of the Nazi Holocaust, and Israel's euphoric 1967 victory against a united Arab army gave even greater impetus to use Hanukkah as a celebration of Jewish pride and survival. Attention to the relevance of Jewish values as part of the American ethos could be measured by both the proliferation of Jewish Studies departments that sprang up in major prestigious universities and the appreciation granted by the Catholic Church through Vatican II to the role of Judaism as Christianity's "elder brother."

Companies capitalizing on the increased ethnic pride produced a line of commercial products that touched on every facet of Hanukkah gift-giving and celebration, including availability of Hanukkah gift wrapping paper, ribbons depicting names and symbols of Hanukkah, and blue-and-white streamers for party decorations. Gift-wrapping displays at department stores included Hanukkah paper. Stores placed Hanukkah menorahs alongside miniature Christmas trees in their window displays. The Hanukkah spirit became part of the nation's Christmas shopping season. During this period, Jews and other Americans acknowledged Hanukkah as a holiday to be celebrated publicly alongside Christmas. In this revitalized climate, families began to think about celebrating Hanukkah without the need to reference Christmas. Ironically, Rabbi Mordecai Schreiber, B'nai B'rith's Jewish educational director (1977), stated: "Now, the national office of the B'nai B'rith Youth Organization is leading a movement to take all signs of Christmas out of Hanukkah."[43]

Philip Goodman's *The Hanukkah Anthology*, published in 1976, reflects Hanukkah's expanded role in Jewish life.[44] The book contains rich examples of stories, poems, and dramatizations that can be used by adults and children. As if to show that Hanukkah has been magnified not only in the United States but in other countries as well, Goodman describes how

Hanukkah is celebrated in other lands and in other settings, from Riga to Jerusalem, from World War II battlefields to the kibbutz in Israel. Particularly poignant are stories from the ghettos and concentrations camps of World War II; these depict how the menorah gave hope to so many who were living in subhuman conditions. Wartime "V-mail" correspondences used the Hanukkah miracle as a metaphor for the Allies anticipated victory over the Axis.[45] As an example, Rabbi N. Witkin of New York sent a V-mail to Chaplain Ralph Moses Weisberger on which there was a drawing of a Maccabee with spear and shield lighting a menorah. The caption over the image says, "The Spirit of the Maccabee Lives On . . ." and underneath reads, "Hanukah Greetings from the Persian Gulf Service Command."[46]

By the 1970s, it was no longer popular for American Jews to have Christmas trees in the home. When the novelist Anne Roiphe revealed how meaningful the Christmas tree was in her youth and now had become to her children, she struck a negative emotional chord in many Jews who reacted strongly to her embrace of Christmas.[47] Roiphe eloquently addressed the sacredness of the tree while dismissing the lighting of the menorah as an anachronistic custom rooted in superstition. What irritated readers was not just her description of the glee with which she decorated the tree in her home but also how she used the occasion to celebrate assimilation and universalism and to castigate Judaism as being parochial. Her words, tinged with anger and contempt for Jewish practices, irritated many, including those who also decorated trees in their homes. Sharon Gamsin from Brooklyn, New York, responded with surprise at Roiphe's extreme rejection of Hanukkah and asked why Jews have to choose one celebration over another. "I, like many other assimilated Jews," she remarks, "have come to celebrate an ambiguous holiday season." She explains that she "will have a Christmas tree because it's fun and pretty and makes the house smell great" and also a menorah. "Why ignore and reject my own history when I can have a bit of both?" Gamsin asks.[48]

In 1979, *The Jewish Press*, a New York Orthodox Jewish newspaper, even called for a boycott of the *New York Times* for printing Roiphe's op-ed piece, going so far as to claim that the paper fostered anti-Semitism for printing Roiphe's comments disparaging Judaism.[49] Apparently, negative reaction to her article, including threats made upon her life, forced Roiphe to reconsider the arguments she made in 1978. She had a change of heart, as reflected in the title of her article "Taking Down the Christmas Tree," which she published in 1992. Roiphe apologized. She stated that she misjudged her readers and her own true feelings about Judaism. She displayed, by her own admission, ignorance about the history of Hanukkah and had naively adopted an assimilationist ideology without thoroughly thinking through the consequences of her attitude. "I hadn't understood," she wrote, "that, growing up in the forties, I had absorbed the anti-Semitism of the culture, and that's why I thought that people who spoke with accents were peculiar, that Jews were outsiders. I wanted to be inside with the others. . . . I didn't realize that assimilation had a dark side. . . . I now realize that assimilation can produce an identity that is shallow, materialistic, rooted, and anxious. Assimilation can deprive a person of the pleasure of belonging and the vitality that comes from real knowledge about and interest in that person's own community."

By the time of Roiphe's confession, Hanukkah was no longer the minor holiday that she remembered. Hanukkah had reached a high level of public awareness, in part, due to its commercial sophistication. A 1995 invitational show in San Francisco had on display 125 menorahs, with prices ranging from $350 to $3,000, and made from a myriad of materials, including fused glass, stainless steel, acrylic, graphite, circuitboard, marble, Plexiglas, and wax.[50] In 1997, holiday greeting card manufacturers estimated that eleven million Hanukkah cards were sold in hundreds of designs. The dreidel, made originally of lead, and later wood and then plastic, is now manufactured in crystal, porcelain, stained glass, and sterling silver, suitable not just for use but also for display. Today's dreidels rotate at the push of a button, light up or sing out, jog on little plastic feet, and shoot out of a toy gun. Dreidels have become highly sought-after collectibles, and dreidel-collecting clubs now exist in cities across the United States.

New Fads and Innovations

Specialty Hanukkah novelties have also been created for and marketed during the Christmas season. For example, a chess set, for sale at J. Levine's Books and Judaica shop in Manhattan, is called the "December Dilemma." Christmas figurines comprise the set for one team and, Hanukkah figurines comprise the opposing team. Danny Levine, current owner of J. Levine's, defends the groupings: "The set pits the Christmas tree against the dreidel, Santa Claus against the Israeli flag, the 'bar mitzvah boy' against the priest. . . . They're multicultural, and they're not fighting, they're playing."[51] Also representative of this new merchandise is a set of three-dimensional wrap-around paper eyeglasses for sale at Jewish bookstores around the United States. The cost of the glasses is nominal at $2 per pair. The miracle

Figure 2.1. Detail from December Dilemma chess set, ca. 2004. © Jewish Museum Berlin, photo: Jens Ziehe.

of these glasses is when they are donned at night the glasses transform Christmas (or any other holiday lights) into six-pointed Stars of David lights.

Hanukkah's coming of age was forecasted in a late twentieth-century survey showing Hanukkah celebrations as increasingly popular for all Jews in the United States. Sociologist Bruce L. Berg reported in 1988 that both a majority of traditional and nontraditional Jews across the United States lit Hanukkah candles: 96 percent by Reform Jews, 87 percent by Orthodox, 79 percent by Conservative, and 70 percent by non-practicing Jews.[52] Historian Elizabeth Pleck wrote: "There was no single creator of the American Hanukkah nor was the holiday associated with a specific Jewish organization or with Zionism. . . . The growth in the popularity of Hanukkah was not an effort to recapture a lost Jewish heritage, but instead an attempt to make a Jewish festival competitive with the dazzle of and allure of a major Christian holiday. The Jewish rediscovery of Hanukkah was not a protest or critique of Christian culture so much as a form of flattery, a recognition that Jewish children needed a seasonal holiday which could compete with the tinsel and trinkets of Christmas."[53]

At the same time as the renewed interest in and popularization of the celebration of Hanukkah itself, which was widespread and far-reaching, new cultural activities and pursuits evolved throughout the United States. On a national level, in 1996, as a result of a letter-writing crusade led by Myrna Holtzman of New York the U.S. Postal Service issued the first Hanukkah stamp depicting nine candles in a variety of colors.[54] The stamp was so popular that it was reissued in 1997 and each year thereafter, with a new dreidel design added in both 2004 and 2009.

Grassroots campaigning was successful in another venue. In 1997, nine-year-old Mallory Blair Greitzer and her father wrote repeated letters to the management of the Empire State Building in Manhattan requesting that the color of the building's tower lights be changed in honor of Hanukkah. This request was steadfastly rejected on the basis that the management's policy limited the lights to honor each religion on one day per year. (The landmark's lights are blue and white for Israel Independence Day.) Mallory's father then wrote to Leona Helmsley, the management company's owner. Against the advice of her staff, Helmsley granted Mallory's request. In celebration of Hanukkah in 1997, the Empire State Building was (and each year thereafter has been) set alight with blue and white.[55]

The American popularization of Hanukkah even reached outer space. From December 2 through December 13, 2003, U.S. astronaut Jeffrey Hoffman, who is Jewish, made his fourth NASA flight as a crewmember on the Space Shuttle *Endeavour*. During this flight, the Hubble Space Telescope (HST) was captured, serviced, and restored to full capacity through a record five space walks by four astronauts, including Dr. Hoffman. To celebrate Hanukkah in the space ship, Dr. Hoffman brought with him a dreidel and a menorah. He spun the dreidel for a live audience watching via satellite on a television network sponsored by the Hasidic Lubavitch movement.[56]

Among the new Hanukkah fads that were spawned in the beginning of the twenty-first century was a dreidel game called "No Limit Texas Dreidel" (NLTD). In 2007, during a car trip, Jennie Rivlin Roberts and her husband created a game without the use of cards, "players bet, raise or fold depending on the strength of their dreidel hand."[57] Since the time of its introduction, the sales for NLTD have skyrocketed from 1,500 copies sold in its initial year to sales averaging 10,000 copies per year to date. The deluxe version of the game, which includes two bags of *gelt* and ten temporary tattoos, sells for $49.95. When asked if adding an element of poker to the spinning of the dreidel was kosher, Rivlin Roberts, the game's founder, stated: "Dreidel is a gambling game. I've talked to rabbis about it. If you're gambling for fun and it's not taking away time and money from your family, it's fine. . . . And of course we are playing for chocolate, so it's not a sin."

In 2007, the Major League Dreidel championship was created. Described as an exciting "amped-up Hanukkah party and battle royale," players compete for the longest dreidel spin. From the championship's inception until 2012, the league has grown from 32 competitors to 120, with events scheduled in New York, San Francisco, Denver, and Miami. Eric Pavony, Major League Dreidel's founder and self-styled "knishioner" allows that this "is not your rabbi's dreidel."[58] Traditionally, each player spins the dreidel and relies primarily upon luck to win. Pavony's perspective of the game is that the focus is on the length of the spin and not on how the dreidel lands. Each round of spinning is on "progressively smaller surfaces" so that skill is more of a factor than luck.

At present, the league's primary championship venue in New York City is the Knitting Factory, a music venue in Williamsburg that has been transformed for the night into a Hanukkah haven for Hasmonian hipsters. Between spinning bouts, Gods of Fire, a heavy metal act, plays such songs as "The Quest for the Latke Oil" and "Taking the Temple." Competitors, who adopt pseudonyms such as Spindiana Jones, Goy Wonder, Spinona Ryder, Debbie Does Driedel, and Jewbacca, spin the four-sided top on a now patented and mass-produced board called the "spinogogue." The entrants stoop over the spinogogue boards, "cracking fingers and stretching their wrists." The prize is a crystal dreidel-shaped trophy. The 2007 champion, Pamela "Pamskee" Goldman, arrived with a bull's-eye depicted on her spinning wrist. The goal of every competitor was to trounce Pamskee's world record spin of 17.8 seconds. All the while, the "mid-twenties crowd shouts, high-fives and swigs such Jewish-themed beers as Genesis Ale and Messiah Bold." Every competitor seemed to have a unique technique: "Tasmanian Dreidel spins with his whole body. Dre-idol has covered his fingers with wax and plans to spin the top upside down. But Pamskee sets the standard. She uses only the barest of movement with her fingertips to get her world record spins." As the competition advanced toward midnight, two players remained: Pamskee and "Virtual Dreidel."

To the chants of the crowd ("spin, spin, spin"), Virtual Dreidel won the competition and received the trophy. His identity was revealed as Howard Pavony, the father of the game's creator. Howard, descrying any inference of nepotism, cited that the "clock does not lie."

Major League Dreidel presently has a one-night season, although Eric Pavony would like to see it lengthened. In reflecting upon his creation, Pavony points to the educational value of this new Hanukkah game: "I think Major League Dreidel can do some good, like open the eyes of people who have never experienced Hanukkah. And, it's a good vehicle to get people who don't celebrate their Judaism excited." Pavony has other Hanukkah-themed games in process: "Gelt Roulette" and "Target Tops."

Hanukkah has clearly come of age. The December 2–8, 2010, edition of *TimeOut New York*, a weekly magazine publication that lists cultural happenings in the New York City area, mentions the following Hanukkah cultural activities at prominent venues: The Eight Nights of Hanukkah with Yo La Tengo, Sephardic Music Festival, Young Friends of the Museum (of Jewish Heritage) Hanukkah Party, Menorah Horah, Latkes and Vodkas with Gary Shteyngart, Latke Festival 2010 at City Winery, and Major League Dreidel. The magazine also listed public menorah lightings by Chabad in both New York City and Brooklyn. Similarly, throughout the United States, American Jews now have a wide variety of Hanukkah entertainment choices reflecting its broad-based popularity.

Hanukkah music continues to be created. In a 2003 concert in New York, the Klezmatics, a popular Grammy Award–winning Klezmer band, performed Hanukkah songs that showcased a selection from the many lyrics written from 1949 through the early 1950s by Woody Guthrie, the iconic American folk troubadour and songwriter. The lyrics had lain fallow and long forgotten in Guthrie's archives until their discovery in 1998 by Woody's daughter Nora Guthrie. Nora asked the Klezmatics to write original music for the lyrics, which fuses strains of Klezmer music with American folk and bluegrass. The 2006 album, *Woody Guthrie's Happy Joyous Hanuka*, comprises many different songs, including "Happy, Joyous Hanuka" and "Hanuka Tree." Two of the eight songs, "The Many and the Few" and "Hanuka Dance," had lyrics and melodies penned entirely by Guthrie. The songs were in part biographical. Woody was married to Marjorie Mazia, a Jewish dancer with the Martha Graham Dance Company who was the daughter of Aliza Greenblatt, an activist and Yiddish poet. Nora remembers, "For Hanukkah actually, we had a hat—we didn't get presents—but we had a hat with different amounts of Hanukkah gelt, and every night we'd pick out five cents or twenty-five cents of gelt. My mother

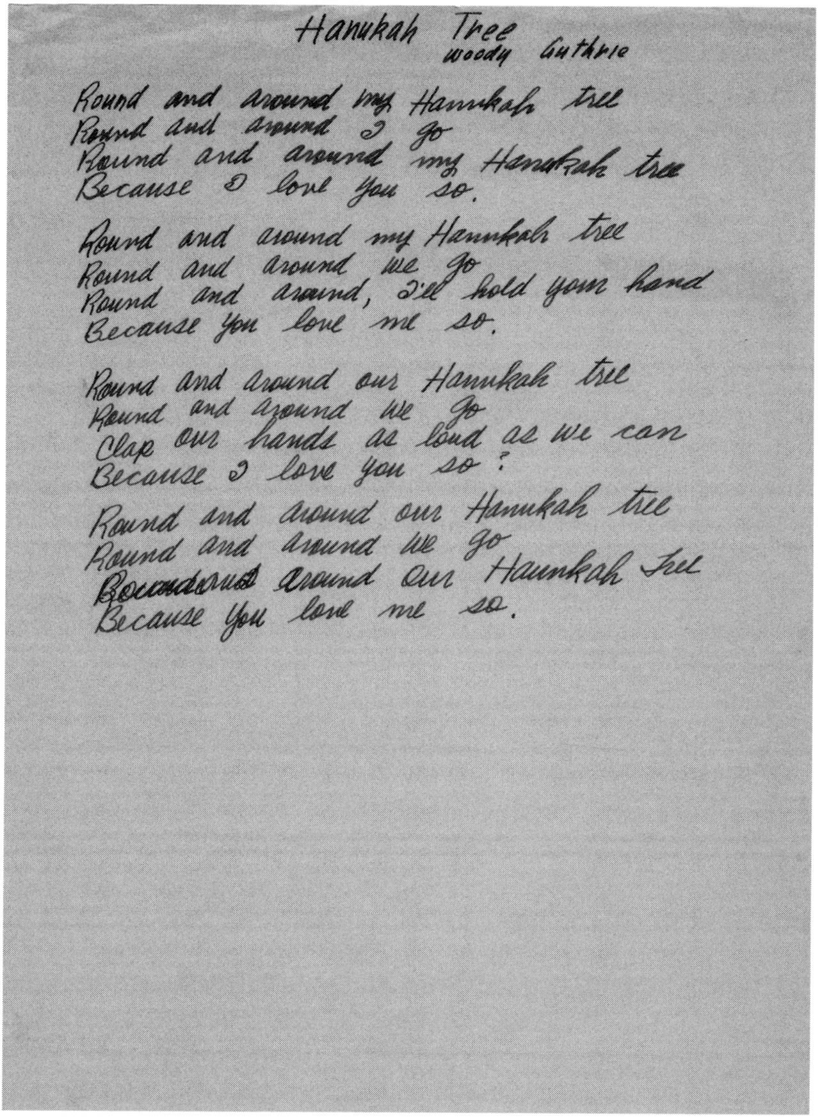

Figure 2.2. Woody Guthrie's original handwritten "Hanukah Tree" song lyrics, ca. 1949. Courtesy of the Woody Guthrie Archives. Copyright © 2002 Woody Guthrie Publications, Inc.

played piano, and we used to sing and dance every night."[59] At the 2003 debut concert with the Klezmatics at the 92nd Street Y in Manhattan, folk legend Arlo Guthrie, Woody's son and Nora's brother, joked that as children they would dance "around the Hanukkah tree." "Happy Joyous Hanuka" counts down each candle on the menorah ("Seven for the sons of

Hannah that died / Six for kings and the tricks they tried / Five for the brothers Maccabee"), while "Hanuka Tree" has a lively simple melody ("Round and around my Hanukah tree / Round and around I go / Round and around my Hanukah tree / Because I love you so"). According to Nora, most of Woody Guthrie's Hanukkah songs seem to be written in November or December within five days of each other "because he had bookings in December for children's Hanukkah parties in assorted Brooklyn community centers." As was his wont, Woody would "write songs only for the gig a few days before and then go on to other songs for other gigs." For the Guthrie family, a family of improvisers not of traditions and for whom the approach to religion was "all or none," the tree was a "Christmas tree, a Hanukkah tree, and a holiday tree. It was a fluid thing!"

In the spirit of the modern technological age, new songs are also popularized through internet media such as YouTube. One recent example during Hanukkah in 2010 is the YouTube sensation "Candlelight" featuring an all-male a cappella singing group from Yeshiva University in New York City.[60] Parodying the music of the hip-hop song "Dynamite" by Taio Cruz, the lyrics of "Candlelight" refer to latkes, candles, and a telling of the Hanukkah story. The YouTube video for the song had been viewed more than three million times in the three weeks since its release in the early part of December 2010 (and by the beginning of 2012 the song had been viewed more than seven million times). Demonstrating its unbelievable popularity among grammar-school-aged children, the video was shown, less than one week after it release, during a Hanukkah assembly at the Abraham Joshua Heschel School in New York City. All the children in attendance knew the words and music and sang along.

Largely symbolic, but indicative of Hanukkah's popularity even in states with small Jewish populations, Idaho's Governor Dirk Kempthorne signed a proclamation on December 1, 2004, making December 7, 2004, National Menorah Day in the state of Idaho. The governor declared that "the message of Chanukah resonates quite powerfully with the fundamental principles of American life, as this nation was founded on the principles of hope and religious freedom." The proclamation reads, in part:

WHEREAS, This year marks the 25th anniversary of the National Menorah which was first lit in 1979 with President Jimmy Carter and given its name by President Ronald Reagan in 1982; and

WHEREAS, Chanukah, the Festival of Lights, is among the most widely celebrated of the Jewish holidays;

NOW, THEREFORE, I, DIRK KEMPTHORNE, Governor of the State of Idaho, do hereby proclaim, December 7, 2004, to be national Menorah Day in Idaho.[61]

As a sign that the holiday of Hanukkah had become a symbol of religious liberty for all Americans, the largely non-Jewish citizens of Billings, Montana, used the menorah as a means to fight anti-Semitism and bigotry that gripped the town in 1993. In December of that year, Isaac and Tami Schnitzer, a Jewish family, placed a Hanukkah menorah in their window. An anti-Semitic town resident hurled a cinderblock through the Schnitzers' window and threatened other families and institutions displaying menorahs. The townspeople decided to take a collective stand against bigotry and, through a campaign waged by the *Billings Gazette* and the town's sheriff, families and businesses were asked to display pictures of menorahs in their homes and jobs. People responded enthusiastically; by the time the campaign concluded an estimated 10,000 people had answered the call. This communitywide protest dramatically decreased the incidence of hate crimes in that town.[62]

The Americanization of Hanukkah from the statehouse to the nation's capital is further evidenced by the unprecedented popularity of the holiday song entitled "Eight Days of Hanukkah," written by U.S. Senator Orrin Hatch, a Utah Republican with an affection for Jews and a love of Barbra Streisand.[63] A video of the song originally debuted via *Tablet*, an online Jewish cultural magazine, just prior to the beginning of Hanukkah in 2009. The production of this song was a multicultural endeavor. Hatch's collaborator, Madeline Stone, is a Jewish songwriter from the Upper West Side of Manhattan who specializes in Christian music. "I'm a pretty liberal Democrat," Stone said. "But it became more about the music and the friendship for me and Orrin." Furthermore, the song was performed by Rasheeda Azar, a Syrian American vocalist from Indiana. Senator Hatch spoke of "Eight Days of Hanukkah" as a "gift to the Jewish people." Hatch described his ultimate goal: Barbra Streisand performing one of his songs. "It would be good for her and good for me," Hatch said, "while acknowledging that given her outspoken liberalism, that union might require another miracle."

By the beginning of the twenty-first century, Jews in America embraced Hanukkah as a symbol of religious freedom and an antidote to Christmas. Hanukkah's attainment of this status, especially in the public arena, did not emerge without controversy. The push to display menorahs in civic spaces was challenged in court cases because it purportedly violated the separation of religion and state. Nonetheless, Hanukkah was accepted by the non-Jewish population in the United States as the Jewish Christmas, rich in traditions and customs and centered on children and the family. And in the eyes of Jews in America, Hanukkah had come of age. Hanukkah achieved, like Christmas, major holiday status through its inclusion in the public school and the shopping mall, in the home and, indeed, all the way to the White House.

CHAPTER 3

WE EAT CHINESE
FOOD ON CHRISTMAS

During Elena Kagan's United States Supreme Court confirmation hearings of 2010, at a particularly contentious moment, South Carolina Senator Lindsey Graham directed the discussion to the 2009 Christmas Day bombing attempt on a Detroit-bound airliner. Graham then asked the candidate where she was on Christmas Day. Justice Kagan famously answered, "You know, like all Jews, I was probably at a Chinese restaurant." Her comment provoked laughter and reduced the level of tension in the room. Recognizing that some in the room might be unfamiliar with the custom, Senator Charles Schumer of New York then explained how Jews had a special affinity with eating out at Chinese restaurants on Christmas because they were the only restaurants open in New York City. A popular joke reflects on this affinity for Jews to eat in Chinese restaurants: "The Jewish people are 5,000 years old, and the Chinese people are 3,000 years old. So what did the Jews eat for 2,000 years?"

Chinese restaurants became a favorite eatery for Jews who emigrated from Eastern Europe to the United States and to New York City, in particular, in the early twentieth century. Chinese cuisine was an inexpensive and exotic alternative to the more familiar and expensive foods served at Jewish delicatessens.[1] It was a happy coincidence that Chinese restaurants stayed open on Christmas Eve, thus giving Jews across the United States a natural venue in which to partake of their own versions of Christmas dinner. "Eating Chinese" on Christmas soon became a national sensation that defined Christmastime activity for Jews all over the United States.

The origin of this venerated Jewish Christmas tradition dates to the end of the nineteenth century on the Lower East Side of New York City. Jews found Chinese restaurants readily available in urban and suburban areas in America where both Jews and Chinese lived in close proximity.[2] The first

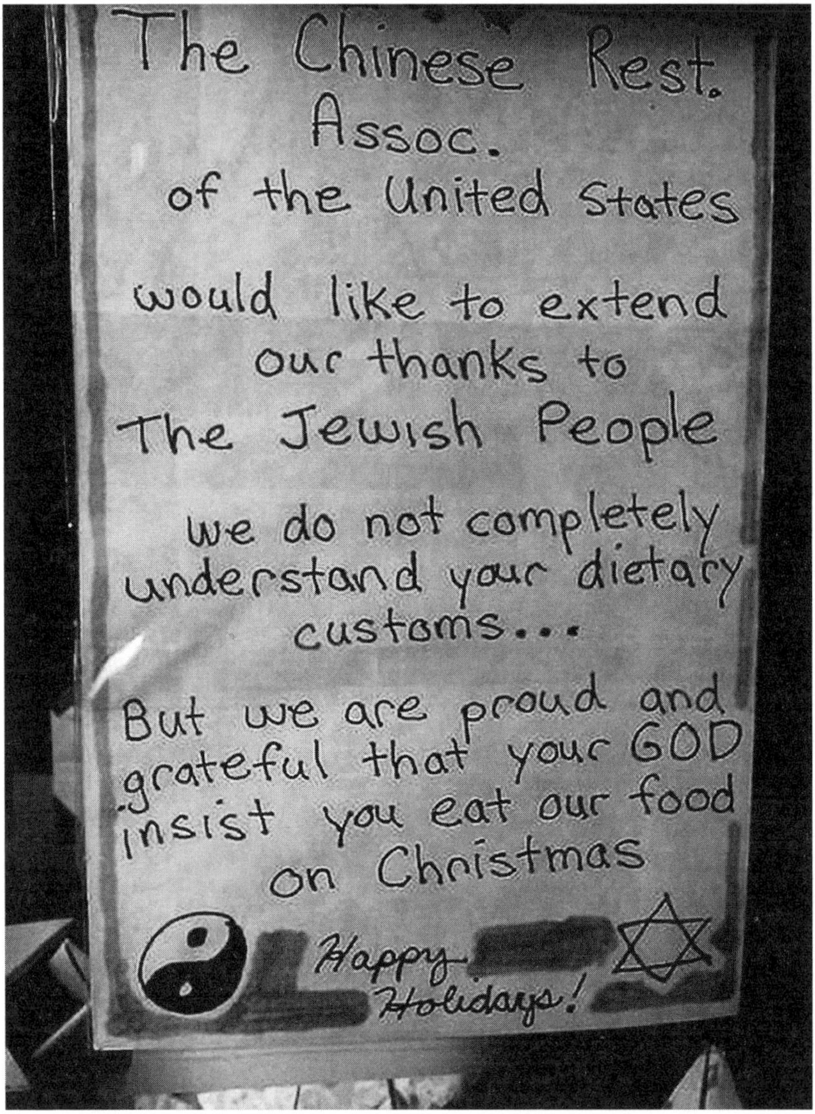

The Chinese Rest.
Assoc.
of the United States

would like to extend
our thanks to
The Jewish People

We do not completely
understand your dietary
customs...

But we are proud and
grateful that your GOD
insist you eat our food
on Christmas

Happy
Holidays!

Figure 3.1. Sign in a Chinese restaurant. Plaut family collection.

mention of this phenomenon was in 1899 whereby the *American Hebrew* weekly journal criticized Jews for eating at nonkosher restaurants, singling out in particular Jews who flock to Chinese restaurants.[3] In 1903, the Yiddish-language newspaper the *Forward* coined the Yiddish word *oysessen*—eating out—to describe the growing custom of Jews eating outside the home in New York City.[4]

By 1910, approximately one million Jews had settled in New York City, constituting more than one quarter of the city's population. Delicatessens were favorite venues for Jewish immigrants in the United States who found not only foods familiar from their home countries but also foods that only the affluent could previously afford. Replacing the cafes and cake parlors of the Lower East Side in the 1930s, delicatessens served a standard Jewish fare that was based on deli meats, "oversized portions, mustard in paper cones, and wise guy waiters."[5] The noted author Alfred Kazin summed up the importance of the deli for the Jewish psyche: "hot spiced corned beef, pastrami, rolled beef, hard salami, soft salami, bologna, frankfurter 'specials' and the thinner, wrinkled hot dogs always taken with mustard . . . and now, as the electric sign blazed up again, lighting up the words Jewish National Delicatessen, it was as if we had entered into our rightful heritage."[6] Although most of these delicatessens were kosher, some began to serve what came to be called "kosher style"; that is, they offered familiar kosher meats with the addition of nonkosher combinations, such as mixing meat and milk. These delis allowed Jews to wean away from their stricter in-home kosher use to eating nonkosher food outside the home. In time, kosher-style delis added nonkosher foods and allowed patrons a wider choice, providing, as historian Hasia Diner notes, "the familiar with the new."[7]

Soon, immigrants were exposed to non-Jewish ethnic foods and tastes. In the neighborhoods in which Jews first settled, Chinese restaurants were plentiful. A 1936 Lower East Side publication, *East Side Chamber News*, reported that at least eighteen Chinese tea gardens and chop suey eateries had recently opened in the heavily populated Jewish area. All were within a short walking distance of Ratner's, the famous Jewish dairy restaurant in Manhattan.[8] Some of these Jews, tailoring their kosher dietary practices, remained strict in home observance but became flexible with the foods they ate outside the home. The feminist author Letty Cottin Pogebrin relates that her family, which kept kosher in the home, ate nonkosher food outside the home when she was growing up in the 1950s: "At home, my mother obeyed the Jewish dietary laws; she bought her meat from the kosher butcher and maintained separate sets of dishes and cookware for meat and dairy meals. However, in the homes of people who did not keep kosher, we ate meat with milk—Chicken a la King, for instance—and in restaurants we ate *trayf*, ritually unclean foods like pork or shellfish."[9] Many children of immigrants rejected dietary restrictions, which they believed to be impractical and anachronistic. By the end of the twentieth century, after only one hundred years, immigrant Jews were more familiar with sushi than with

gefilte fish, a transition from the more traditional diet of their forebears
that Chinese restaurants facilitated.

Moreover, the Chinese accepted Jews and other immigrant and ethnic
groups as customers without precondition. There was no inherent
anti-Semitism to overcome when entering the restaurant because
Chinese owners and waiters had no history of prejudice toward Jews.[10]
Not having yet mastered the English language, immigrant Chinese
restaurateurs, as Philip Roth perceptively comments in *Portnoy's
Complaint*, thought that the Jew's Yiddish-inflected English was the King's
English.[11] Furthermore, Jews chose Chinese restaurants over other ethnic
cuisines, such as Italian, because Christian symbols were absent in these
venues. The Chinese restaurant was, as sociologists Gaye Tuchman
and Harry Gene Levine point out, a "safe *treyf* " (safe nonkosher food)
environment in which to enjoy a satisfying and inexpensive meal made
with ingredients that were desirable and familiar to Eastern Europeans,
including onions, garlic, and vegetables.

Comfort and anonymity can also be found in the foods served, which,
while not being kosher per se, are disguised through a process of cutting,
chopping, and mincing. Pork, shrimp, lobster, and other so-called dietary
abominations are no longer viewed in their more natural states.[12] Pork, for
example, wrapped and hidden inside a wonton looks remarkably like that
of Jewish *kreplach* (a dumpling). Also, the absence of milk in Chinese
cuisine shields Jewish patrons from observing meat served with milk,
a violation of kosher laws. In general, Chinese food eased the transition
from kosher to acceptable nonkosher eating.

The younger generation enjoyed asserting its independence from family
tradition.[13] Felix Mayrowitz, a resident of Brownsville, New York, commented in 1928 that he observed young Jews frequenting one of the six chop
suey houses lining the streets of Pitkin Avenue. Mayrowitz wrote: "The
standard order is a dish of roast pork as an accompaniment to shrimp chow
mein. Thus do the children of Brownsville symbolize their revolt from
the outworn beliefs of their fathers!"[14] For children of immigrants, eating
Chinese foods not only broke with kosher dietary restrictions but also
added a level of "sophistication and worldliness."[15] It was important for
them to demonstrate a cosmopolitan spirit as a sign of successful adaptation to American culture.

The war between chop suey and gefilte fish did not go unnoticed in the
Jewish press. The daily Yiddish newspaper *Der Tog* ran an article in 1928 in
which the reporter commented on this culinary tug-of-war between the
eating habits of the old world and the new world. "Down with Chop Suey!

Long Live Gefilte Fish!" was the battle cry sounded and backlash waged by those defending traditional cultural habits.

"Eating Chinese" became so popular that Jews regularly patronized Chinese restaurants. The weekends were popular occasions. Neil Postman, who grew up in Brooklyn in a heavily populated Jewish area during the 1930s and 1940s, remembers that his family routinely ate at the local Chinese eatery on Friday nights: "Every Friday night, my brother Jack, sister Ruth, and I had this routine of going to the Chinese restaurant. . . . The dinners were thirty cents each, and the tip was a dime. We'd get egg drop soup, an egg roll, and chow mein. And then a little bowl of ice cream with a fortune cookie."[16] Molly Katz wrote in her 1991 humorous guidebook that Jews typically ate at Chinese restaurants on Thursday and Sunday nights: "Chinese treats may be enjoyed anytime, but there are two nights on which Jews flock to Chinese restaurants: Thursday (because it's the housekeeper's night off) and Sunday (because we just do)."[17] Jews patronizing Chinese restaurants for Sunday lunch and supper ran parallel to after-church meals organized in the homes of church-going Americans.[18] By the beginning of the twenty-first century, the custom of eating Chinese food had spread across the country and was considered to be a venerated Jewish tradition, especially dim sum dining for Sunday brunch. In fact, the Chinese restaurant had become a place where Jewish identity is made, remade, and announced.[19]

"EATING CHINESE" IN JEWISH HUMOR

The incongruity of Jewish families and friends partaking of exotic Chinese foods became the source of much humor.[20] Humorist Molly Katz noted how attached Jews were to eating Chinese foods: "For no reason that has ever been clear to anyone, Jewish people adore Chinese food. . . . As foreign as caffeine and cream are to our bodies, soy sauce is our cure. Never mind chicken soup; when Jews need comfort, solace or medicinal nourishment, we dive for moo shu pork."[21]

Borscht Belt comedians used Chinese food as grist for humor in the 1950s, when comparing old and new world traditions. "Jews always look for Chinese restaurants," goes one joke, "but how often have you heard of a Chinese looking for gefilte fish?"[22] The move from the delicatessen to the Chinese restaurant spawned a joke widely circulated in the 1960s in which patrons attempt to order items from an unfamiliar menu. A customer orders egg foo young: "Tonight you're out of luck," said the waiter. "We used up the last egg an hour ago, and we don't have any young left either." "In that case," said the customer, "just bring me a bowl of the foo."[23]

One well-known comedy skit involved comedian Buddy Hackett who performed an impression of a Chinese waiter delivering food at the Concord Hotel. He recounted to his Jewish colleague Alan King how he developed a skit based on Jews ordering at a Chinese restaurant:

> HACKETT: One night we went for Chinese. There was a waiter named George there. I got up and started yelling fake Chinese at him down the dumbwaiter. On stage, it got screams. In the beginning I used to put rubber bands around to make Chinese eyes, but a few years later I decided that was offensive. And I didn't need it.
>
> KING: No, everyone knew, we all went to Chinese restaurants then, [choosing] one from column A, one from column B.[24]

Also, beginning in the 1950s, the experience of eating at Chinese restaurants was the butt of Jewish jokes on television shows showcasing Jewish comedians. The novelty of types of foods eaten, the contrast to kosher dietary traditions, and the manner in which Chinese food is consumed are staples of Jewish humor. A 1955 Sid Caesar television skit presented on *Caesar's Comedy Hour* was situated at a Chinese restaurant called the Golden Pagoda. The skit illustrates the difficulty of a Jewish patron's trying to master the art of eating with chopsticks. A pair of businessmen jostles their unwilling friend, Bob, into a Chinese restaurant. "I only have thirty minutes; we could have had a sandwich," he protests. His frown turns to glee when he turns to see a plate of steaming Chinese food being carried by a waiter nearby: "Chinese food! Oh boy! Ping Pong Goo! Ding Dong Skoo!" he declares. When their food is delivered, Bob is distracted by one old friend and then another and is unable to get a chopstick in edgewise. He is left to salivate as his lunch partners polish off the entire meal.[25] The skit illustrates how disparate Chinese portions can appear on one's plate, with a variety chosen by guests to be shared with others. The communal manner of eating Chinese food made it all the more enjoyable to Jewish customers. The skit also highlights the discomfiture of encountering a new method of eating—chopsticks.

Similarly, a skit on the widely popular television show of the late 1950s, *The Steve Allen Show*, features Mr. Neville Nosher (a play on the Yiddish word meaning "one who relishes eating"), a character who is a connoisseur of food, sent to review a Chinese restaurant. A neophyte patron asks him, "Is it very exclusive?" "Oh yes," Nosher responds. "Tonight they threw out a couple for ordering the family dinner. They weren't married." Nosher then instructs the audience in the preparation of "special Chinese sauce," a concoction of soy sauce, plum sauce, and hot mustard that he renders inedible by his liberal use of mustard. "The ensuing roars of the audience suggests many of them had made the same mistake."[26]

Many decades later, in an episode of a 1990 television show, *Brooklyn Bridge*, Chinese food turns out to be the one activity that parents of dating interfaith teenagers, Alan and Katie, have in common. The relationship is distressing to Alan's immigrant grandparents and Katie's father, an Irish American policeman. The teenagers, believing communication can overcome prejudice, persuade their families to meet. The grand meeting takes place at the Flower Garden Restaurant. The Irishman, Mr. Monaghan, when placing the order for his family of "squid appetizer, oxtail soup, pork kebabs, shrimp in lobster sauce, and flaming octopus rings," earns the scorn of Alan's grandmother. "We're not ready to order, Danny," she tells the waiter. "It takes us longer because we care about what we eat." The Jewish parents, the Silvers, settle on a simple order of five platters of chicken chow mein. The evening threatens to unravel when the Silvers are unable to summon a Hebrew prayer to match the Monaghan's rendition of grace before meals. The families also fail to find a single acquaintance in common ("You mean you don't know Sol Moscovitz?" Mr. Silver asks in amazement). Tensions finally ease after Alan's grandfather tastes the Monaghans' oxtail soup. Soon, the families are exchanging priest and rabbi jokes. Chinese food becomes the common denominator that links these two families and helps transcend ethnic and religious differences.

In a 1990 television episode of *Seinfeld*, entitled "The Chinese Restaurant," Jerry, Elaine, and George attempt to dine at Hunan on Fifth Avenue in Manhattan. Their seating is delayed by the arrival of regulars like "Mr. Cohen," whom the maître d' "hasn't seen in a few weeks."[27] This delay implies that Jews who are loyal patrons of Chinese restaurants are regarded as insiders while those who haven't yet achieved regular status at the establishment remain outsiders. One manner, therefore, in which Jews achieved acceptance in American society was by proving that they were no longer outsiders; they had successfully adopted a foreign cuisine as their own.

EATING CHINESE FOOD ON CHRISTMAS: A SACRED TRADITION

For American Jews, eating Chinese reaches its pinnacle on Christmas. Jews flock to Chinese restaurants on Christmas not only because they are open while other restaurants are closed but also because Jews regard eating

Chinese food as a special occasion. At the same time that most American families gather to participate in the ritualized Christmas holiday family meal, Jews in America are celebrating a secular day in a highly charged popular ritual of eating Chinese and, more recently, other Asian ethnic foods. Over the years, Jewish families and friends gather on Christmas Eve and Christmas Day at Chinese restaurants across the United States to socialize and to banter, to reinforce social and familial bonds, and to engage in a favorite activity for Jews during the Christmas holiday.

Eating Chinese food has become such an important part of Jewish life on Christmas that the media frequently report on people's experiences, which prove to be varied and quite sophisticated reflecting a myriad of regional choices.[28] A sampling of opinions was posted to Ed Levine's blog *New York Eats* when he wrote a column entitled "Chinese Food, Christmas Day, and the Jews: Where Can We Go for Old-School Chinese?" Levine rhetorically asks, "So where can we go for good Cantonese or Chinese-American food today? Sichuan restaurants somehow don't cut it (eating twice-cooked pork on Christmas Day doesn't seem right), so it would seem as if our options are limited. Shanghainese food is terrific, but eating soup dumplings and Lion's Head on December 25 just isn't the same. So what are we left with?"[29] Levine follows his query by suggesting six places to eat in the New York area; he offers a range of choices, from dim sum to noodles to wonton soup. In response, readers posted blog entries that compared and contrasted their experiences and identified their favorite places. A Detroit Jew reflected on the Chinese restaurants in Detroit that he frequented: "Chinese was a well-honored tradition in Detroit as well. Although the places weren't as crowded as the dim sum places I went to last year, the good Chinese places in suburban Detroit could all easily hold a few *minyans*." A New Yorker's blog entry summarized the scene many a Jew encounters on Christmas Eve: crowds and long lines. "Last night C-town [Chinatown] was pretty packed . . . lines out the door at Joe's Shanghai and its sister restaurant Joe's Ginger—same at Ping's. NY Noodletown was pretty packed too, but at least the line was not out the door. I never knew it would be so packed on Christmas Day, but it is madhouse." Another entry from a New Yorker shows how certain Jews choose to combine deli and Chinese food: "I think Christmas is my favorite Jewish holiday. This year, at midnight on Christmas Eve, we had *matzoh* ball soup, chopped liver, *cholent*, pastrami, and *kasha varnishkes* at the Second Avenue Deli. For lunch on Christmas Day, we had Peking duck in Chinatown at (where else) Peking Duck House. Both restaurants were packed."

Some Chinese restaurants have become so revered by members of the Jewish community that they have been given nicknames. The Golden Temple Chinese restaurant on Beacon Street in Brookline, Massachusetts, home to a sizable Jewish population, is very popular throughout the year. It is known among local Jews simply as "the Temple," according it a level of sacredness normally reserved for the synagogue.[30] The Golden Temple's finest moment is Christmas Eve. *Saveur* magazine reports that "while Christians are digging into Christmas goose, the other half of the Judeo-Christian equation is waiting in a two-hour line [at The Golden Temple] to order Beijing duck."[31]

Even Orthodox Jews in the United States have borrowed a page from their secular brethren in frequenting Chinese, albeit kosher, restaurants on Christmas. Over the years, kosher Chinese restaurants have become popular and supply venues for Orthodox Jews seeking meaningful activity outside the home during Christmas.[32] By 1990, there were fifty-one kosher Chinese restaurants nationwide, and since then the number has grown.[33] The challenge for kosher Chinese cuisine is to approximate Chinese cooking without using pork or shellfish. The kosher industry has solved this problem by producing imitation nonkosher products using kosher ingredients, a category known as "imitation *treyf*," making it by design "safe."

At kosher Chinese restaurants, such as the Shalom Hunan in Brookline, Massachusetts (now closed), an Orthodox Jew could eat eel, shrimp, and pork—all made with vegetarian substitutes. Located on Brookline's Harvard Street in the heart of Jewish Boston, the kosher Shalom Hunan attracted during Christmas an overflow crowd of predominantly kosher diners.[34] The Chinese manager of Shalom Hunan commented that the biggest restaurant crowd of the year was always on Christmas.[35] Unlike their forebears, Orthodox Jews do not harbor feelings of isolation on Christmas. Yet, similar to feelings espoused by secular Jews, they do not find Christmas relevant. One affable middle-aged man described it succinctly, "It's a nice holiday, just not mine."

The tradition of Jews eating Chinese food on Christmas Eve is so pervasive that it has been the catalyst for many a Yuletide parody. "*Erev* Christmas" was written by veteran storyteller Bruce Marcus and Lori Factor (now Factor-Marcus) and published by the *Boston Globe* newspaper in 1993. These two Boston-area Jews chronicled their personal Christmas Eve quest for Chinese food with some measure of comic license, adding to the large canon of verse by satirizing the well-known poem, "A Visit from Saint Nicholas" by Clement Clarke Moore.

Erev Christmas [Christmas Eve]

'Twas the night before Christmas, and we, being Jews,
my girlfriend and me—we had nothing to do.
The Gentiles were home, hanging stockings with care,
secure in their knowledge St. Nick would be there.
But for us, once the Chanukah candles burned down,
there was nothing but boredom all over town.
The malls and the theaters were all closed up tight;
there weren't any concerts to go to that night.
A dance would have saved us, some ballroom or swing,
but we combed through the papers; there wasn't a thing.
Outside the window sat two feet of snow;
with the wind-chill, they said, it was fifteen below.
And while all I could do was sit there and brood,
my gal saved the night and called out: "Chinese food!"

So we ran to the closet, grabbed hats, mitts, and boots—to cover our
    heads, our hands and our foots.
We pulled on our jackets, all puffy with down,
and boarded the T, bound for Chinatown.
The train nearly empty, it rolled through the stops,
while visions of wantons danced through our *kopfs*.
We hopped off at Park Street; the Common was bright,
with fresh-fallen snow and the trees strung with lights,
then crept through "The Zone" with its bums and its thugs,
and entrepreneurs pushing ladies and drugs.
At last we reached Chinatown, rushed through the gate,
Past bakeries, markets, shops and cafes,
in search of a restaurant: "Which one? Let's decide!"
We chose "Hunan *Chazer*," and ventured inside.

Around us sat others, their platters piled high
with the finest of fine foods their money could buy:
There was roast duck and fried squid (sweet, sour and spiced),
dried beef and mixed veggies, lo mein and fried rice.
There was whole fish and *moo shi* and shrimp *chow mee foon*,
and General Gau's chicken and *ma po* tofu . . .
When at last we decided, and the waiter did call,
we said: "Skip the menu!" and ordered it all.
And when in due time the food was all made,
it came to the table in a sort of parade.
Before us sat dim sum, spare ribs and egg rolls,

and four different soups, in four great, huge bowls.
And chicken wings! Dumplings! And beef teriyakis!
And fried scallion pancakes—'cause they're kinda like latkes.

The courses kept coming, from spicy to mild,
and higher and higher toward the ceiling were piled.
And while this went on, we were aware
every diner around us had started to stare.
Their jaws hanging open, they looked on unblinking;
some dropped their teacups, some drooled without thinking.
So much piled up, one dish, then another,
my girlfriend and I couldn't see one another!

Now we sat there, we two, without proper utensils,
while they handed us something that looked like two pencils.
We poked and we jabbed till our fingers were sore,
and half of our dinner wound up on the floor.
We tried—How we tried!—but, sad truth to tell,
ten long minutes later and still hungry as heck,
we swallowed our pride, feeling vaguely like dorks,
and called to our waiter to bring us two forks.

Then we *fressed* and we feasted, we slurped and we munched;
we *noshed* and we supped, we breakfast and lunched.
We ate near to bursting and drank down our teas,
and barely had room for the fortune cookies.
But my fortune was perfect; it summed up the mood
when it said: "Pork is kosher, when it's in Chinese food."
And my girlfriend—well . . . she got a real winner;
Hers said: "Your companion will pay for the dinner."

Our bellies were full and at last it was time
to travel back home and write down this rhyme
of our Chinatown trek (and to privately speak
about trying to refine our chopstick technique).
The MSG spun 'round and 'round in our heads,
and we tripped and we laughed, and gaily we said,
as we schlepped all our leftovers home through the night:
"Good *yom tov* to all—and to all a Good Night!"[36]

This parody lampoons several recurring themes pervasive in the Jewish affinity for Chinese food: the Jewish penchant for Chinese food on Christmas, the ineptness of eating with chopsticks, a lack of understanding of what foods are being referred to because of their Chinese names, and the passion with which they are eaten. Selecting "Hunan Chazer" as the restaurant of choice reflects the irony of Jews eating nonkosher food, called in Yiddish *chazer*, or pig. The boisterousness of the evening is described by the food that kept coming ("The courses kept coming, from spicy to mild, and higher and higher toward the ceiling were piled"), which was contrasted with the boredom they experienced at home on Christmas Eve. The couple's euphoria is symbolized by the MSG that was present to heighten the couple's awareness: "The MSG spun round and round in our heads, and we tripped and we laughed. . . ."

Bruce Marcus and Lori Factor-Marcus described their composition:

> We began "*Erev* Christmas" on December 24, 1992—one year to the day before it was published on the op-ed page of the *Boston Globe*—on the back of a placemat in a restaurant in Boston's Chinatown. In those days, the *Boston Globe* published Clement Clarke Moore's "A Visit from St. Nicholas" on the front page every December 24th. That poem was our inspiration; we decided to write a spoof that described how we spent our Christmas Eve . . . We took some flak for "Erev Christmas." After it was published, a few people took us to task for representing non-traditional Jewish dietary habits. Most, however, seemed to take our doggerel in the playful spirit in which it was written. And lastly, when asked if this is a true story (and sometimes even when we are not asked), we explain to folks that we remember there being little or no snow on the ground on Christmas Eve, 1992, and we actually do know how to use chopsticks.[37]

The first performance of the poem by Marcus was at a Jewish Storyteller's Coalition. Marcus's performance of "*Erev* Christmas" has become part of the American Jewish folk tradition through its widespread dissemination by e-mail, print media, and YouTube.

Other parodies, including some that have appeared on YouTube, mimic the function of Chinese restaurants to save Jews from being bored on Christmas. In 2006, Brandon Walker composed the enormously popular song "Chinese Food on Christmas," as reflected by the high number of visits to this YouTube video.[38] In 2006 more than 583,000 guests visited the site, while in 2007 three times as many vistors generated more than 2,000 comments. By 2011, the song had 1,800,000 viewings. In the lyrics of his YouTube parody, Brandon wakes up on Christmas Day and sees a Christmas tree barren of presents because Santa Claus was not going to appear in a Jewish house. Brandon sings, "What's a Jew to do on Christmas?" The answer is: "I eat Chinese on Christmas because there ain't much to do on Christmas." Once at the restaurant, he joins a band that turns this culinary experience into a Jewish celebration, complete with stereotypical Jewish music, a Jewish wedding dance (lifting the groom off the floor while seated in a chair), and the blowing of the shofar (ritual ram's horn). The song's music and dance address the depth to which eating Chinese food has become integrated in the American Jewish psyche and how happy Jews are to be immersed in activities on Christmas Eve and Day.

Kung Pao Kosher Comedy: Jewish Comedy in a Chinese Restaurant on Christmas

Jews who ate at Chinese restaurants on Christmas across the United States formed a loosely extended yet temporal community that took its Jewish identity seriously. It didn't take long for one enterprising comedian and self-proclaimed Chinese food enthusiast to conceive of the idea of adding entertainment to the eating experience. Quite simply, it started as a joke. In October 1993, a stand-up comedian named Lisa Geduldig, who resides in San Francisco, California, was hired to perform at what she thought was a women's cabaret evening at a comedy club in South Hadley, Massachusetts. When she arrived at the venue, Lisa realized that she had, in fact, been hired to tell Jewish jokes at the Peking Garden Club, a Chinese restaurant. On her website, Lisa Geduldig relates how she told an old summer camp friend, Tobi Sovak, about the irony of combining an evening of Jewish humor and Chinese food.

In San Francisco, a couple months after this conversation, Lisa inaugurated the first Kung Pao Kosher Comedy as an evening of Jewish stand-up comedy in a Chinese restaurant on Christmas. To create a Jewish atmosphere, every year the organizers saturated the Chinese restaurant venue with Jewish themes, music, symbols, and performances. To add to the holiday ambiance, the Chinese restaurant was decorated with recognizable Hanukkah props, including dreidel piñatas and inflatable decorations that look like matzo balls and bagels, blow-up dreidels sitting atop restaurant vases, and streamers and banners in the Israeli flag colors of blue and white. When Hanukkah overlapped with Christmas, guests joined together and lit Hanukkah candles, chanted blessings, and sang Hanukkah songs.

When Kung Pao Kosher Comedy's founder Lisa Geduldig conceived of the event, she hoped to create a hermetic Jewish environment where guests could focus on Jewish tradition and identity and bypass Christmas. "Jewish people," Geduldig said, "feel alienated that time of year and just like to have something to celebrate, instead of hiding under the covers until the end of December. . . . I mean you get very Christmas-ed to death from November

27 on," she admitted. "I'm not, like, anti-Christ or anything. You just feel like a stranger in a strange land for the entire month of December."[39]

Lisa, with the help of sympathetic Chinese restaurant proprietors, recast the restaurant into a carnivalesque Jewish feast where patrons view Hanukkah decorations, listen to Jewish music, and are entertained by Jewish comedians. To add to the Jewish authenticity of the evening, Lisa ensures that the evening's sights and sounds are communicated using a sprinkling of Yiddish words and Yiddish proverbs translated into English and inserted in fortune cookies. For example, one proverb states: "Better the bite of a friend than the kiss of an enemy." Lisa also predicates her appeal to the charitable nature of people during the holiday season by asking Jews to give *tzedakah* (charity), a prominent Jewish value exercised in the spirit of seasonal giving.

Lisa's vision has proven highly successful. Since its inception in 1993, the Kung Pao Kosher Christmas event has increased every year, and now, after two decades, Jews consider it to be an annual Christmastime tradition. It has also been replicated in American cities with sizable Jewish populations. That first year, Lisa expected 250 people to come. To her surprise, more than four hundred patrons queued up outside the Chinese restaurant to gain admittance. Crowds have reached into the thousands and peaked at three thousand in 1997 when the popular comedian Henny Youngman came to perform at the New Asia Chinese restaurant in San Francisco's Chinatown.

Appealing to a cross section of Jews and Jewish organizations from the San Francisco Bay area, the show's reputation has attracted people from as far away as Vancouver, Tucson, and New York. They come to an event headlined as "Kung Pao Kosher Comedy," a title that merged familiar Chinese and Jewish words. "Kung Pao" is known to patrons of Chinese restaurants as a style of food preparation. "Kosher" lends an air of Jewish authenticity to the event, even though the foods served are not, in fact, certified kosher. Geduldig makes a point to let everyone know that shellfish is, in fact, being served ("kosher walnut prawns") so that those who abstain for dietary reasons will be forewarned. In her monologues Lisa mentions that pork falls under the category of "safe *treyf.*" "You know how Jews aren't supposed to eat pork, right?" Lisa asks. "But . . . there's a small unknown clause in the Torah that says if it's wrapped in a wonton, it's ok." Said, tongue-in-cheek, Lisa puts out a "*treyf* alert," letting people know that there is no pork on the menu. "But one dish has shrimp (because your hostess loves shrimp)." Lisa avoids the problem of forcing nonkosher foods on guests by providing an alternative vegetarian menu at buffets served for the dinner shows.

The reputation of this novel event spread quickly throughout the Bay area and picked up sponsors from Jewish and non-Jewish organizations. For example, Congregation Emanu-El of San Francisco has often sponsored the official Kung Pao Kosher Comedy t-shirt and fortune cookies served for dessert, and the Workman's Circle has advertised prizes of two thirty-minute videos in Yiddish (with the humorous titles. "Why *Shlep* [drag] to the Gym?" and "*Tsures* [trouble] in the Kitchen?") to raffle winners. The Jewish Community Federation asked on its promotional flyer: "Is kosher sweet and sour pork an oxymoron? Not Sure? Call. . . ."

Publicity also capitalized on the incongruity of combining Jewish ethnic and Chinese cultures. One newspaper opined that "Kung Pao Kosher Comedy is becoming a Christmas tradition in the vein of San Francisco traditions that combine the odd and the ball to best effect."[40] Another paper commented: "It's no secret that Jews face tough sledding when Christmas comes to squat like the jolly King Kong winter events. Many a Bay Area Jew, however, has been saved by the annual Kung Pao Kosher Comedy show."[41]

Loyal followers and interested parties peruse a website on which can be found information on pricing and scheduling for the upcoming December shows. The website descriptions are communicated humorously using Yiddish-phrased English words to attract potential patrons to a night of comedy. The site www.koshercomedy.com, for example, is listed as being on the *World Vide Veb* (an alliteration using Yiddish-inflected English). For several years, the show sent postcards to entice patrons to reserve early. One postcard depicted a crowd lolling around a swimming pool in a Catskills resort, a scene setting the context for a relaxed and fun-filled Kung Pao Kosher Comedy event. The site promised to offer guests a gastronomical feast reminiscent of the great Jewish restaurants and popular Jewish foods. Fictitious directions to Kung Pao list: "From New York City, go to Yonah Shimmels and get Lisa one dozen knishes, go to Kiev and get her some blintzes, go to Zabar's and get her anything."

Lisa Geduldig's business card and promotional literature also melds Chinese and Jewish symbols. The event's logo comprises a typical take-out container on which is drawn Jewish stars on both sides inscribed with the following motto: "Spend a traditional Jewish Christmas in a Chinese Restaurant." The graphic design used on her stationary, dinner menu, and publicity combines the "kosher font" (which resembles Hebrew and Torah calligraphy) and "comic book II" (a font resembling Chinese calligraphy).

Those who work the shows are given Yiddish names. Lisa (the self-proclaimed *meshugganah* [crazy] producer and Mistress of Ceremonies) and Lawrence (the *meshugganah* publicist) put out a call for one hundred volunteers who are known as *shverer arbeiters* (Yiddish for hard workers). A volunteer *macher* (volunteer coordinator) oversees the *shverer arbeiters*. The liaison to the performers (or as Lisa is wont to call her, the "Vanna White" of the show) and Lisa's main assistant is called *Bubbelah* (an affectionate name for grandmother). Additional assistance is provided by a sound *maven* (knowledgeable person), a lighting *mensch* (person of good reputation), a *Vorld Vide Veb* mistress, and a *Will Kvetch* (will call) *mensch* who handles tickets on hold. These volunteers are acknowledged and thanked in the program. Additionally, "special *mensch*-ion" (a play on the word *mensch*, meaning moral person) is made for certain companies and individuals that have provided additional services.

With Yiddish setting the linguistic stage for a Jewish evening, the organizers blend Jewish and Chinese symbols on a playbill, modeled on ones prepared for Broadway shows. On the front cover is the event's logo, a dreidel with the Hebrew letter "*shin*" (standing for the Hebrew word *shahm*, meaning "there"—Israel) and a pagoda. Two chopsticks protrude from the top left side of the open takeout container. The chopstick on the right has a banner at the top with the name "Kung Pao Kosher Comedy." To the right of the pair of chopsticks and popping out of the takeout container is a black design in the shape of Jewish star. Embellished on the star are the words "Hot and Sour."

San Francisco is known to be socially and culturally progressive. Chinatown in San Francisco is one of the largest Chinese neighborhoods outside of China, the perfect setting for this Jewish Christmas carnivalesque event. Chinatown's vibrant business concerns, popular restaurants, and eager sidewalk fruit and vegetable vendors are open for business on Christmas. People of Chinese descent, as well as other Americans, come and go in droves as they busily engage in neighborhood life.

San Francisco has a relatively small, marginalized, and assimilated Jewish community.[42] Lisa has reflected on how Jews are more marginalized in San Francisco simply because it's not New York City: "San Francisco is not such a Jewish city, so it's even more alienating and even more subversive . . . people have no idea that it's Yom Kippur. When you walk down the street in New York, everything is closed. The schools are closed. If you're not Jewish in New York, you're Jewish by osmosis. If you're not Jewish in San Francisco, you're not Jewish!"[43] The city does not have any distinct Jewish neighborhoods, though Jews over the years have occasionally gravitated to Chinatown to shop and to establish a Jewish presence. The popular glatt kosher Sabra Grill restaurant, established in 1996, sits inside Chinatown's decorative gate. Antique shops, owned by expatriate Israelis and specializing in European and Asian art, have at various points in time operated in the Chinatown vicinity.

Kung Pao Kosher Comedy is successful because Jews in San Francisco seek a social setting in which guests can celebrate their Jewish heritage and affirm their identity. Kung Pao attracts crowds that are highly conscious of their Jewishness. Lisa estimates the audience to be at least 85 percent Jewish, ranging from hip to Orthodox.[44] A handful of Jewish interfaith couples and even Chinese-Jewish couples attend. The audience ranges in age from twenty to ninety years. Most are affiliated members of the Jewish community—from secular, cultural, educational, and religious organizations; some are politically progressive, including a mixture of gay and straight patrons. For Lisa and her guests, Kung Pao Kosher Comedy is a burst of Jewish fresh air during the Christmas season. San Francisco is also a city well known for showcasing avant-garde performers, among them Lisa Geduldig.

At Kung Pao Kosher Comedy, Jewish stand-up comedians entertain audiences during six to eight consecutive shows that span three to four days. Three comedians perform at each showing, drawn from a mix of men and women, straight and gay. Through the years, comedians such as Shelley Berman, David Brenner, Henny Youngman, and Freddie Roman have all headlined at Kung Pao. Also represented is a younger generation of comedians who range in age from twenty to forty-five, such as Lisa Kron in 2003 and Jonathan Katz in 2009.[45] Lisa Geduldig is aware that the world of comedy has historically been dominated by men. It is a badge of honor for her that new female comedians are making their mark and are present on the stage at Kung Pao Kosher Comedy.

Kosher Comedy on Christmas: Jewish Humor Helps Overcome the Holiday Blues

At the heart of Kung Pao Kosher Comedy are comedic performances that serve as an extended commentary on the status of Jews at Christmas time and their quest to find relief from a Christmas-dominated holiday season. "When I say six words—Jewish comedy, Christmas Eve, and Chinese restaurant," Lisa remarks, "people smile and it clicks."

Comedians who perform at Kung Pao Kosher Comedy make audiences smile by relating their experiences of Christmas and Hanukkah. One year, comedian Cathy Ladman told how the Hanukkah gift her parents bought her fell short of expectation. "When I was a kid, my friends thought I was lucky. 'Wow, Hanukkah's eight days, you get eight gifts.' Wrong. My parents would give me one gift and rip it into eight pieces."[46] Cathy, in another show, picked up on this theme of frustration, indicating that Christmas gifts may disappoint. "Mary gets gifts from the Wise Men," which in her opinion are useless gifts, very much like Jewish children get for Hanukkah: "Myrrh. Oh how wonderful. Myrrh. You can never receive enough myrrh. I had hoped for a cradle, but they brought myrrh. I hate the wise men. They bring such lousy gifts."[47]

Satire is used to describe the overly commercialized Christmas holiday. In one performance, the comedian Scott Blakeman asks, "Did you ever notice that on television they say 'We want to wish a Happy Chanukah to our Jewish friends' and a week later they say 'Merry Christmas to all' and there are lots of Christmas sales but never a Chanukah sale? 'We bought enough merchandise to last one day and it's lasted eight days— it's a miracle.'"[48]

Lampooning both Hanukkah and Christmas bypasses tension often experienced by Jews for being different and marginalized during the holiday season. Comedians raise awareness of the challenge of having to recognize Christmas as important to American society while at the same time desiring to escape its influence. At Kung Pao, humor is the chosen vehicle employed by a Jewish minority to confront a holiday season dominated by the Christian majority. Humor is a weapon comedians use to take cultural revenge on Christmas, thereby symbolically robbing the holiday of its ability to intimidate. One repeat patron, a forty-two-year-old doctor, explained: "I am an outsider. It is someone else's birthday party and I'm not invited. . . . We all commiserated about living through and being an outsider for one month a year. . . . I will attend the Kung Pao show next year because I belong to the group . . . it's heartening to hear someone say these things publicly, as they are not very PC [politically correct]."

Unmistakably, in two short decades, Kung Pao Kosher Comedy, a Christmastime innovation, has become a cultural tradition that introduces Jews in America to a new and humorous way of encountering Christmas. Through these performance vehicles, a new cultural reality is created in which Christmas simply does not matter. The audience emerges from Kung Pao Kosher Comedy as an extended family that shares moments of laughter, poignancy, vulnerability, and triumph. After an evening of redeeming laughter, it is funny and unexpected for the master of cere-monies to call out as the comedy banquet ends, "See you next year; next year in Jerusalem." This bellow, taken from the conclusion to the Passover meal, contains a realization that after the show ends, the temporary relief, joy, and camaraderie also comes to an end. After all, the next morning, people will wake up, and, outside, it will still be Christmas. Next year it will be necessary to once again reassemble, seek temporary haven from the Christmas season, and collectively share an alternative cultural tradition of affirming and proclaiming Jewish identity in the face of Christmas.

Kung Pao Kosher Comedy's Impact on Creating New Jewish Traditions on Christmas

Kung Pao Kosher Comedy has become a model for other similar Christmas Eve Jewish comedy banquets and has set a trend for Jewish social gatherings across the country. Over the years, Jewish organizations in American cities have copied Lisa Geduldig's event format by hosting a Christmas Eve dinner of Chinese food followed by a Jewish comedy show; however, none of these have the staying power of Kung Pao Kosher Comedy. For example, the Brandeis University Women's Chapter of San Jose, California, named its event "With Eggrolls You Get Laffs." This San Jose event took place for a few years, from 1995 through 2000, at a Chinese restaurant buried in a strip-mall shopping center. In 1997, the San Jose Jewish comedy banquet attracted between 150 and 200 patrons who paid $37.50 per person, of which $8.00 was tax deductible. The event sold out and yielded a small profit, which, in turn, was donated to the Brandeis University library.

The Jewish Community Center (JCC) in the District of Columbia also hosted an event called Kung Pao Comedy, paying homage through its name to the San Francisco original. The Washington, D.C., event, which took place on Christmas Eve in the years 1996 and 1997, was held at the Jewish Community Center in Washington. Advertisements for the JCC event appeared one week before Christmas of 1997 in the district's Jewish newspaper. The advertisement presented the following question: "What do you call hundreds of people eating Chinese food and laughing hysterically? Kung Pao Comedy." Of the event, the local Jewish newspaper wrote: "It's the perfectly hilarious thing to do on your otherwise dull Christmas Eve. One of the most recognized (and often joked about) traditions in the Jewish canon has nothing to do with synagogue, Israel or even, the Torah. Give up? It's the annual, 'Let's go out for Chinese food and a movie because it's Christmas Eve and we have nothing else to do . . .' The Washington, D.C., Jewish Community Center reinvents this time-honored combination of the Jewish community's great loves: live comedy and Chinese food."[49] By virtue of dietary demand, the foods served at the Washington event were kosher, which differentiated it from the "kosher-style" menu of the San Francisco original. Ticket prices were $26 for members and $40 for nonmembers, respectively. A review which appeared in the *Washington Post* after the December 1996 show carried the headline "God Jest Ye Merry Gentlemen at Jewish Comedy Show, Having a Little Fun with Christmas."[50] Of the event, the reporter, Marc Fisher, wrote: "It's Christmas Eve, the streets are empty, and many Jews figure their Christian friends are at home, eating ham and rehearsing uncomfortable silences for the next day's family gatherings. So what's a Jew to do? . . . Not a problem. Everything a Jew needs on Christmas is taken care of right here—Chinese food and comedy."[51] Rob Kutner opened the comedy show by saying: "Good evening, I want to be the first this evening to wish you a Merry—oh, never mind. The real reason we're here tonight is it [stinks] to be a Jew on Christmas Eve in America. Imagine if Jews got their hands on Christmas. Okay, we're supposed to be nice on Christmas. But, precisely how nice? And I ask you, imagine the concept of 'Silent Night.'"[52] The audience roared imagining the contrast between the uproarious evening and the usually silent night to which Jews are typically subject. The rabbi, who was wearing an Abbot and Costello tie, promoted the idea of Jews looking at this event from a Jewish perspective: "Here we are tonight, as usual, trying to see the non-Jewish world entirely through Jewish eyes. And of course, to us, it's a conspiracy. They give us the day off and there's nothing to do."[53]

By 2012, the tradition of a live performance of Jewish comedy, often coupled with Chinese food on Christmas, had become commonplace across the United States. In Philadelphia, on Friday night, December 24, 2010, the Gershman Y sponsored the second annual "Moo Shu Jew Show." An evening of Jewish comedy set in a restaurant in Philadelphia's Chinatown, this sold-out "Meshuggena" event, advertised as being "created for Jews to enjoy at Christmas time, where Jews feel most at home in a Chinese restaurant," featured a six-course banquet and several of "the funniest comedians from New York."[54] Additionally, the New York City Stand-Up Comedy Club "The World," in Times Square, hosted the show "Jewish Christmas Eve Comedy."[55] At nearby Caroline's comedy club on Broadway, New York's best Jewish comedians have been appearing at Christmas during each of the last ten years. In 2010, from December 22 to 25 a show, called "The Chosen Ones," featuring two performances each night, invited customers to "come celebrate the festival of lights with a festival of laughs" with New York's top Jewish comedians. The club urges people "to skip the Chinese food and a movie on Christmas Eve and come to Caroline's."[56] Another New York comedy venue, the Comic Strip, advertises its annual two Christmas Eve shows of "A Kosher Christmas Eve": "NYC funniest Jewish comedians doing schtick . . . guaranteed funnier than Chinese food and a movie."[57]

A different kind of subversive comedy act on Christmas comes in the form of *Jewmongous*, a traveling comedy concert by songwriter Sean Altman. Altman reflects on his Christmas concert, which occasionally features songwriter and singer Cynthia Kaplan, saying "We are all in on a joke, it's somebody else's big night—we've crashed the prom and took over the champagne room. There's a delicious feeling of naughtiness, of engaging in the forbidden."[58] *Jewmongous* makes regular appearances throughout the United States, including Joe's Pub in New York City, the Birchmere in Alexandria, Virginia, the Iron Horse Café in Northampton, Massachusetts, the Tin Angel club in Philadelphia, Club Passim in Cambridge, Massachusetts, the Skokie Theater in Skokie, Illinois, and Hooker-Dunham Theater in Brattleboro, Vermont. He has toured seven European cities and even Asia. (Altman fondly recalls his gig for Congregation Kehillat Beijing.) In 2011, Altman's second tour of Israel included a performance at Jacob's Ladder, Israel's major folk festival and a dozen other concerts nationwide.

Kung Pao Kosher Comedy and the multitude of similar events like it that are now organized across the United States reflect a new, positive attitude by younger American Jews toward the Christmas holiday season. These Jews unabashedly express their feelings, reflecting a new openness to challenge Jews to ignore the influence of Christmas on American society. A younger Jewish generation wants to be active during the Christmas holiday, to celebrate and be festive about Jewish community and personal identity. The success of new cultural traditions like Kung Pao Kosher Comedy helps Jews overcome historic contradictions faced by earlier generations of American Jews. Jews attending comedy shows on Christmas Eve reflect a Jewish community that is able to overcome feelings of being an outsider to holiday celebrations.[59] In previous generations, American Jews had no choice other than to participate in Christmas or reject it. Now Jews can substitute a new Jewish cultural reality whereby Christmas is not an isolating force. Organized comedy events during the Christmas season allow Jews to find alternative means to congregate, socialize, and strengthen their Jewish identity. Kung Pao Kosher Comedy and similar social events across the nation, such as singles' balls and klezmer concerts, signal the arrival of a new era in the Jewish response to Christmas, one in which the holiday of Christmas plays a secondary role to the interests of a thriving and self-aware Jewish community.

The successful impact of Kung Pao Kosher Comedy (and other similar Christmastime entertainment directed at Jewish patrons) is reflected in press reports calling it an important Jewish "Christmastime tradition," relevant for those who do not celebrate Christmas. Furthermore, the press acknowledges the value of American minority groups at Christmas searching for alternative seasonal celebrations that are humorous and social. Indeed, Americans today are comfortable embracing both the religiously reverent and creative expressions of alternative December holiday festivities.

Until recently, those Americans who rejected Christmas, including Jews, were considered outsiders. By joining together on Christmas at entertainment venues across the United States to celebrate and proclaim Jewish identity, Jews achieve the special status of insider, representing those who seek alternative, acceptable means to celebrate the holiday season. As one young Jewish woman observed while waiting to enter a Kung Pao Kosher Comedy performance, "I want to be with other Jews celebrating, doing something that's not Christmas, that's 'un-Christmas.' I want to feel like an insider, not an outsider. Being here at Kung Pao Kosher Comedy, I don't feel like an outsider."[60]

CHAPTER 4

"'TWAS THE NIGHT BEFORE HANUKKAH"

REMAKING CHRISTMAS THROUGH PARODY AND POPULAR CULTURE

The humorous assault on the character of Christmas represented by Kung Pao Kosher Comedy's biting humor reflects a whimsical and subversive strain in American society. Observers of popular culture capitalize on contrasting religious and secular aspects of Christmas to exaggerate Christmas's benefits and faults. Christmas lends itself to parody and even caricature because the holiday incorporates elements from many different nationalities and cultures. Christmas is also continually reinterpreted by different generations of Americans to reflect ever-changing social and cultural viewpoints. The more American society becomes amenable to the involvement of members of diverse ethnic and religious groups, the greater the license writers, artists, and entertainers take in reshaping the meaning of Christmas for American society.

Jews, at once excluded outsiders and consummate insiders in the American success story, played a considerable role in this remaking of Christmas. As prominent writers and entertainers in America, Jews worked to neutralize Christmas from two different perspectives. First, they sought to recreate Christmas as a reflection of patriotic pride, devoid of any religious meaning and full of the qualities of home, children, and goodwill. Accordingly, in the public mind, Christmas was celebrated for its sentimental impact rather than its historical meaning. In the twentieth century, this dichotomy's far-reaching consequences led to deemphasizing mention of either Christmas or Hanukkah and to offering inoffensive seasonal rather than Christmas-specific greetings. Second, Jews satirized Christmas by proclaiming any emphasis on home, children, and goodwill to be overly conformist and idealistic. Artists satirized and parodied Christmas, thereby revealing a deeper Christmas malaise among the general population, including both Jewish and non-Jewish Americans. Viewing Christmas through the lens of popular culture and parody crystallizes the development and interplay of these two perspectives.

IRVING BERLIN'S "WHITE CHRISTMAS"

Irving Berlin (1888–1989), one of the greatest American composers and lyricists, can be credited with penning the most popular Christmas song of all time, "White Christmas." Philip Roth, in his book *Operation Shylock*, offers kudos to Berlin for secularizing Christmas through his best-selling song. Roth writes: "God gave Moses the Ten Commandments and then he gave Berlin 'Easter Parade' and 'White Christmas' . . . and what does Irving Berlin brilliantly do? He de-Christs them both! . . . He turns Christmas into a holiday about snow. . . . H*e turns their religion into schlock*. But nicely! . . . If supplanting Jesus Christ with snow can enable my people to cozy up to Christmas, then let it snow, let it snow, let it snow."[1] Of course, as Jody Rosen perceptively remarks in his book *White Christmas: The Story of an American Song*, Berlin's achievement in turning attention away from the religious aspects of Christmas was purely unconscious. Rosen explains that Tin Pan Alley artists had been rewriting the American songbook since the 1920s.[2] Largely immigrant and Jewish, writers, performers, and producers of Tin Pan Alley recreated an image of America that was filtered through an outsider's perspective. By focusing on the folk and ethnic elements of America's holidays, they painted a sentimental portrait of their value in reinforcing American patriotism and pride.

Representing the sandwich generation between World War I and World War II, Berlin prolifically created a panoply of patriotic songs and Broadway shows. His magnum opus was "God Bless America," which he wrote in 1938. It was his good fortune that "White Christmas" would burst onto the musical scene when the United States entered World War II. "White Christmas," although written as part of a holiday cycle for the 1942 movie *Holiday Inn*, was actually composed in 1941 and held back for the appropriate moment when Berlin could secure Bing Crosby to record the song. Even though it seemed impossible for "God Bless America" to be topped by any song, Berlin bragged to his steadfast arranger Helmy Kresa that "White Christmas" would be the greatest song ever written.[3]

For Berlin, the power of Christmas was in projecting an idealistic world for which Americans longed. The idea of "White Christmas" came to Berlin when he was working in Hollywood during the Christmas season and could not be with his family to celebrate. Berlin was married to a non-Jew and celebrated Christmas at home. While in California, he composed an opening stanza to "White Christmas" that expressed his disappointment at missing his family and the snow that swathed the Christmas season on the East Coast. These lines were ultimately cut out of the now classic version of the song. Fortuitously for Berlin, soldiers sent off to war shared the same anxiety and homesickness. When "White Christmas" was released as a record in May 1942, it became an instant hit, even six months prior to the Christmas season. Berlin worried that the song would lose its appeal by Christmastime. But when soldiers going to or coming back from war heard "White Christmas," they instantly embraced it as the embodiment of all that was good about America and all that they left behind. Record sales soared, and "White Christmas" became the greatest Christmas song of all time.

"White Christmas," demonstrating the genius of Berlin, was part of a popular culture that drew on the emotions and tastes of the times that included patriotic fervor. Tin Pan Alley had already moved away from blackface minstrels and into folk themes that capitalized on describing the qualities that made America great: home, family, love, hard work, and a conforming allegiance to the United States of America. To bring out these qualities in song and Broadway performance was to depict the absence of these traits and the longing for them. Christmas songs, plays, and movies catered to these themes, the best known of which were *Holiday Inn*, *White Christmas*, *Miracle on 34th Street*, and *It's a Wonderful Life*.

Implicit in Roth's turgid remarks about Berlin's "White Christmas" song is the idea that popular culture manipulates people's tastes. Though musical tastes often follow cultural trends, mass entertainment thrives on introducing the cutting edge and creating new fads. Irving Berlin was known for riding this wave with a vengeance and selecting the appropriate singers to convey his patriotic messages. "White Christmas" required Bing Crosby to carry the simple words into the memorable phrases with his "dreamy . . . sentimental crooning."[4]

As opportunistic as Berlin was in attempting to sell large quantities of sheet music and records, he had his pulse on the emotional impact of the holiday on Americans of the time. For all Americans, whether Christian or Jew, the December season of Hanukkah and Christmas evoked strong feelings of idealism, of a world at peace in which families could celebrate the holiday spirit together. For Americans who celebrate Christmas, idealized images abound to convey this spirit: family and friends trimming trees, waiting for Santa bearing gifts, exchanging greeting cards, sitting down to a family feast, caroling, building snowmen, and sledding. For Jews, seasonal joy was accomplished through lighting menorahs, spinning dreidels, singing Hanukkah songs, and opening presents. These images captured people's imaginations, and holiday symbols could be seen in store windows, magazine advertisements, and greeting cards. "White Christmas" supported and drew sustenance from the universal, positive ambiance that pervaded the holiday season, reflecting everything that was right with the country. In the worldview of Irving Berlin and his fellow composers, Christmas was a celebration of the potential for joy that must be reclaimed each year.

Irving Berlin was not the only Jew to have found an opportunity in the American Christmas season to express the mood of the country. From 1945 and into the present, American Jews composed some of the most beloved Christmas songs, many of them reaching canonical Christmas status. American Jewish composers are responsible for major holiday hits: Johnny Marks wrote "Rudolph the Red-Nosed Reindeer" (1949), "I Heard the Bells on Christmas Day" (1956), "Rockin' around the Christmas Tree" (1958), and "Holly Jolly Christmas" (1965); George Wyle cowrote "It's the Most Wonderful Time of the Year" (1963), Mel Torme composed "The Christmas Song" ("Chestnuts Roasting on an Open Fire," 1944), Jay Livingston and Ray Evans produced "Silver Bells"(1950), Mitchell Parish coauthored "Sleigh Ride"(1950), and Sammy Cahn and Jule Styne wrote "Let It Snow, Let It Snow, Let It Snow"(1945).[5]

Of particular interest is the song "Rudolph the Red Nose Reindeer," whose lyrics were originally composed in 1938 by Robert L. May in the form of a narrative poem. May, who was an advertising copywriter for Montgomery Ward and who was facing a number of personal and financial challenges, wrote the song to give hope to his four-year-old daughter while her mother, his wife, lay dying of cancer: "May described in story form not only the pain felt by those who were different but also the joy that can be found when someone discovers his special place in the world."[6] Constant retelling of the story to May's daughter resulted in embellishment and refinement to the original. May then produced a handmade book to present to his daughter. At a holiday party hosted at Montgomery Ward, May was pressed to share his Christmas tale. Observing that everyone in attendance wanted a copy, the head of the company felt that it would be a huge promotional hit. By 1946, Montgomery Ward had given away six million copies of the book, all to children who came to the stores to sit on Santa's lap. Product and toy deals followed the book's success. The book was then adapted into a song by Johnny Marks (May's brother-in-law, a prolific composer in his own right), who facilitated its recording by Gene Autry, albeit reluctantly, in 1949. It became the second-best-selling Christmas song of all time. May's biography indicates that he identified with the shunned Rudolph because he was teased as a child for his small stature and thinness. His adult life had also been difficult as the family faced financial ruin under the burden of his wife's medical expenses. Ace Collins, who catalogued the history and stories behind popular Christmas songs, derives from this song the lesson that it takes "courage to be different."[7]

The theme of overcoming hardship underlies much of the power of the Christmas season. Popular media capitalizes on the failings of modernity and heralds the Christmas season as a promise of salvation. Poverty, war, urban plight, minority status, and greed—conditions inimical to a progressive society—can be assuaged by casting a fantasy net around a particular period of the year. During Christmas and Hanukkah, greed is transformed into charity, societal and familial dysfunction into harmonious relationships, diversity into unity, anonymity into caring, and aggressive feelings into peaceful contemplation. The popular culture surrounding Christmas and Hanukkah ensured that novelty and commercial success would coincide with American ideals. The marketing of Christmas and Hanukkah to the American public through vehicles of entertainment and commerce provided for an appeal to popular taste to elicit holiday joy.[8]

A perusal of the ever-successful Radio City Music Hall's *Christmas Spectacular*, ongoing since 1933, demonstrates that the very songs and images created by Irving Berlin and other Jewish composers and artists continue to infuse Christmas with the glamour of a world transformed by good wishes and universal peace.[9] Evergreen trees, snow, Santa Claus, reindeer, children, and stockings emerge as recognizable images from a burst of visionary zeal to unite a country and a world fraught with disappointment. To the consternation of religious devotees, these symbols and images have come to embody American tradition, as old as the country itself and as representative of Christmas as Jesus.

Popular Christmas celebrations return time and time again to the forms and themes articulated by Irving Berlin and his colleagues because a strong American ethos overrides societal conflicts and tensions. Modern renditions of these popular songs have been recorded on Christmas holiday albums by such music superstars as Neil Diamond, Barbra Streisand, Barry Manilow, Carole King, Simon and Garfunkel, and most recently Bob Dylan and Paul Simon, all of whom were born into Jewish families.

The Development of a Satirical
Approach to Christmas

While Irving Berlin and his fellow lyricists were in the process of reshaping popular cultural attitudes toward Christmas by stressing its ties to patriotism, others chose to reveal a more cynical side of Christmas. A growing number of entertainers catered to the attitudes of those who did not share in the euphoria of the Christmas season. Comedians played off the disjunction between religious and secular impulses and traditional and commercial holiday images. Their weapons were not nostalgic songs or redemptive movies, but comedic routines and satirical stories that examined how tastes in popular culture were being manipulated to erode cherished American values. Jews in the interwar and postwar eras were just as involved in this critical perspective as they had been in heralding America as an ideal. In their own way, they took control of Christmas, not by embracing it, but by parodying it, thereby reducing its significance for those who could not fully share in its observance.

The earliest and most consistent material for parody is the figure of Santa Claus. As he took modern shape in Clement Moore's verse "'Twas the Night Before Christmas" and in Thomas Nast's visual images of the 1800s, Santa was clearly not an ordinary human being.[10] His elf-like stature depicted with a chubby belly only helped to elevate his magical capabilities, which included not only being able to distinguish which children were naughty and which were nice, but sneaking into and escaping out of chimneys in the homes of these children. As later developed by the political cartoonist Nast, Santa's girth grew as did his size into a grandfatherly figure sporting a long white beard and wearing a red coat with white collar and cuffs, white-cuffed red trousers, and black leather belt and boots. Santa's role as beneficent gift-giver ensured that his reputation would remain intact, even though his exaggerated features served as grist for the humor mill for many years to come. Santa was likewise co-opted by the advertising industry, which rendered his role as pitchman for profit makers even more incongruous with his roles of mythical gift-giver and peacemaker.[11]At the same time as Santa became a cherished icon of the American Christmas, replicated in store windows and street corners, his portly figure was often caricatured. Santa was portrayed as the robber baron, who pretended to offer people what they need but in fact encouraged them to buy goods in quantity to increase his company's profits (hence the symbolism of a large stomach). The legendary American and Jewish humorist, the literary figure Sidney Joseph Perelman (known by his nom de plume S. J. Perelman), penned a short story entitled "Waiting for Santy," a playlet that was published in the *New Yorker* magazine on December 26, 1936. "Waiting for Santy," a depression-era parody of Clifford Odets's play *Waiting for Lefty*, examined proletarian rhetoric in the context of a revolt in Santa's workshop on the eve of Christmas led by Jewish revolutionary elves. Perelman played upon the relationship between employer (in this case, Santa as chairman of his toy factory) and employees (Santa's workers), who were being short-changed and mistreated.[12] Because Jews played a prominent role in developing unions and improving conditions for workers, Perelman's Christmas playlet rang a responsive chord. Santa's beneficence toward children during the Christmas season was grounded in the claim that he made his fortune on the back-breaking labor of his employees. Counter to the popular image of happy elves, Santa's gnomes in Perelman's playlet were unhappy and expressed their dissatisfaction behind Santa's back.

The gnomes Riskin and Ruskin, a wordplay on Jewish surnames, mirror Jewish involvement on both sides of the picket line. Riskin is the instigator, casting aspersions at Santa: "A parasite, a leech, a bloodsucker—altogether a five-star nogoodnick!"[13] In response, Ruskin calls Riskin a "Karl Marx." Riskin responds by hurling labels at Ruskin, calling him "scab, stool pigeon, company spy." Santa's workers are depicted as producing fake toys, consisting of "snow queens painted on flexible flyers." Panken, the gnome who works like a slave and asks no questions, points out the artificiality of Santa's handiwork to the fatalist Briskin and hands him a wax fruit that he had painted. Briskin castigates Panken for complaining but doing nothing to alleviate his plight, unlike Rivkin who is consciously trying to get "tight" with the boss and improve his standing. Who does he think he is, queries Riskin—"J. Pierpont Rivkin"? Here is an allusion to the robber baron who pretends to be generous when, in fact, he makes his fortune on the exploited labor of the less fortunate. Rivkin pretends to be Santa's heir by wooing Santa's daughter. However, in doing so, Rivkin realizes he is complicit in Santa's phony status. When Santa becomes ill, he offers Rivkin both his own position and his daughter, thereby transforming his future Jewish son-in-law into the boss, the Santa Claus, on Christmas Eve.

Perelman's parody was the first of many that relied on the comedic nature of Clement Moore's description of Santa and his reindeer. Given the popularity of Clement Moore's poem and the ease with which it could be caricatured, it is not surprising that "'Twas the Night Before Christmas" would become the most parodied of all Christmas literature. Illustrations of this genre go back as early as 1938 and continue through the 1940s and 1950s, becoming common by the end of the twentieth century.[14] By 1965, a parody of Clement Moore's poem appeared in Marie Jaffe's witty Yiddish translation of the poem entitled "Erev Krismes" (Christmas Eve).[15]

"'TWAS THE NIGHT BEFORE HANUKKAH" PARODIES

Santa Claus was particularly attractive to Jewish children who saw facsimiles of him in shopping malls and in store windows and who believed that he was responsible for the gifts that Christian children received. Although the Hanukkah holiday expanded over time to include gifts for Jewish children, the absence of a Santa-type figure was sorely felt.

That lacuna was filled in 1981 by Daniel Halevi Bloom, creator of a local news weekly in Juneau, Alaska. Bloom offered Jewish children an opportunity to write to Santa at his North Pole address in the guise of Bubbie and Zadie (Yiddish for "Grandma" and "Grandpa"). These familiar and loving grandparental figures are those typically credited with spoiling Jewish children through year-round gifts. Unlike Santa, Bubbie and Zadie's giving is not tied to judging who is naughty or nice. The role of this fictional Bubbie and Zadie (as it is for Santa) is to help parents become aware of what gifts their children want at holiday time. When Bubbie and Zadie enter the home on the first night of Hanukkah, as described in Bloom's 1985 children's book *Bubbie and Zadie Come to My House: A Story for Hanukkah*, they are accepted with familiarity despite the fact that they have magical powers. Rather than material presents, the fictional Bubbie and Zadie bring "good luck" and "a good heart."[16] In 2006, the book was reprinted in a twentieth-anniversary edition with newly colored illustrations. Reviews of the book posted online vary in tone and response. One reviewer likened the figures of Bubbie and Zadie to "being Santa Claus in a beard and dress," to which Bloom responded: "Bubbie and Zadie are not Santa Claus and have no relation to him. But I respect [his] opinion on this, and say go in good health, sir!"[17] Another reviewer states, "This book is a classic. It belongs in every Jewish (and half-Jewish) home in America. Daniel Halevi Bloom is a modern day Bing Crosby!"[18]

Ultimately, Bloom's Bubbie and Zadie were fictional characters too closely grounded in reality and not enough in fantasy. In popular culture they were therefore not entirely successful as counterparts to Santa. It was much easier to parody Santa and to create a Jewish counterpart who would mimic Santa, albeit with a Jewish twist. Early examples of this genre painted the Jewish Santa as a reluctant antihero—part *nebbish* (timid simpleton), part *schlemiel* (dolt). By the 1990s, this Jewish Santa persona became much more forthright and, at times, aggressive.

Stanley Adams and Sid Wayne combined their talents in 1962 to offer one of the first examples of this category of parody in their music record album "'Twas the Night Before Chanukah."[19] The 1960s saw a growing movement toward Jewish pride and identity that allowed for greater freedom to laugh at the incongruity of a secular season that masqueraded as a religious holiday. While most selections on this record album were song parodies, "'Twas the Night Before Chanukah" continued the spoken tradition, sprinkling verses with Yiddish words and phrases familiar to immigrants and their children.

The opening stanza, as in all such parodies, begins with the signature "'Twas the Night Before Chanukah" where everyone and everything was quiet. However, instead of stockings, underwear (*gatches*) is drying by the fire because grandfather (*zeyde,* an alternate spelling of zadie) had fallen in *chazerei* (dirt). The children were having thoughts of *halavah* (a Middle Eastern sesame candy), the mother wore a *babushkah* (scarf head covering), and the husband sported a *yarmulke* (religious head covering). In comes a portly Santa-like figure with a long white beard who is identified as Pinkus (a well-known Jewish name, whose biblical namesake acted as a zealot for God). Pinkus enters with a pushcart pulled by eight tiny reindeer, all which have been given common Yiddish surnames, such as Ginzburg, Burnstein, and Shapiro. When Pinkus arrives into this Jewish home, family members question his identity and origin. They surmise that he must be from the North Pole, but he answers satirically, "strictly from Miami Beach" (where there is a large Jewish population). At first thinking him *meshuge* (crazy), the family members become more comfortable in his presence, and this Jewish Santa-like figure helps them trim their Hanukkah "bush" and prepare dreidels, *kneydels* (matzoh balls), and knishes. In return, Pinkus receives a seltzer with a small dish of cherry preserves. The conclusion has the listener in stitches, as this Jewish Santa has difficulty going up the chimney—like a *feigele* (a little bird), a comic, albeit pejorative, euphemism for a homosexual.[20] All poems that parody "'Twas the Night Before Christmas" also parody the last line ("Merry Christmas to all and to all a good night!") by substituting its corollary "Happy Hanukkah to all, and to all a good *Yom Tov* [Happy Holiday]."

A later transitional version of "'Twas the Night Before Chanukah" parodies Santa from the outset, moving from a *meshugane* (crazy) generic character to Max Klaus who gains his validity from being an Orthodox Jew, sporting a wide beard and *peyes* (sidelocks).[21] Unlike the earlier example, in which the family is just waiting for Hanukkah to begin, this family is in the midst of a party scene in which participants are glimpsed *fressing* (eating heartily), a famous Jewish pastime. The family has trouble understanding why an old man is on the roof, an *alte kakker* (a curmudgeon). He must, the family surmises, be either a thief or a *schnorrer* (freeloader).

It is clear to the family in this version that this harbinger brings anything but cheer. He appears to be always complaining about traveling and the pressures that he undergoes from being barraged by requests from children throughout the world. In keeping with the dictates of good hospitality, Mr. Klaus is offered a glass of tea. The tea accords him the time to recount his woes. And although Mr. Klaus (a typical Jewish name) complains that he is too old for this job, he admits that he still makes a decent living and would probably be back the following year. He parts uttering the traditional holiday greeting: "*Gut Yontif*" (Happy Holidays).

In yet another version of this seemingly ubiquitous parody, the stranger, again a religious person wearing a *yarmulke*, is thrilled to be in a Jewish home, and his hosts are excited to have him.[22] He is clearly one of them, speaking Yiddish and known by the recognizable Jewish and Hebrew name of "Shloimey," from the Hebrew name Shlomo (Solomon). As a welcome guest he gets more than a glass of tea, namely a meal guaranteed to satisfy (chopped liver, *knaidlach*, and *kreplach*). Sitting down at this festive meal reminds everyone of the Passover seder meal, to which Shloimey says he will return. Why he will make his return visit on Passover is not indicated other than the familiar reference to the return of Elijah in the coming year. On this occasion of Hanukkah, he is more than pleased to be able to leave a toy. This gesture mirrors the gift that children receive for bargaining after having stolen the *afikomen*, the last piece of matzoh to be eaten at the Passover seder meal. The more Shloimey hangs around, the more acceptable he seems to be, until he becomes a fixture of the Hanukkah story in the same way that Santa is commonplace in most American homes. The message is clear: the Jewish family has its own holiday benefactor.

The triumph of the 1967 Israeli war in the Middle East produced new heroes. One example is Moshe Dayan, a legendary Israeli army general, who becomes Santa's replacement in Jerome Coopersmith's whimsical *A Chanukah Fable for Christmas*.[23] In this version, which begins with the trademark "'Twas the Night Before Christmas," a young Jewish boy pines for a Santa to bring him presents. The guest who visits is Moshe Dayan dressed in red velvet, with one eye covered by a black patch and sporting a soft army cap. This Santa-like figure rides through the sky on a dreidel with a Star of David at the top's peak. Moshe Dayan transports the boy throughout the world, showing him how people celebrate the holiday season in their own way. The message is that the Jewish child need not be jealous of Christmas because each and every religion has its own unique December holiday and its own folk heroes.

THE STAND-UP COMEDY TRADITION

Jews in America have played a vital role in joking about American life since vaudeville took America by storm in the early 1900s. In his book *The Haunted Smile: The Story of Jewish Comedians in America,* Lawrence Epstein remarks that "Jews played a prominent role, serving as comedians, booking agents, stage managers, and theater owners."[24] Centered in New York where many performers with a Jewish background lived, vaudeville was attractive to Jews as an avenue for success. Jews showed talent for comedy, in part, because of their history of survival, calling for use of imagination, wit, humor, and adaptation to new surroundings. Many Jews who found their start in vaudeville performances became beloved figures in American comedy. By the 1940s and 1950s, comedians such as George Burns, Milton Berle, Phil Silvers, George Jessel, Fannie Brice, Ed Wynn, Eddie Cantor, Jack Benny, the Marx Brothers, and the Three Stooges became household names when television entered the living rooms of American families.

As the consummate outsider, the Jewish comedian was constantly peering into American culture, standing on the cusp between assimilation and Jewish identity. Excluded from mainstream society following World War I, the Jewish comedian was forced to hone his skills in exclusively Jewish settings, such as in the New York Catskills, where an entire immigrant generation laughed at the comedian's failures and successes in adopting America as if it were his or her own. The list of famous comedians who began their careers in the Catskills is extensive. Comedians such as Red Buttons, Danny Kaye, Alan King, Buddy Hackett, Henny Youngman, Jerry Lewis, and Joan Rivers, many of whom changed their names, developed their styles and routines in this hermetic environment.[25] Ironically, as American culture embraced Jewish comedians as representatives of the American immigrant experience as a whole, these same comedians were careful not to draw too much attention to their own distinctiveness and backgrounds. Sprinkling their vignettes with Yiddish phrases, gestures, and inflections was sufficient. Jokes about the sacred seasons of Christmas and Hanukkah remained, at that time, taboo.

With the onset of the social and cultural revolutions of the 1960s, Jewish humor helped to facilitate minorities' expressions of pride in their roots and their ability communicate more directly about overcoming societal pressure to assimilate. Comedians such as Lenny Bruce and Jackie Mason began to speak openly about their Jewishness and to use conscious distinctions between Jews and non-Jews in their comedy routines. Bruce, whose acts were certain to offend everyone, humorously delineated the difference between Jews and gentiles, Jews being "hip and urban" while "goyim" (gentiles) are not.[26] In this famous comparison, Bruce foreshadows Adam Sandler's listing of prominent Jews in his 1996 "The Hanukkah Song," but Bruce divides Jews and gentiles not by their birth or by conversion but by their level of "hipness": "I'm Jewish. Count Basie's Jewish. Ray Charles is Jewish. Eddie Cantor is goyish . . . Hadassah, Jewish," he quipped. "Marine Corps—heavy goyim, dangerous. Pumpernickel is Jewish, and, as you know, white bread is very goyish."[27]

Jackie Mason was another comedian who, beginning in the 1960s, explained the difference between Jews and gentiles, using a Yiddish-affected English to frame his comedy. Mason remarked in his routines that he has frequently been told that he is "too Jewish" and would only succeed if he dropped his accent. His comparisons of Jewish and non-Jewish behaviors were provocative for the time. For example, Mason joked that Jews were incapable of mugging anyone: "When a thief demands, 'Give me your money or I'll kill you,'" Mason begins, "a Jew cannot say, 'I'll kill you.' A Jew would have to say, 'Listen, you don't have to give me all your money . . . maybe you got a few dollars now, a few dollars later.' There are Jewish muggers . . . but they're not called muggers. They're called lawyers.'" While this humor hinted at the self-deprecation that would later define Woody Allen's career, it also presents the Jews as being more refined and clever, part of a professional class that is highly esteemed and about whom new stereotypical images are fabricated.[28]

During the 1960s, religious, ethnic, and minority groups, actively asserting their roles in American society, created an environment where members of each of these respective groups welcomed learning, and even laughing, about each other. A series of jokes about the interface between these groups circulated in the guise of encounters between the clergy of the three main religions: Protestant, Catholic, and Jewish.[29] The jokes began with the same introductory formula: "There was a priest, a minister, and a rabbi . . ." and ended with the rabbi outsmarting his colleagues. During this period, not only did Hanukkah become the subject of a great deal of interest among non-Jewish Americans who were exposed to Hanukkah songs in Christmas (or holiday) pageants and on television specials, but also non-Jewish Americans were marrying Jews in increasing numbers. Americans became more curious about Hanukkah and Jews more relaxed about the threat of Christmas to their Jewish identity. This was a period characterized by parody about the two holidays, when comedians could comfortably joke without fear of offending celebrants of either holiday.

By the end of the twentieth century, there was greater willingness to critique one's own religion and heritage, to point out oddities as seen from the perspective of a sympathetic audience. Comedians in American society, many of whom were Jewish, began to mine Jewish material for subjects of humor; they found little material to be taboo and out of bounds. Whereas comedians of the 1930s, 1940s, and 1950s in the United States were careful about what they said when they performed in front of Catskill audiences, by the 1960s it was common to hear disparaging remarks about religion and ethnicity.[30]

At the same time, idioms of humor became more strident and laced with vulgarities and language that previously had been considered taboo. The period between the 1960s and 1990s witnessed generations of young people disenfranchised from American society and from religion. Members of those same generations championed the rights of women, people of color, and a myriad of ethnicities to equal treatment and access, in not only the law but also popular culture. While society still maintained a veneer of respectability for minority and ethnic groups, comedians were more likely to highlight the prevalence of hypocrisy in society, particularly with respect to influential political and religious figures who grounded their viewpoints in religious themes.

The transition from taboo to abandon when speaking about one's own religion can be viewed by comparing Henny Youngman, a first-generation Catskill performer, with Freddy Roman, a third-generation baby-boomer Catskill performer. Indeed, by the time Freddy Roman reached the attention of wider American audiences, the Catskills had ceased being a haven for Jewish gatherings and entertainment. It is both interesting and telling that Youngman and Roman were both headliner performers at Kung Pao Kosher Comedy where they displayed contrasting styles of Jewish humor.

Henny Youngman, king of the one-liner, was invited to Kung Pao Kosher Comedy in San Francisco as an exercise in nostalgia designed to recreate a bygone era in Jewish comedy.[31] Its organizers appreciated Henny Youngman's status as a headliner and his potential to draw large audiences. Indeed, 3,000 people came to hear him in 1997 during his four shows. This was the largest audience ever to attend Kung Pao Kosher Comedy, and it was his last performance. He died one month later. At the Kung Pao show, of Youngman's more than one hundred one-liners, none related to either Jewish subjects or personality traits. Many of Youngman's jokes stereotyped minorities, with a particular focus on women. His jokes were outlandishly anachronistic and immediately drew the ire of the audience.[32]

In contrast, Freddy Roman, who performed a year later, based his repertoire almost entirely on Jewish scenes and incidents. Roman's jokes also reflected a different period and generation, one in which Jews frequented the Catskills, grew older together, and ultimately moved to retirement homes in Florida. His jokes, unlike Youngman's, were somewhat relevant to a modern audience because listeners could understand the hardships that their parents had endured and the comedic ways in which their parents' lives grew stagnant and predictable. Roman's style involved describing a particular scene and then inserting an incongruent behavior. His language was neither vulgar nor inclusive of expletives. Roman's jokes showcased the foibles of others and were never directed at himself. For example, when comparing the fixed date of Christmas on December 25 with Hanukkah's fluctuating dates on the lunar calendar, Roman remarked that Hanukkah came out "either too late or too early, but never on time!"[33]

Both Roman and Youngman can be contrasted with a younger generation of comedians who now regularly appear at Kung Pao Kosher Comedy. Their respective styles are unabashedly egocentric, viewing everything in relationship to their own life experiences. For this generation, living in an age where religion, family, and society are all acceptable subjects for conversation and, sometimes, ridicule, comedic routines are more about the dysfunctional and edgy aspects of life. Jewish heritage is just one of the many identities that American Jewish comedians weave in and out of their routines. Complimentary one moment and derogatory the next, Jewish life experiences are viewed to be relevant, as a part of a worldview that is comforting under certain circumstances but burdensome under others. Jokes and monologues, influenced heavily by popular comedians such as Jerry Seinfeld and Jon Stewart, present trivialities rather than the significant aspects of Jewish life in America. These trivialities are then elevated to an increased level of importance by the comedian in "routines, filled with small observations."[34] This brand of humor, no matter how mundane the topic, is laced with irony and sarcasm, demonstrating that the dutiful application of societal values may produce irony, hypocrisy, and cultural miscue.

The young comedians showcased at Kung Pao Kosher Comedy in San Francisco take an increased license with language and subject matter and are not embarrassed to offer their full, unadulterated critique of Christmas. Kung Pao's Mistress of Ceremonies Lisa Geduldig opens her monologues with a reflection on how Jews seek opportunities to dismiss Christmas as irrelevant. The tenor of the monologue is that if Christians cannot give

Hanukkah equal time, then Christians should keep their holiday to themselves and not force everyone around them to acknowledge it. This monologue is typical of Geduldig's style: "I am tired of people greeting me throughout the month of December, saying 'Merry Christmas.' What will I say the next time someone says 'Merry Christmas,' 'Fuck you?' . . . Or to the question, 'What did you do for Christmas?' I'd say something like, 'What did you do for the Lag Ba'omer or Shemini Atzeret [Jewish holidays unfamiliar to the non-Jewish public]?'"[35] When asked about her use of profanity to subvert Christmas, Lisa explained that she enunciated what every Jew is thinking. "You know, I hate Christmas. My people hate Christmas."[36]

Dan Lewis stressed in his 1998 performance at Kung Pao that Christmas and attendant symbols have strong negative connotations for Jews in America:

> Let's be honest. We are pissed off. Hanukkah didn't catch on like we thought it would. We lit candles and put on a hat. Nobody came over. There's no Rudolph the red-nosed rabbi for us. We put up a Santa Claus one year, but ever since I have been that tall [pointing to his height] I am afraid of that fat bastard coming down my chimney. Santa Claus: "He sees you when you are sleeping; he knows when you are awake. You better watch out. You better not shout [said in a whining, nasal tone] you better not cry, I'm telling you why. Santa Claus is coming to town" . . . and he's got a knife, sitting in a van, drunk on egg nog, snatching kids.[37]

In the nexus between Christmas and Hanukkah, Kung Pao Kosher Comedy developed its comedic tenor with Christmas as the backdrop and with Jews laughing at Christmas. Jokes were also directed at Hanukkah. Jaffe Cohen, who performed at Kung Pao Kosher Comedy in 1995, irreverently satirized the theme of miracles said to have occurred on Hanukkah: "While other kids were celebrating Christmas, my father tried to build up Hanukkah. He said it was a miracle that one day's worth of oil lasted for eight days. I wasn't impressed. My mother was proving that same miracle with pot roast."[38]

Similar biting humor directed against Christmas and Hanukkah reached audiences in greater measure when comedic performances moved to the medium of television. Shows like *Saturday Night Live* and *South Park* broke new ground in openly dealing with the December dilemma and in mocking the pretensions of those who subscribed to the most ritualistic aspects of either Christmas and Hanukkah.

COMEDY PERFORMANCES ON TELEVISION

Television brought the Jewish comic genius to mass audiences throughout America. *Saturday Night Live*, as Ariel Kaplan explained, combined the shock comedy of *National Lampoon* "with a more sophisticated Jewish style of humor, led by a group of very talented Jewish writers under the tutelage of producer and writer Lorne Michaels."[39] *Saturday Night Live*, which began its long continuous run on NBC in 1975, developed a reputation for tackling previously taboo subjects. Such skits as "Hanukkah Harry," "Jewess Jeans," and the 1988 game-show parody "Jew, Not a Jew," satirized the Jewish embrace of popular culture in which Jews mimicked society while contributing their uniquely Jewish perspective to the process of cultural exchange. The effect of this period was to allow both the writers of *Saturday Night Live* and performers of the 1990s, such as Adam Sandler, to be more open about their Jewish identities and to parody every aspect of Jewish life, from extreme assimilation to strong religious attachment.

Comedian Adam Sandler's 1994 "Hanukkah Song," which appeared for the first time on *Saturday Night Live*'s "Weekend Update" (on December 3) was an immediate hit. Written by Sandler with *Saturday Night Live* writers Lewis Morton and Ian Maxtone Graham, ostensibly for Jewish kids who might feel left out of the Christmas celebratory mood, the songwriters offered a song that served as a "who's who" of Jewish actors and celebrities, both real and fictional, who celebrated Hanukkah. During the 1990s, when political correctness forced members of religious groups to downplay their uniqueness, the lyrics suggested that Jews take pride in celebrating Hanukkah because popular actors were not embarrassed to claim that they were Jewish. Sandler also broached another controversial subject when he included in his list those actors who were half-Jewish and even quarter-Jewish, implying that they were to be included in the Jewish fold (even though they are not considered Jewish by Orthodox or Conservative denominational standards).

Officially released as a cut on the album *What the Hell Happened to Me?* in 1996, the Hanukkah song hit number eighty on the Billboard Hot 100 and number twenty-five on the U.S. Modern Rock Charts.[40] The song attained commercial success not because it gave voice to Jews who sought public affirmation for Hanukkah, but because of its comedic tone. Particularly resonant with audiences was Sandler's use of a juvenile, nasal voice (which would become his trademark) and his appending humorous suffixes to words in order to make them rhyme with "Hanukkah."

Over the years, Sandler revised the lyrics and performed the song in his stand-up comedy act. While successive versions of the Sandler song include greater numbers of Jewish, half-Jewish, and quarter-Jewish stars who celebrate Hanukkah, the final stanzas of each version interject a modicum of humor via their references to controversial subjects: drinking and smoking drugs, for example. Sandler allows for their intake, presumably, as a way to celebrate both Hanukkah and the euphoric discovery that so many stars are Jewish. In fact, the original version of the song as sung on *Saturday Night Live*'s "Weekend Update" admonished the listener from partaking in "marijuanikah"; however, subsequent versions revoked any reticence. In later versions it was okay to smoke "marijuanikah" and to drink excessively in "Tijuanaka." The song was considered comedic and, therefore, harmless enough to be heard by children, despite its seeming endorsement of illegal activities.

A similar satirical ode to the benefits of Hanukkah over Christmas is presented in a 1999 television episode of Comedy Central's *South Park* entitled "A Lonely Jew on Christmas."[41] The boy Kyle laments, in language laced with expletives, that Santa Claus bypasses his house, that he must eat kosher latkes instead of ham, and that he has to sing a Hanukkah song (whose title is a gibberish paraphrase of Hebrew) instead of "Silent Night." An anonymous voice soothes Kyle's apprehension by pointing out that Hanukkah has none of the undesirable elements of Christmas, such as having to sit on Santa's lap, being around inebriated family members, and having to feel obligated to give charity. The suggestion, like that made by Adam Sandler, is that Kyle should be proud of his Jewishness at all times of year, especially Christmas.

South Park, however, is not known for its tame use of language and subject matter. In a scene in which Kyle is teased because his mother refused to let him participate in a Christmas play, the play's director offers Kyle a chance to sing a non-Christmas song. Rather than selecting a typical Hanukkah tune, as might have occurred in many public schools, Kyle composes a subversively farcical response using a scatological theme. "Mr. Hankey, the Hanukkah Poo" is the title of a character whose bathroom habits are turned into a form of protest.[42] Comprehending the degree of Kyle's animosity to Christmas, the school principal and the mayor conclude that they need to remove Christmas symbols deemed offensive by Kyle and replace them with generic ones. Through Kyle's actions, these authorities also reach an understanding that it is oppressive to force Jewish students to participate in Christmas pageants and concerts year after year and that doing so may cause great psychological harm. In fact, Kyle is diagnosed with a fecal disorder and is placed in a psychiatric ward. Kyle is let out when Hankey speaks to the town's people and scolds them for forgetting the universal spirit embedded in the holiday season. According to this episode of *South Park*, those who champion one religion over the other will, euphemistically, be sullied and ruin the holiday for others.

HANUKKAH HARRY BECOMES AN AMERICAN FOLK HERO

Hanukkah humor reached its zenith with the introduction of a made-for-television Jewish counterpart to Santa Claus, Hanukkah Harry. If Santa was readily available to most American children, Jewish children had no corresponding hero with which to identify. Precedence had already been set with the creation of Santa's various Jewish counterparts, such as Uncle Max, first used in children's books for Hanukkah, and Mr. Klaus and Shloimey, named as antiheroes in parodies of "'Twas the Night Before Christmas."

In the hands of the writers and performers of the groundbreaking television satirical show, *Saturday Night Live*, Hanukkah Harry emerged as Santa's most enduring Jewish counterpart. Hanukkah Harry was first introduced in a 1989 episode of *Saturday Night Live* in "The Night Hanukkah Harry Saved Christmas" as a positive figure who had earned a reputation as a trustworthy Jewish Santa.[43] So well-respected was Harry that when Santa became ill just prior to Christmas and was unable to fulfill his duties, he called upon Harry to take his place. Hanukkah Harry ably substitutes for Santa until the non-Jewish children he visits realize that Harry has distributed practical gifts—slacks and socks (typical presents for Jewish children)—and not the gifts that they had hoped to receive. After their initial disappointment, the children realize that Hanukkah Harry was only trying to help out under difficult circumstances. They ultimately appreciate Hanukkah Harry's willingness to assist Santa, in the same manner as fellow Americans are thankful to Jews who willingly volunteer to substitute and perform their jobs on Christmas Day. As for the *Saturday Night Live* episode, while Santa may have had the better gifts, Hanukkah Harry had the altruistic motive, teaching that holiday spirit is more appealing than the crass commercialism to which many children, Christian and Jewish, are subjected.

Just when one is left to believe that Hanukkah Harry has reached a modicum of success, the rivalry between Santa and Harry reaches epic proportion in the minds of imaginative comedians. Some have envisioned Harry winning in a combat between the two giant holiday superstars.

Hal L. Singer's 2002 music release on compact disc "I Saw Hanukkah Harry Beat Up Santa" offers one such episode and a motive of jealousy for the fisticuffs that are about to ensue.[44] Harry instigates the rivalry by "haunting Christmas like the ghost of Christmas past." Santa "bashes in Harry's Caddy" and "Harry jumps in his Caddy and he was mad as heck," resulting in his taking "off after Santa to break his jolly neck."

Without any pretext, Hanukkah Harry gets even with Santa Claus for Santa's control of the Christmas airwaves. The scene takes place in front of Morrie's deli, presumably so that Hanukkah Harry will have support and justification for his retribution on Santa. His use of a Cadillac car to inflict harm hearkens to a time when this automobile was considered to be a status symbol among immigrant Jews. The message is clear: Santa's hubris will ultimately contribute to his undoing.

These two roles of Hanukkah Harry, supportive and combative, are recorded as entries in the Internet *Urban Dictionary*, a source of humorous definitions found in the urban environment.[45] The first definition of Hanukkah Harry is that of a "very funny guy that helps Santa Claus and lives in Israel." His brother, Santa Cohen, helps as does his sister, Yenta Claus. The siblings have a cousin named *Schmanta* Claus, and they all love Hanukkah. The second definition posted in *Urban Dictionary* for Hanukkah Harry is "the Jewish equivalent of Santa Claus" when "Hanukkah Harry wipes Santa Claus's ass."

As portrayed in American Jewish popular culture, Hanukkah Harry illustrates that Hanukkah is just as important as Christmas. Once this parity was achieved through the humor of Jewish artists, satire became the vehicle of choice. In the fantasy world facilitated by the then-new YouTube internet medium, a Hanukkah bird drops presents from his high vantage point, along with bird waste. Introduced through YouTube, in 2006, the comedian and rapper Eric Schwartz (aka Smooth-E) presented a scene centered upon a bird dressed in blue that delivers presents over the course of eight nights from his home in Boca Raton, Florida.[46] Apparently, Hanukkah Harry trained him. The bird's sole recognizable trait is his "blue and white turd," although a news helicopter sights the bird sporting a yarmulke. Reminiscent of Big Bird, the beloved television character of *Sesame Street* fame, this Hanukkah bird is considered cute and responsive to children's needs. The cuteness is undermined, however, by the bird's limitations; he does not talk, and he cannot be seen.

Eric Schwartz's message in this rap, as well as in his other YouTube entries ("Chocolate Coins" in 2006 and "Hanukkah Hey Ya" in 2008) is that Jewish children have no reason to envy Santa. They have so many

Figure 4.1. Hanukkah Harry, at SantaCon, a mass gathering of people in Santa Claus costumes, parading publicly on New York streets. Washington Square, Greenwich Village, New York, 13 December 2009. Copyright and photo: Joshua Eli Plaut.

"cool" rituals, games, and gifts that they deserve to be called heeb hoppers. Unlike children who celebrate Christmas, they never have to worry about whether they were naughty or nice, nor need they request any presents directly from a Santa while seated on his lap. This Hanukkah bird can neither read a gift wish list nor be seen by children. But the presents for all eight nights continue from an endless and miraculous source of gifts.

Both Hanukkah Harry and the Hanukkah bird now appear in popular cultural celebrations during the month of December. Beginning in 1994,

Figure 4.2. Jews for Santa, at SantaCon, Greenwich Village, New York, December 13, 2009. Copyright and photo: Joshua Eli Plaut.

every year on a specified weekend date in December in cities throughout the United States and the world, thousands of young people sporting Santa costumes converge on a central gathering place. The focus of the gathering is multifold: rooted in a flash mob and featuring both spontaneity and creativity, the participants meet to publically parade, to rove, and to barhop, clearly having a good time all the while spreading, albeit bawdy, cheer and goodwill. A website called SantaCon.info provides information about several of the gathering sites in the Northeastern United States, as well as historical context and the prospect of purchasing cheap Santa suits and

Figure 4.3. Mrs. Hanukkah Harry and Mrs. Santa Claus, at SantaCon, Greenwich Village, New York, 13 December 2009. Copyright and photo: Joshua Eli Plaut.

other Santa paraphernalia. In New York City alone, thousands of Santas converge from all directions in Washington Square Park in Greenwich Village. This street gathering always includes a few people dressed in blue-and-white robes as Hannukah Harry and as Mrs. Hanukkah Harry. Occasionally, dreidel and menorah costumes appear, and even, on rarer occurrences, a person surfaces dressed as a blue-and-white bird, a clear reference to the Hanukkah bird of Youtube fame.

THE MUSICAL SATIRE TRADITION

The anxiety associated with adjusting to living as a religious minority in a majority culture is also expressed in the tradition of holiday musical parody. The topic of assimilation proves a popular subject of humor among comedians who delight in pointing out the hypocrisy of those who abandon their heritage and yet retain trappings of their immigrant culture. Importing Yiddish words into popular American tunes exemplifies this first genre of musical parody and leads to hilarious results. The parodies of Mickey Katz in the 1940s and 1950s and Allan Sherman in the 1950s and 1960s entertained both immigrants and their children.[47] Born in Cleveland, Ohio, to European parents, Katz took American folk tunes and turned them into Yiddish farce, continuing in the venerable tradition established by Jewish entertainers who were sensitive to the struggles of immigrant parents and their children. Jewish vaudeville tunes capitalized on Jewish stereotypes.

Katz incorporated stereotypical Yiddish personalities into recognizable situations—eating at a deli, searching for a mate, and negotiating the familiar Jewish neighborhood of the Lower East Side. He then exaggerated their significance through the mode of comedy *shtick* (farce) that characterized his tunes. At a time when Americans wanted to assimilate in the 1940s and 1950s, to discard Yiddish in favor of English as their main language, and to move away from crowded immigrant environs for the suburbs, Katz saw this repositioning as a premature abandonment of immigrant cultural values. Through selecting popular American tunes, Katz reminded his listeners that they could not so easily shed their traditional Jewish attitudes and behaviors. Although Jews laughed at his jokes, they were simultaneously embarrassed by his unabashed references to immigrant neighborhoods and delicatessens. In one of his most popular pieces, "Duvid Crocket, King of Delancey Street" ("home of gefilte fish and kosher meat"), Katz mocks the heroism of the backwoodsmen (itself a Disney fiction), exaggerates the trivialities of immigrant Jewish life, and transforms the Jew into an anti-hero for whom stories of America's greatness are themselves myths to bolster an artificial national uniformity.[48]

Allan Sherman accomplished a similar feat with his musical parodies of the 1950s and 1960s; he needed neither to present himself through a strictly Yiddish idiom nor to sprinkle his performances with frantic *shtick*.[49] His audiences were just as often non-Jews who saw in Sherman someone who was perceptive to the anxieties of Americans who felt stifled by the blandness and uniformity of the 1950s and who were searching for opportunities to express their individuality. Satirizing popular tunes, particularly Broadway show tunes, Sherman reminded his audience that the composers and performers they admired were Jews whose theatrical genius came from their ethnicity, despite the best efforts of these entertainers to hide their Jewish roots. Sherman's goal was to mock the pretense of an all-inclusive American culture that was too blind to recognize the many ethnic strands of which it was composed. Sherman alluded to this in his satire of those who regard themselves as "blue bloods." The voice we hear is of the knight, Sir Greenbaum, singing to the strains of "Greensleeves":

Said he: "Forsooth, 'tis a sorry plight that engenders my attitude
    blue-ish."

Said he: "I don't want to be a knight. That's no job for a boy who is
Jewish."[50]

In Sherman's 1963 parody of "The Twelve Days of Christmas," he enu-
merated silly, impractical, and sometimes obsolete gifts. These gifts included
an obsolete Japanese transistor radio, green polka-dot pajamas, a calendar
book with an insurance man's name on it, a simulated alligator wallet,
a statue of a lady with a clock where her stomach should be, a hammered
aluminum nutcracker, a pink satin pillow embroidered with the words
"San Diego," an indoor plastic birdbath, a pair of teakwood shower cloths,
and an automatic vegetable slicer. Sherman listed as his gift to himself
for the twelfth day of Christmas, a desire to exchange all the other gifts.
Sherman was satirizing both the tradition of Christmas gift-giving, as well as
mocking through parody the materialism and commercialization of the
holiday.[51]

By the 1960s, when Sherman composed his now famous "Hello
Muddah, Hello Faddah (a Letter from Camp)," Americans had become
doubtful about what constituted heroism in American society and what
were its most compelling virtues. If "brawn and physical prowess" were
not to define the American character, then perhaps Jews could offer
intellect, wit, and passion. Jewish humor played an important role in
allowing Americans to become acquainted with members of minority
groups and to see the Jew not as the occasional outsider but as the social
representative of minorities that aspire to be American yet retain their
ethnic identities.[52]

Following in Katz's and Sherman's footsteps, a group known as "Stanley
Adams and the Chicken Flickers" composed and performed the first
collection of musical parody devoted to Hanukkah in 1962.[53] Taking
popular Christmas carols, such as "Deck the Halls" and "Twelve Days
of Christmas," Stanley Adams, with the help of Sid Wayne, composed
"The Eight Days of Chanukah," and "Deck the Halls with Matzoh Balls."
Similar to those of Mickey Katz, their songs were sprinkled with Yiddish,
a technique used to convey the irony of taking well-respected Christmas
music and turning it into a Hanukkah farce. The incongruity of a Jewish
Santa (foreshadowing Hanukkah Harry of the 1990s), with family digesting
deli foods instead of traditional Christmas fare and decking the halls with
matzoh balls instead of Christmas ornaments, brought laughter to listeners
who, even if they did not understand all the Yiddish expressions, appreciated the juxtaposition of incongruous images. Through these parodies,
Santa lost his luster, Christmas traditions became irrelevant, and Jews

could envision not having to be captivated by the allure of ubiquitous Christmas symbols.

More than thirty years later, in 1998, What I Like About Jew (the comedic duo of Sean Altman and Rob Tannenbaum) followed in this vein by performing the original song "Hanukkah with Monica."[54] Another What I Like About Jew original, "(It's Good to Be) a Jew at Christmas," focused upon the positive aspects of Hanukkah: "It's clear that we're the chosen ones: we got eight nights, they got just one," the fun of consuming exotic Chinese food on Christmas Eve, the freedom to walk anywhere on Christmas because the streets are empty, and the pride in knowing that Americans were worshipping a person who was born a Jew. So, "Yes, it's good to be a Jew at Christmas" because "you know that Christ was born a Jew, which means that Mary was one too." "It's good to be a Jew at Christmas" and, therefore, "Don't you wanna be one too? It's good to be a Jew at Christmas."[55]

What I Like About Jew represents a modern reaction to and clear departure from the holiday parodies of Mickey Katz, Allan Sherman, and Stanley Adams. The difference between the two groups of comedic performers is that Altman and Tannenbaum (who each pursue separate careers now in the same genre) write their own songs, adding a layer of lewdness unavailable to earlier comedians. "Hanukkah with Monica" turns the intern's sordid affair with President Bill Clinton into a bawdy holiday romp. The key lyrics rhyme with Hanukkah and scenes depicting Hanukkah paraphernalia are given sexual overtones. The subtext of this plot and one reason for the success of this farce relied upon the bad publicity generated from Lewinsky's Jewishness. "And every day she's in the news is one more bad day for the Jews. How long must we suffer through the blues?" The lyrics mockingly and irreverently address a presidential scandal by elevating the episode into an issue for the entire American Jewish community.

Similarly, What I Like About Jew gives credit to Santa's forgotten reindeer (a Jew, of course) for being the brains behind Santa's popularity. In their "Reuben the Hook-Nosed Reindeer," Reuben's "bulbous semitic beak" typecasts him as a Jew.[56] In one vein he is a nice Jewish boy version of Cinderella who "cooks blintzes for Blitzen, does Santa's taxes, and cleans his hooves every week." He's also the consummate behind-the-scenes guy who makes Santa's Christmas enterprise run like clockwork: "He checks the oil, rotates the tires, wraps the presents, and packs the sleigh. He checks the road map, rewinds the Streisand tape, he packs a thermos of consommé." Santa also depends on Reuben's stereotypically keen shopping

Figure 4.4. *Hanukah with Monica* album cover, 1998. Artwork used with permission of Sean Altman and Rob Tannenbaum of the band What I Like About Jew.

skills: "He gets a separate receipt for the milk and the meat, pays wholesale for toys." According to Sean Altman, "in Reuben's mind, of course he would keep separate receipts as he's an anal retentive mensch, the perfect accountant!" Reuben is indeed a nice Jewish reindeer who "went to Yeshiva, [but] won't chase beaver; mahjongg is 'his' reindeer game." In this musical tale spun by What I Like About Jew, Jews underlie the success of Christmas.

Sean Altman is now performing as the comedic song act Jewmongous, a satiric tour de force that includes his songs "My Phantom Foreskin," "Be My Little Shabbos Goy," and "Taller Than Jesus," a send-up of John Lennon's oft-misunderstood statement that the Beatles were "bigger than Jesus."[57] His most provocative song is "Christian Baby Blood," an Irish bar-room chantey that explodes the myth of the blood libel, the ancient accusation that Jews drink the blood of Christian babies. Altman says: "My mother was worried about that one. She said, 'Aren't you afraid people will think you're serious—that Jews really drink the stuff?' I'm singing in a rollicking Irish drinking song in a fake Irish accent about the joys of drinking Christian baby blood. Who could think I'm serious? And that's when I think I'm most successful, when I'm poking fun at a stereotype and deflating it."[58]

Altman draws a distinction between the comedy of his youth and of his parents' generation. Altman deems his comedy a clear departure from that of Woody Allen, Mel Brooks, and Alan Sherman; he is trying neither to assimilate nor apologize, and the characters in his songs are neither stereotypically wimpy nor victimized. "That generation of Jewish comedy borders on self-loathing; if anything my material is self-aggrandizing. The comparison that most annoys me the most, though, is Allan Sherman. He's a parodist, writing new lyrics to existing songs, and the results are 'cute.' I'm a career song-writer and God help me if my Jewmongous songs are ever 'cute.' I'd rather be compared to Lenny Bruce: biting, occasionally outlandish but always smart and thought-provoking." Altman confesses that "Jesus takes a bit of a beating in my act because he's a convenient, easy scapegoat. Like the saga of the Boston Red Sox, Babe Ruth, and the New York Yankees, Jesus was 'our star,' our heavy hitter. We let him get away, he started a dynasty with our competitor and we were left wandering in the desert for untold years. It's our own 'curse of the Bambino.'"[59] In 2010, Jewmongous's "Blame-a da Jews," a musical exploration of the ancient papal roots of anti-Semitism, became a popular YouTube video. "I hit my mark on that one," Altman says. "The song is a sarcastic commentary on anti-Semitism, its roots in the Catholic Church, and how some people literally blame the Jews for every woe: a crappy job, a lousy economy, bad weather or a hang-nail." Strong parallels have been drawn between Altman's subversive musical parody and the comedy of his hipster contemporaries, Sacha Baron Cohen, Jon Stewart, Sarah Silverman, and *Heeb* magazine.[60] Altman has also been deemed to be "racy and funny and smart and affectionate, written for a generation of fully assimilated Jews who grew up on punk rock and *South Park* [written by Trey Parker and Matt Stone]."[61]

By using parody to comment on the pervasiveness of Christmas in American society, Jews can advantageously communicate a range of attitudes, from assimilation defense to cultural pride. Jews are able to depict through parody a Christmas holiday that seemingly masquerades as a holy day but is actually a commercial ruse to make people believe that giving gifts and spreading good cheer can transform a competitive world into a harmonious one.

In the popular media, neither Hanukkah nor Christmas threatens anyone. The holidays are celebrated as examples of entertainment and celebration intended to fill the season with feelings of cheery good wishes.

During World War II, when many soldiers served away from American shores, Christmas tunes helped promote feelings of patriotism, taught lessons of tolerance, and facilitated a vision of a world where differences did not divide. Jews, in particular, whose minority status prevented them from embracing Christmas, developed humorous formats for reducing, if not redefining, its significance. Through satirical songs, written parodies, comedic performances, television skits, and YouTube rants, Jews imagined a world in which Hanukkah was at least as important as, if not more important than, Christmas. In the best of possible worlds, Christmas would be irrelevant for American Jews.

In the hands of skilled comedians, providing Christmas with a Jewish context decreased its importance, thereby making Christmas images appear odd and anachronistic. Santa wears a prayer shawl (*tallis*), Rudolph becomes Reuben, and reindeer antlers appear as menorah lights. In the hands of satirists, Santa, Rudolph, and reindeer lose their luster and even evince a cynical side. Their foibles and missteps beg for Jewish intervention through the help of Hanukkah Harry or Reuben the Reindeer who make their Christmas counterparts appear misguided. In this comedic world-view, Hanukkah has so much more to offer Jews than Christmas: familiar Jewish foods and Yiddish expressions, key ingredients for a celebration that Christmas lacks.

America's Jews have reacted to their exclusion from Christmas in a manner similar to how they have reacted to their exclusion from a country club—by building a better one of their own.[62] However, in so doing, Jews have demoted both Christmas and Hanukkah, mixing both in a popular culture concoction that asks little of each holiday and begs only that those who participate have fun and laugh at their own seriousness. The role of Jewish parody has helped to ensure that Christmas not be taken too seriously and that the celebrations of other religious, ethnic, and cultural groups be accorded equal respect and opportunity. On Christmas Day, throughout the United States, many American Jews, while adopting a very different and serious attitude toward Christmas, volunteer to serve holiday meals at nursing homes, hospitals, and food pantries. The dynamics of this 150-year social arrangement plays an important role in the American celebration of Christmas.

CHAPTER 5

THE CHRISTMAS MITZVAH

'TIS THE SEASON TO BE GIVING

One Christmas morning, Uzzi Raanan rose early from his Los Angeles home and put on his work clothes. Uzzi was not headed to his job. On this particular day, he intended to distribute food to the homeless and gifts to the needy. For Uzzi, a Jew who does not celebrate Christmas and who might otherwise stay at home, this day was an opportunity to contribute charitably to help non-Jews.[1] Under the auspices of the Jewish Federation Council of Greater Los Angeles, Uzzi linked up with four hundred other Jewish volunteers to help the homeless in area shelters, to distribute food and toys, and to renovate old buildings.

Charity and gift-giving are integral parts of the Christmas holiday season. For more than 150 years, Americans have attached special significance to giving and volunteering on Christmas as ways of fulfilling the holiday's spiritual mission.[2] Whether gifts are earmarked for children, for friends, or for organizations supporting the needy, benefactors and recipients are mutually bound to each other through civic and religious obligation. Charitable agencies call on citizens to open their hearts and their checkbooks to help the disadvantaged during this period. Annually, the Salvation Army, one of the earliest proponents of charitable giving at Christmas, trumpets a need for volunteers to sort food, wrap presents, and ring bells. The United Way broadcasts a quest for volunteers to serve holiday dinners and spend time with those who are alone during the holiday season.

According to the Red Cross, the disparity between the rich and the poor across the United States is most glaring on the day before, the day of, and the day after Christmas.[3] Newspapers throughout the country report on the myriad of social service efforts organized by large and small charitable agencies and often praise volunteers for exemplary services. One newspaper advertises: "Give a gift of yourself for a good cause, a few hours of your time or donations of clothes, food and toys that can make a world of difference to those in need and to non-profit organizations on shoestring budgets." The Salvation Army advertises "'Tis the season to be giving."[4]

By consulting newspaper lists, those wishing to volunteer can select from many sites that welcome volunteers, and they can choose appealing tasks for which assistance is required. City newspapers, such as the *New York Times*, sponsor their own programs to support favored charities that provide food, housing assistance, medical care, and social services to the poor.[5] *New York* magazine's annual holiday gift issue includes a section for suggested gifts "that make a difference."

City governments also promote opportunities for giving. In California, the volunteer center of San Diego County maintains a database of five thousand volunteer possibilities in one hundred locales at Christmas. Requests are for Christmas carolers, entertainers, gift sorters, food distributors, and donations of money.[6]

Companies and businesses sponsor toy-drives in conjunction with public Christmas charities and foundations. The Starbucks coffee chain, for example, publicizes its "Holiday Angels" toy drive to help terminally ill children in the community. "Simply bring a new, unwrapped toy to your local Starbucks by December 17," announces a flyer. "Donate a toy, delight a child."[7] During the holiday season, the Texas-based Seafood Supply Company, distributor of quality seafood to the restaurant retail industry since 1974, sponsors a program called "Santa's Sleigh." The program supplies enough tuna, swordfish, and halibut to provide more than 44,000 meals to agencies served by the San Antonio Food Bank.[8] Every December, the Massachusetts Institute of Technology Public Service Center organizes a "giving tree" by which MIT students, staff, and faculty provide gifts to needy children in the Cambridge and Boston area. Working with more than fifteen local agencies, the MIT Public Service Center and the Pan-Hellenic Association collect gifts requests from more than 1,500 children.[9] The military also assists toy drives throughout the country, and soldiers volunteer to distribute gifts for children in hospitals.

The genesis of America's call to give to the needy on Christmas can be found in the early 1800s when rapid industrialization created a visible poor and indigent population. Churches that typically took on responsibility for supporting the needy became overwhelmed. Newspapers, local officials, reformers, and state legislators called on the wealthy to help alleviate poverty. At Christmas, the plight of the poor tugged on the heartstrings of those who had the means to celebrate. The Protestant philosophy known as Social Gospel, which considered wealth to be a sign of God's blessing, also carried with it an obligation to share with those less fortunate.[10] The commercialization of Christmas highlighted the contrast between what many considered crass materialism with an abject poverty that prevented the poor from fully enjoying the holiday.

The British author Charles Dickens gave a literary name to the selfish person who refuses to be compassionate on Christmas. In his 1843 composition *A Christmas Carol*, Scrooge, the last name of an employer who responded "humbug" when anyone asked for donations, became a symbol of selfishness and greed. He kept his employee Cratchit in near servitude and turned a deaf ear to Cratchit's plea for help for his disabled son, Tiny Tim. Scrooge had a change of heart when he was visited by the spirits of Christmas past, present, and future—visions that portrayed him as a selfish human being whose only hope of not dying alone and forgotten was to become sympathetic to those in need. Ebenezer Scrooge then made up for years of dispassion by giving a raise to his employee, Bob Cratchit, by helping Cratchit's son, Tiny Tim, and by being generous with those who asked for charitable donations.

During the 1840s, Dickens's story became enormously popular, even outselling the Bible in bookstores throughout America. Readers became heightened to the importance of being beneficent on Christmas, and the press used the book's emotional power to mobilize citizens to help alleviate the pressing needs of the poor.[11] An 1876 article in the *New York Times* wrote that "there seems to be no reason why everybody, including all the possible Bob Cratchits and Tiny Tims in the great Metropolis, should not today have the happiest of 'Merry Christmases.'" The times are hard, the article admitted, but charitable institutions stand ready to supply food, toys, fruits, and candies for children all over the city. Apparently, employers heeded the call because the paper writes that "never before were there so many purchases by employers who desired to reward faithful employees."[12] Echoing Dickens, a flood of morality tales written at the time identified "worthy paupers" in need of rescuing from circumstances of "dire misery."[13]

New York intellectual and journalist Margaret Fuller publicized the benefits of giving to children on Christmas.[14] In 1844, she brought gifts to children at the New York Asylum for the Deaf and Dumb on Christmas Day.[15] Her ebullience at seeing the faces of smiling children caught the public's attention and turned charitable giving to children into civic ritual.[16]

Following Fuller's example, New York's charitable agencies institutionalized formal open houses on Christmas Day for the affluent to meet the impoverished children. Examples include the Mission House, located in the worst slum of the city, and Randall's Island, home of the municipal hospital, insane asylum, and almshouse. Throughout New York City, indigent children received attention, gifts, and festive meals, gestures that made their substandard living arrangements a focal point.

Soon thereafter similar attention was directed to indigent adults. The Salvation Army, an offshoot of the evangelical missionary group from England that aided the poor, organized charitable giving to poor and homeless adults in the 1880s.[17] The army hosted a spectacular charitable event at Madison Square Garden for twenty thousand men and women where, as the press describes, "the hungry and homeless were fed at tables on the arena floor, under the glare of electric lights."[18] Rich and poor came in from different entrances, their differing statuses clearly demarcated and duly acknowledged.[19] This was "a charity event on an industrial scale," a *New York Times* article observed, designed to lead to "the bridging of the gulf between the rich and poor." Although some complained that the poor were exploited to make the rich look good, the Salvation Army made it clear that the real motive was to treat the poor with loving "heartiness." Funds needed for these dinners were raised by unemployed men who were hired to dress up like Santa and solicit contributions on street corners.[20] Soon politicians demonstrated their goodwill by hosting Christmas dinners for their constituents who were "down-and-out." Tammany Congressman Timothy D. Sullivan was one of the first to do so at the turn of the twentieth century, followed by his son who carried on the tradition for more than twenty-five years.[21] In 1911, at the sixteenth annual Bowery dinner, six thousand indigents enjoyed the feast.[22]

Individual charitable acts were not enough to combat poverty. Professional charitable organizations mobilized civic giving on large and extended scales. City agencies appointed caseworkers qualified to assess the needs of the poor. The New York Association for Improving the Condition of the Poor prioritized assistance to the needy, while simultaneously ensuring that panhandlers and the counterfeit were not included. In 1912, the *New York Times* initiated a narrative about the "100 Neediest Cases" and openly requested donations for specific extended needs. The New York Association for Improving the Condition of the Poor assisted the *New York Times'* effort by eliminating the panhandlers, choosing the cases, and preparing the stories.[23]

EARLY JEWISH PARTICIPATION IN CHRISTMAS CHARITY

Jews, who often had to sit on the sidelines while their many American neighbors celebrated their December holiday, saw in this outpouring of

Christmas charity an opportunity to be part of a new American tradition. Forty years after Margaret Fuller's crusade began an avalanche of charitable works, the Jewish community followed suit. In an 1885 article printed in the Cincinnati-based *American Israelite*, the author acknowledged that Jews had enthusiastically endorsed charitable giving to their non-Jewish neighbors. "It is the custom here, as in other cities," the author wrote, "to provide a hearty meal for all the poor children of the vicinity during the Christmas holiday. . . . Many of our Hebrew families, recognizing that the movement was to make children happy, set aside all question of faith and doctrine and contributed very liberally in money and material."[24]

The great Jewish codifier and philosopher Moses Maimonides, writing in the twelfth century, had already sanctioned giving to non-Jews when he said, "One must feed and clothe the heathen poor together with the Israelite poor for the sake of [communal] peace."[25] Jews, of course, were no strangers to organizing charitable works. The Jewish concept of *tzedakah*— performing charitable acts of righteousness and justice—is a fundamental biblical commandment that has historically been practiced wherever Jews have resided. Maimonides codified the Jewish community's age-old obligation to the poor by writing, "You are commanded to give the poor person according to [the poor person's] needs. If [a poor person] has no clothing, [the poor] should be clothed. If [the poor] has no household furnishing, these should be bought for [the poor]. . . . You are thus obligated to support [the person's] needs."[26] As far back as the sixth century, the Talmud teaches that the concept of tzedakah encompasses gifts of both monetary value and time, "a gift of one's self."[27] The following rabbinic pronouncement provides examples of both these modes of giving: "These are the principles whose fruits a person enjoy in this world but whose principal remains intact for him in the world-to-come. They are: honoring father and mother, acts of kindness, visiting the sick, providing a bridal dowry, burying the dead, devotion in prayer, and making peace between our fellowmen."[28] In the Jewish religion, as in most religious traditions, the act of giving benefits not only the recipient but also the donor. As an anonymous sage put it, "they who feed the hungry feed themselves too, for charity blesses one who gives even more than one who takes."[29]

Charity among Jews in the United States through the early 1800s was localized in synagogues organized for the purpose of taking care of newly arriving Sephardi Jews. As a result of the large-scale German Jewish immigration beginning in 1820, philanthropic organizations were formed to assist *landsman*—fellow countrymen—to establish societies based on town of origin. As the Jewish population grew, charities were filtered through institutional agencies that transcended regional interests.[30] The Jewish communities of Cincinnati and Philadelphia were the first to develop institutional philanthropy, followed by Jews in New York.[31] In 1819, Rebecca Gratz, the American-born descendant of German immigrants, established the Hebrew Female Benevolent Association of Philadelphia, the first independent Jewish charity in America.[32] The association offered food, clothing, shelter, fuel, an employment agency, and traveler's aid to Jews in distress. Another compelling reason for assisting Jews from within the community emerged: during periods of anti-Semitism Jews found it uncomfortable to use non-Jewish charitable organizations because of the intensive proselytizing by agency staff.

Jewish charitable efforts were further facilitated by the synchronization of the Jewish holidays with American shopping cycles and national holidays. Folklorist Barbara Kirschenblatt-Gimblett observes: "Among German Jews, holding social events with charitable objectives became an important way of observing Jewish holidays . . . nowhere was this more clear than in the annual charity fairs held just before Christmas . . . using the form of the charity fair for Jewish ends."[33]

The first widespread Jewish charitable volunteer activity on behalf of fellow citizens in the United States took place during the American Civil War, spanning four years beginning in 1861. The privations of the Civil War inspired an unprecedented outpouring of aid and assistance to soldiers and their families who remained at home.[34] Jewish welfare societies, social organizations, as well as synagogues and individuals provided war relief across the United States. Jewish women's societies in Cincinnati, Charlotte, Mobile, New York, Philadelphia, Pittsburgh, and Rochester prepared bandages, gathered donations for assistance to soldiers' families, sewed and knitted garments for soldiers, packed food cartons, organized benefits for sanitary commissions, and even volunteered in hospitals at the bedsides of injured soldiers.

By the end of the nineteenth century, the Jewish community was strong enough to consider joining in the charitable Christmas fever that swept the nation. Instances of Jews giving to non-Jewish causes were regularly mentioned in Jewish and general newspaper publications. Hy King Jr., president of the Washington Hebrew Congregation in the District of Columbia, sent a letter on December 22, 1884, to the organizer of a local Christmas collection along with a wagonload of presents. He wrote that he hoped his donation of Christmas presents would "gladden the hearts of the poor little ones" and agreed that "your noble charitable work should appeal to all creeds."[35]

This letter and accompanying gifts made a most favorable impression on the Christmas Club, the host agency. An anonymous note written in the aftermath praised Jewish volunteers as being "the largest and most munificent contributors to the Christmas Club."[36] On January 6, 1888, the same paper reported that a certain J. Jonas, a former alderman from Chicago, donated baskets of roast beef and chicken from his own food store to feed six hundred people. Azmed, the pseudonym of a correspondent to the *American Israelite* from New Orleans, noted in 1891 that many benefactors of Christian charities were Israelites.[37]

American Jewish charitable efforts soon began to focus not just on monetary aid but also on relieving fellow Americans from their work so that they could instead spend Christmas Day with family. On December 29, 1927, an editorial in the *American Israelite* reported on the feelings of reciprocity that pervaded between Americans who celebrated Christmas and Jews working in the New York City Post Office. Jews agreed to substitute for their colleagues at work during Christmas, and non-Jews offered to work for Jewish employees on the Jewish high holidays of Rosh Hashanah and Yom Kippur.[38] The same reciprocal relationship occurred in hospitals, the military, and government agencies. The *American Israelite* of December 28, 1944, noted that "Jews ask extra duty so Christian buddies may observe Christmas" and described an arrangement by which American Jewish male and female soldiers and military personnel relinquished time off for four consecutive years during the Second World War so as to help members of other religions. Jewish personnel volunteered to stay on military bases to allow their Christian colleagues to celebrate the holiday with family back home. Reform Rabbi David I. Cedarbaum, a chaplain in the armed forces, championed the value of helping his Christian soldier brethren in a 1944 Hanukkah sermon, "We esteem your beliefs and your customs. We will help you observe them."[39] This tradition continued after the war. In 1958, Rabbi Hank Skirball, then serving as a chaplain at the U.S. Army base in Baumholder, West Germany, volunteered to be the officer on duty on Christmas.[40]

Beginning in the 1960s and continuing until the present, this generosity of spirit intensified and extended on an individual basis to helping those outside of one's immediate work environment. In 1970 Gerald and Lucille Sands of Needham, Massachusetts, decided to spend Christmas Day in voluntary service at Saint Elizabeth Hospital in Brighton and the Pine Street Inn in Boston, services which they continued for seventeen years. Gerald was motivated, in part, by the conviction that Jews should relieve Christians at their work so that they can attend church or spend the holiday with family.[41]

From the 1950s onward, Jewish organizations initiated a collective communal effort and widely publicized requests for volunteers to substitute for fellow workers on Christmas. In December 1964, Bernard Korzennik of Temple Beth El in Hartford, Connecticut, for example, called upon fellow synagogue members to volunteer in area hospitals to replace paid workers who could stay at home to celebrate Christmas. Following Korzennik's example of thirty years of volunteerism, Jewish volunteers fed patients, pushed meal carts, and worked at reception desks and ward desks throughout the hospital in a spirit of what the congregation's *Weekly Bulletin* called "neighborliness."[42] Under the auspices of Temple Beth El's Men's Club and Senior Youth Group, and in cooperation with other synagogue groups in Greater Hartford, volunteers were asked to serve as hospital aides at local hospitals on Christmas Day in 1965, allowing non-Jewish workers "to enjoy their sacred holiday with their families and friends."[43] The hospital administrator Sister Mary Madeleine was elated to have assistance from the temple, as reflected in her note of thanks that praised volunteers for exhibiting the spirit of cooperation that gave a "tremendous boost to our personnel on duty, as well as to our patients."[44] Thirty-eight years later, Temple Beth El's tradition continues and has been refashioned and expanded into a monthly program currently called "Nourishment for the Soul: A Dinner for Hartford Children at Charter Oak Cultural Center." One Monday night per month, volunteers from Temple Beth El prepare and serve dinner to fifty Hartford children and their families.

The momentum for synagogue- and organization-lead volunteerism on Christmas Day gained force in the late 1960s. In 1967, Jewish War Veterans of Philadelphia visited the local Veterans Administration hospital on Christmas and provided relief for the hospital staff. The Dallas Jewish Interbrotherhood Committee began a "Holiday *Mitzvah*" program in 1971 that attracted more than three hundred volunteers to replace non-Jewish workers at sixteen Dallas area hospitals. In Atlanta, the B'nai B'rith Gate City Lodge recruited 170 Jewish volunteers as "pinch hitters" to replace non-Jewish workers.[45]

In 1972, the Men's Club of Detroit's Temple Beth El staffed Providence Hospital's admitting office, emergency room, gift shop, and information desks "so that Our Lady of Providence League and Red Cross volunteers who regularly handled these posts, could stay home and celebrate Christmas."[46] The temple group worked December 23, 24, and 25, an effort that prompted one local newspaper's comment: "Brother, that's brotherhood." Proud of its members' volunteerism, Temple Beth El's bulletin happily reported: "With each holiday, our *mitzvot* seem to expand into ever-growing opportunities to serve." By 1974, women had joined the men in volunteering at Providence Hospital.[47]

In 1974, three reform synagogue brotherhoods in Cincinnati (Rockdale Temple, Temple Shalom, and Isaac M. Wise) substituted for workers at Cincinnati's Bethesda North Hospital. The temple brotherhood coordinator of this event considered this instance to be the first organized effort of this nature in Cincinnati. The coordinator was aware of a similar effort in Philadelphia in which thirteen synagogue brotherhoods organized nine hundred volunteers to work in sixteen area hospitals.[48]

From the late 1980s and continuing to the present day, from Thanksgiving through January, synagogues and Jewish organizations throughout the United States set up wintertime collections, generally in the form of clothing and toy drives. Their goal is simple: to enhance fellow Americans' celebration of Thanksgiving, New Year's Eve, and, above all, Christmas.

AMERICAN JEWS VOLUNTEER TO PLAY SANTA CLAUS

Perhaps the most interesting and ironic form of Jewish volunteerism during Christmas-time is the phenomenon of the Jewish Santa Claus. In a limited sense, this title is bestowed on Jewish volunteers who act generously, very much like Santa Claus would. More commonly, this description refers to Jews who volunteer to wear Santa garb and act in character. A Massachusetts *Needham Times* newspaper article refers to the performance of these two aspects of Santa's persona: "Santa takes on different forms. For the needy in Needham this year, as with every other year, Santa is more than one person."[49]

The *Patriot Ledger* newspaper of Quincy, Massachusetts, portrays the Lamb family as acting Santa-like when volunteering: "The Lamb family has no experience playing Santa Claus," the *Ledger* writes. "But it doesn't take long for the Jewish foursome to spread Christmas cheer. In little more than an hour, Susan, Paul, and their two daughters completed what has become their personal holiday tradition, delivering hot dinners and warm wishes to elderly people alone in their homes."[50]

Beginning in 1969 and ending in 1996, Albert Rosen of Milwaukee volunteered annually to replace workers on Christmas Eve and Christmas Day. After a chance encounter with a man who bemoaned that he had to work on Christmas, Rosen called a local radio station and asked the disc jockey to announce that "a Jewish man wanted to work for a Christian on Christmas."[51] Rosen, substituting for Christian strangers at work, performed their duties on Christmas. He volunteered as a police dispatcher, bellman, switchboard operator, television reporter, chef, convenience store clerk, radio disc jockey, and gas station attendant. To be most productive, he trained for each position in advance of Christmas. While not directly referred to as Santa, an Associated Press story dubbed Albert Rosen a "Jewish elf," as if he were one of Santa's helpers. Albert Rosen was eulogized on December 2, 1998, as acting "Christ-like" because of what he did for others. His story served as inspiration because Wesley Davis, an African American friend of Rosen's, took his place several weeks later to fulfill a promise Al had made to answer telephones at a home for the blind on Christmas Day. "Al would have wanted that," said Davis.

A celebrated case of acting like Santa Claus was the response of Aaron Feuerstein, the Jewish owner of the large textile factory Malden Mills in Methuen, Massachusetts. His factory burned to the ground in 1995, two weeks before Christmas. Aaron Feuerstein decided to continue to pay salaries to and health benefits for his twenty-five hundred employees until partial production resumed at the mill. He also gave them Christmas bonuses. When asked where he obtained strength and inspiration after the devastation, Feuerstein cited an ancient Jewish quotation that served as his motto: "When all is moral chaos, this is the time for you to be a *mensch.*"[52] For his exemplary efforts, Feuerstein was labeled by the news media as the "Mensch who saved Christmas" for his employees.[53]

In addition to Jews acting generously like Santa, some have donned Santa outfits and played the role of Santa at retail businesses, hospitals, shelters, and private homes.[54] Beginning with the middle decades of the twentieth century, the Jewish-owned Brickman's Department Store in the small community of Vineyard Haven on the island of Martha's Vineyard in Massachusetts began to invite people to serve as Santa during the Christmas season. At that time, Brickman's was the only store on the island to sport a Santa Claus for children to visit during the month of December. Dorothy Brickman, the daughter of the store's founders, explained that her family felt it a civic duty to have a Santa represented in town.[55]

One year, Bernie Issokson, a friend of the Brickman family and a Jewish resident of the island, dressed up as Santa Claus. According to Dorothy, Bernie agreed to dress up as Santa on the very same day that his wife and daughter were attending a Hanukkah party at the only synagogue on Martha's Vineyard. Upon reaching his home, the Jewish Santa Claus discovered that he had forgotten his key and was locked out of his house. He knocked on the door of an elderly neighbor who had made it clear on previous occasions that he did not like living next to a Jewish family.

Having answered the knock at his door, the neighbor did not recognize Bernie dressed up as Santa Claus until he identified himself. From that moment on, the two neighbors were on friendly terms. In this small way, a small town Jew dressed as Santa helped to promote good Christian-Jewish relationships.

The main motivations for playing the role of Santa are to make children happy and to spread holiday cheer and goodwill. Harvey Katz, a Glastonbury, Connecticut, lawyer enjoyed dressing up as Santa Claus. In the early 1900s, Harvey's parents were the first Jewish residents to settle in Glastonbury, a town historically identified with New England farmers. Harvey's parents opened Katz's Hardware Store on Main Street. Eventually, Harvey became a lawyer with a well-respected legal practice in town. He became the first Jewish member of a local bank's board of trustees. As a gesture of goodwill, every year during the 1970s and 1980s, Harvey dressed up as Santa Claus for one afternoon and spread good cheer throughout the bank because of, as he explained, "his love for kids and creating a joyous mood during the holiday season."[56]

Toward the end of his life, comedian Alan King satirically described his encounter with a Yiddish-speaking Santa Claus at the corner of Fifty-seventh Street in Manhattan. The Jewish immigrant from Ukraine justifies to Alan King his "ho-ho-ho" get-up by quipping in Yiddish: "*Men makht a lebn*"—a man has to make a living.[57] A paycheck, however, is not the main reason Jews volunteer to dress up as Santa. Jews who act out the part of Santa do so for altruistic reasons, some for evoking pleasure and others because Christmas was part of their holiday celebration growing up. For people raised from childhood with a Santa tradition, the transition to play-ing Santa Claus in public may be a natural progression. A 1978 *Los Angeles Times* article "Memoirs of a Jewish Santa" reported the story of a man named Jay Frankston who dressed up as Santa Claus in New York for twelve years, from 1960 to 1972.[58] His decision to put on Santa's clothing came after an experience in 1958 of decorating a Christmas tree with his family. For two successive years he played Santa for his Jewish children. The Santa outfit gave Frankston a joyous persona. Wearing a mask, com-plete with whiskers and flowing white hair, the Santa outfit, buttressed by inflatable pillows, transformed him into "a child's dream of Saint Nick." "My posture changed," he admitted. "I leaned back and pushed out my false stomach, my head tilted to the side, and my voice got deeper and richer: 'MERRY CHRISTMAS, EVERYONE.'"[59]

Jay so enjoyed dressing up as Santa that he volunteered to answer letters sent to Santa Claus that were deposited at the main post office in New York

City. He discovered that its third floor was swamped with letters addressed
to Santa Claus at the North Pole. He responded to eight of the letters he had
read and spent $150 of his own money to send telegrams to each of the eight
children. The telegrams announced that Santa was answering their wishes
and would deliver the gifts personally. And so he did. By 1972, Jay was reading ten thousand letters and bringing gifts to 150 children each Christmas.
Publicity about Frankston's good deeds attracted donations, which he then
passed on to charitable organizations to use at Christmastime. Echoing the
sentiments of many Jews who have become involved in bringing cheer to
others on Christmas, Frankston admitted that Christmas belonged to him
and had brought him much happiness through his charity.

A Massachusetts Christmastime Jewish Tradition

As a way to comprehend the richness and recent surge in Jewish
volunteerism on Christmas, it is instructive to consider the depth of
commitment and scope of service offered in one state with a strong history
of Jewish communal involvement. Project Ezra, which started in
Massachusetts in 1985 and has continued to the present, is a highly organized Jewish communal program in the Commonwealth of Massachusetts.
Project Ezra attracts thousands of volunteers throughout Massachusetts
who enlist to help make Christmas Eve and Christmas Day a more cheer-
filled occasion for the hungry, the homeless, and the lonely. Each year, until
recently, the Synagogue Council of Massachusetts announced through its
website a listing of the available Christmas volunteer projects, as well as
photos of past events, to entice new volunteers. In 2011, Project Ezra
celebrated its twenty-fifth anniversary.

In 1985, the Synagogue Council of Massachusetts conceived of Project
Ezra in response to a call for helping the needy on Christmas. The council
acts as an umbrella organization for 120 synagogues from various denominations and Jewish institutions. Project Ezra takes its name from the
Hebrew word *ozer* (help), reflecting the organization's actions in preparing
and serving Christmas dinners in soup kitchens and delivering meals and
gifts to shut-ins during Christmas Day. Executive Director of Synagogue
Council of Massachusetts Alan Teperow indicated that this help assures a
volunteer core to ease the burden of charities overwhelmed with demands
to help on Christmas.[60]

In its first year of operation, the Synagogue Council teamed up with
Father Brian Kelley of the Social Action Ministries of Greater Boston
to identify shelters and food pantries appropriate for interested Jewish

volunteers. The Synagogue Council of Massachusetts matched volunteer responses received from a mass mailing sent to synagogues across the Commonwealth of Massachusetts with shelters and feeding programs. In early December 1986 Teperow predicted such a great response among interested Jews that he would have difficulty organizing enough venues for volunteers to staff.[61]

The program coordinator at that time, Roz Garber, expected to attract 150 volunteers; instead, 600 signed up.[62] Garber, who had never entered a shelter until joining Project Ezra, representing a cross section of Jewish organizations, found the experience of volunteering on Christmas to be very satisfying. Garber relates the euphoria that resulted from this experience: "When my daughter was twelve years old," Garber relates, "I brought her to a shelter to help serve meals on Christmas Day. A woman walked in, and my daughter asked her if she would like some food. The woman responded, 'No, what I really want is a hug.' I stood there and watched my daughter hug this woman. It was the most incredible feeling."[63] Garber reconciled her Jewish identity with her involvement in Christmas by proclaiming that the December holiday season "is a time of giving, a time of peace throughout the world." This ambiance created for her "a spirit that's not necessarily religious that I think we all share."[64]

Grass-Roots Organizing

In its first year, thirty-three Massachusetts synagogues and Jewish organizations participated in Project Ezra, a cross-section of Jewish denominations, Jewish organizations, and unaffiliated Jews. Volunteers were placed at twenty-four shelters and feeding programs run by Boston area churches, including Episcopal, Lutheran, and Paulist groups and social service agencies, such as Little Brothers Friends of the Poor and Willow Manor Nursing Home in Lowell.

Matching venues with Christmastime volunteers requires a high level of organization. Each synagogue appointed a contact person who coordinated with the Synagogue Council office, marshaled its own volunteers, and communicated in advance with the volunteer site. Volunteer supervisors are usually drawn from committees or groups affiliated with congregations, such as social justice groups, men's clubs, ladies' auxiliaries, and youth groups that are charged with the task of organizing, recruiting volunteers, and publicizing the program among synagogue members. Each November and December, newsletters from participating synagogues and Jewish organizations call upon members to volunteer for a "*mitzvah* you'll never forget." Accompanying these notices is Project Ezra's own logo, comprised of Project Ezra's name and a place setting with a chicken dinner and cutlery on both sides.

Even though there is always a favorable response to calls for volunteers, synagogues promote their efforts by appealing to the volunteer's spirit of generosity. A promotional piece from Temple Emanuel of Newton, Massachusetts, for example, pulls at the heartstrings of potential volunteers for Project Ezra by describing the homeless in ways reminiscent of an earlier era's appeal: the homeless people are "looking older than their years, wearing soiled and tattered clothing, holding the hands of ragamuffin children, like something from a Dickens novel."[65]

These yearly appeals are highly successful. One affiliated member of a synagogue in Canton, Massachusetts, reported that her family had read about a program at Pilgrim Church in Dorchester and volunteered on Christmas Day in 1997. They spent three and a half hours setting up and decorating for the annual Christmas meal for 150 people in the church community. These Jewish volunteers wanted "to help people and allow them to have a nice Xmas."[66] Similarly, the Dauer family read the advertisement for the 2008 holiday season and responded by serving food for the homeless at Father Bill's Place in Quincy with a group from their synagogue, Temple Shalom of Milton. Like the family from Canton, the Dauers wanted to deviate from their normal Christmas routine of eating at a Chinese restaurant and going to the movies. "I just feel that I'm so fortunate," said the Dauers' twenty-two year old daughter. "This is the least I could do."[67]

Once committed, volunteers often return year after year. "This has become sort of a family tradition," remarked Liz Oppenheim, a then twenty-six-year-old second-year law student at American University in Washington, D.C. She had visited her parents in Sudbury during college vacation and volunteered with her father for three consecutive years.[68]

Feeding the Hungry: Preparing and Serving Christmas Meals

Project Ezra's programs were mainly centered on preparing, serving, delivering, and cleaning up Christmas Day dinners, which most often occur around noon. Volunteers helped with holiday decorations, especially when the meal is served to a group in a shelter or residence. Project Ezra volunteers also donated, wrapped, and presented gifts. In some cases, Jewish volunteers provided Christmas entertainment, sang Christmas carols, and occasionally orchestrated arts and crafts and recreational projects. Most important, volunteers showed attitudes of caring and concern for the residents.

At the Moreville House Elderly Residence in Boston, for example, volunteers prepared and served dinner and organized caroling and Christmas music for the residents. In the kitchen, Jewish volunteers readied a meal from an assembly line, piling plates high with turkey, stuffing, vegetables, and mashed potatoes. All was awash in gravy. The brimming plates were then passed to an ever-replenishing line of servers. Upon being handed a plate, young and old trotted back and forth from the kitchen to the tables. Halfway through the meal, several volunteers wandered over to the piano. Volunteer Raymond Rosenstock, a middle-aged musicologist, sat down on the piano bench and began to play. Each year he led a rousing rendition of Christmas carols and an occasional Hanukkah melody on violin, piano, and accordion. "Deck the Halls" and "We Wish You a Merry Christmas" were followed by "I Have a Little Dreidel." The other volunteers joined in the spirited singing. The infectious music wafted over the tables. Soon, the residents and the other volunteers joined in. Between mouthfuls, everyone sang! Despite the musical interlude, the volunteers continued to serve and clear away dishes. Finally, it was time for dessert. Ice cream and several varieties of pie drew everyone's attention. The meal ended sweetly.

Preparing food is more than just cooking, presenting, and distributing Christmas meals. There is also an esthetic element that shows a deep well of caring. On Christmas Eve, adults and children from Temple Isaiah of Lexington, Massachusetts, put together food baskets, children wrapped candies, and everybody joined together to add bows to the food gifts. Jeff Goldberg, the temple's social action committee chair, explained the value of pleasing recipients: "It's one thing to get enough protein in people, but you also want to raise the spirit."[69]

It is not just the typical middle-aged synagogue congregants and their young children who are inspired to volunteer at Christmas. Jewish young urban professionals rolled up their sleeves to feed the hungry and homeless in the town of Lynn, located near Salem, Massachusetts. Dan Rooks, an organizer of the yearlong volunteer effort, pointed out that the younger generation may not be as synagogue-minded, but took their parents' teachings on *tzedakah* to new levels. And Christmas provided the perfect opportunity.[70]

Jewish involvement in the many Christmas volunteer efforts has come to the attention of the general media that inevitably treats Jewish charitable participation in a positive light. Jews embracing the spirit of Christmas through volunteerism is regarded as newsworthy by the press, expected but also surprising. The *Boston Globe* stated with glee that "Jewish volunteers spread Yule cheer."[71] And the Boston-based *Jewish Advocate* reported that "Communities Find Jewish Ways to 'Celebrate' Christmas."[72]

Public attention to the goodwill of volunteering breeds enthusiasm and a spirit of ecumenicalism. Boston television station Channel 5 WCVB TV remarked positively on its five o'clock 1996 Christmas Eve broadcast of the spirit of cooperation between various religious and ethnic groups. Reporter Janet Wu noted that "across town it's not just Christians celebrating the true spirit of Christmas" but also Muslims and Jews. Rahim Al-Kaleem, of Naid Quran Mosque joined several of the projects and praised the gathering of different religious groups: "Although we are not Christians per se," he said, "we do buy into the notion of goodwill for all men, regardless of religion."[73]

Displaying a similar spirit, forty Muslims from the Council of Islamic Organizations of Michigan joined the "Mitzvah Day" project in 2009 sponsored by the Jewish Community Relations Council and the Jewish Federation of Metropolitan Detroit to feed the hungry and deliver toys. Victor Begg, chairman of the Islamic council, sought a way for Judaism and Islam to "build bridges of understanding and cooperation" and used Christmas charity as just such a connection.[74] In 2010, the Sixteenth Street Jewish Community Center is Washington, D.C., hosted its annual Day of Service on December 24 (a day early) because Christmas Day fell on the Jewish Sabbath. Its postcard advertisement calling for volunteers proclaims: "One day of service, over 10,000 lives impacted." The Day of Service, attracting one thousand volunteers, is the "capital region's premier volunteer event."[75]

Volunteers feel that bringing their children to volunteer activities teaches a valuable lesson. Sheila Doctoroff, social action chair of Temple Beth El of Belmont, Massachusetts, decided one year to bring her ten-year-old daughter, Jessica, to help serve a Christmas dinner at a church. Before going out to volunteer, mother and daughter had a long talk about the benefits of sharing with people less fortunate. She explained to her daughter that focusing solely on Hanukkah doesn't allow Jewish children to experience what it is to see the other side of life. Christmas provides that opportunity for Jews.

Temple Beth El selected the Pilgrim Congregational Church as a volunteer site, according to Alice Melnikoff, because the church would be a good place to bring children to experience helping an ethnically diverse population on Christmas Day. By helping to cook 250 hot meals Alice's twelve-year-old son, Mark, learned that "a lot of people do not have homes, warm clothes, food."[76] He came to realize that Christmas and Hanukkah are not just religious celebrations or opportunities to receive presents.

Figure 5.1. Publicity postcard for the Day of Volunteer Service, 24 December 2010, sponsored by the Washington, D.C., Jewish Community Center. Courtesy Washington, D.C., JCC.

Working Together to Help the Poor

Beneficiaries of Christmas goodwill comment on the positive impact fostered by interfaith volunteerism, bringing "a ray of sunshine" and serving as "an example of God's people working together in harmony and charity."[77] Writing a letter of thanks to the organizers of Project Ezra, Reverend Park expressed his gratitude on behalf the Paulist Center and their community of homeless and hungry people. He stated in a letter that Jewish volunteers worked tirelessly, which helped many needy to overcome feelings of isolation and division. Their efforts, he wrote, "help to bring together people who worship God in different traditions, but who share the same concerns for humanity."[78]

Some of the most moving volunteer experiences occurred when Project Ezra volunteers visited housebound senior citizens. These shut-ins were pleased not just for the gifts they received but also for the one-on-one contact that made them feel appreciated. One volunteer family of four from Quincy, Massachusetts, visited the same two elderly sisters on Christmas Day during 1995 and 1996. Eighty-nine-year-old Gertrude Bataitis and her eighty-six-year-old sister, Ann, were thrilled to have repeat visitors. "Look, Ann, look what they brought," Gertrude said, carrying the poinsettias into the living room. "Oh, they're beautiful," Ann said.[79]

The family, consisting of two parents and their two daughters, sat and chatted about the sisters' health in the past year and listened to stories about Gertrude and Ann's careers: for forty-two years the former was a Boston elementary school teacher, and the latter was a commercial artist. The elderly sisters found particular joy in conversing with the two young daughters. "Aren't they beautiful children? God love them," Ann said when the family prepared to leave. Gertrude remarked: "You people are lovely . . . thanks a million for making this a beautiful day for us . . . I never talked so much in all my life."[80] The volunteer family hugged the two elderly women and headed for the door. Gertrude then invited her Christmas Day visitors to stop by again.

In addition to the elderly, volunteers also visit those who are infirm. Many of these individuals are AIDS patients. Volunteers supply food, wrap gifts, and exchange photographs and personal life stories. Another elderly housebound woman, Lillian Priest, a resident of Boston's South End neighborhood and age eighty-four, was living on the eighteenth floor of a building. She eagerly anticipated a visit from volunteers from Project Ezra and Little Brothers Friends to the Elderly. "I wait for these holidays to come because then I know I don't have to cook for myself," she said. "Oh, I just love you [volunteers] all to pieces."[81]

Americans who are relieved by Jewish volunteers are also appreciative of their efforts. Laurie Boisvert, the food service coordinator for Father Bill's Place in Quincy, Massachusetts, worked at her job on Thanksgiving Day feeding a holiday meal to hundreds of homeless and needy people. On Christmas Day Boisvert was home with her family in Quincy, opening gifts and relaxing because of the efforts of eighteen members of Temple Shalom in Milton who volunteered to help out. Boisvert remarked that she could leave without worrying about her charges.[82]

THE SPECIAL FUNCTION OF JEWISH VOLUNTEERISM ON CHRISTMAS

Jewish volunteer efforts on Christmas allow Jews the opportunity to participate in Christmas, but in a way that does not detract from their Jewish identity; in fact, their volunteerism reinforces their Jewishness. American Jews engage Christmas in a charitable manner because they translate the Christmas message into the cultural vocabulary of Jewish and American values. Jewish volunteers recognize Christmas as a national holiday devoted to sharing and giving in which they as Jews can participate with pride. Rather than feeling left out of Christmas festivities or bored for lack of something to do as might have occurred in past decades, American Jews are involved in celebrating universal core values of the Christmas holiday season by joining both fellow Jews and other Americans in a shared sense of civic responsibility. Parents teach their children that there are ways to respect the Christmas holiday and be true to Jewish holiday traditions and values. Through volunteering, Jewish adults and children support what many people in America consider the essence of the holiday season—namely, improving the lives of others. While others anxiously wait to receive gifts, volunteers are fulfilled by giving to others.

Volunteering on Christmas overrides religious and ethnic differences and brings all Americans—Christians, Jews, and Muslims—together in common cause. By association with Christmas, the Jewish value of *tzedakah* [charitable acts], originally developed to support the Jewish needy, is able to expand to include anyone whose fortunes prevent them from enjoying the holiday season. For their efforts to give to others outside the faith, the general population accords Jews an elevated status, now seen in American terms as reflecting behavior that is "Christmas-like or "Santa-like." And the holiday of Christmas gains prestige because noncelebrants benefit from its charitable focus.

Historically, Jews have depended on non-Jews to perform certain duties at times when Jews are prohibited by Jewish law from working because of holiday or Sabbath-related restrictions. The Yiddish colloquialism for this non-Jewish helper is *Shabbes goy*. Ironically, a similar relationship has taken root in America in the twenty-first century, a relationship of dependability and reciprocity between Jew and Christian, acted out on Christmas. On Christmas Eve and Day, in large urban centers, the American Jew becomes the *Christmas Yid*, the Christmas Jew. In performing a wide spectrum of charitable acts, Jews assist in aiding non-Jews to celebrate Christmas. Expanding upon German Jewish scholar Franz Rosenzweig's two-covenant theory, Rabbi Harold Kushner wrote: "Christianity needs Judaism to remind it of what pure, uncompromised ethical monotheism looks like. . . . Judaism needs Christianity to remind us that the word of God is not meant to be kept for ourselves alone."[83] Christmas elicits dependability and reciprocity between Americans of all ethnic and religious backgrounds, as expressed on a civic plain during a time when many social service agencies utilize Jewish volunteers who substitute for Christian workers. Consistent with Kushner's words, Christmastime reminds certain American Jews of the need to assume greater social responsibility beyond the boundaries of their local Jewish communities.

Project Ezra's contribution to Christmas volunteerism has been a model of how members of a minority successfully join with the majority to share in a common holiday spirit and idealism. As a result, Jews who volunteer during December do not view Christmas as irrelevant, appropriate only for Americans who celebrate the holiday. These Jews regard Christmas and the December holiday season, including Hanukkah, as a source of abundant joy, and they seek ways to help fellow Americans celebrate their holiday. As a response to Christmas, Jewish volunteerism in December comes closest to sharing in the Christmas spirit. Whether volunteering in soup kitchens or hospitals, visiting housebound elderly people on Christmas Day, dressing up as Santa Claus, or substituting for fellow Americans at their jobs, American Jews have found a way to belong to Christmas without an accompanying twinge of alienation. This Jewish charitable involvement in Christmas giving is one of the most successful responses Jews in America have made to refashioning Christmas as their own. As one newspaper reporter remarked, the "Jewish '*mitzvah*' [in this case, the good deed of volunteering] is a gift of Christmas," and many Americans recognize that Jews are their equal when it comes to Christmas generosity.[84]

Volunteering on Christmas has become an ingrained tradition for Jews in America, a part of the mindset of individuals and the community.

In acknowledgment of the popularity of the annual program in each community, the Synagogue Council of Massachusetts recognized the success of
the grass-roots volunteer activism. Project Ezra achieved its two long-range
goals of directly helping those in need and assisting Christian workers,
who otherwise would be working, to have more time to celebrate their
Christmas holiday. In 2010, after almost twenty-five years of matching
congregations with recipient institutions, Synagogue Council transitioned
control and ownership over Project Ezra to its constituent individual
synagogues. Because participating synagogues have established wonderful
relationships with their partner institutions over the many years of the
program, Synagogue Council decided that it was no longer needed to
coordinate the statewide effort. Now completely synagogue-centered and
without the council's involvement, each synagogue maintains its own
Christmas volunteer projects.[85] Although having been phased out of existence, Project Ezra's name and logo may be used as identification by each
independent organization and synagogue. Despite the lack of a central
clearinghouse, throughout the Commonwealth of Massachusetts, the spirit
of Project Ezra's volunteerism continues with both individual Jewish
and Christian communities benefiting from the positive impact of this
interfaith communitywide annual Christmas activity.

Project Ezra's involvement with Christmas charity was applauded in
1986 at the time of its inception by Massachusetts governor Michael
Dukakis. Writing a letter of gratitude to the organizers of the first Project
Ezra, Governor Dukakis called this Jewish charitable effort "an important
new tradition." These words seemed prophetic. Indeed, both Jews and
Christians experience the positive impact of this annual interfaith community activity throughout Massachusetts and its model for community
action beyond the state's geographic boundaries.

One year later, on December 26, 1987, this sentiment was embraced by
President Ronald Reagan in his Christmastime radio broadcast to the
nation about the subject of voluntarism. In his address, Reagan recognized
that two religious observances, Christmas and Hanukkah, are at the "heart
of America's Judeo-Christian heritage." He also noted that "this is also a
traditional time of merriment and good cheer, a time of family and home
and of Christmas trees and gift-giving." Reagan then linked the holiday
season to a spirit of generosity that he termed "good, old-fashioned
Americanism—neighbor helping neighbor." Citing Thomas Jefferson's
belief that everyone should engage in charity, Reagan asserted that voluntarism is still a strong force in communities throughout America and that
"helping others is just our way, part of our national character. Perhaps it

reflects that we as a people not only enjoy this holiday every year as time off from work but also take to heart the spiritual meaning of Christmas and Hanukkah."[86]

Jewish volunteerism on Christmas has certainly become an established American tradition through which Jews in America have made their presence known. During this joyous season—in which they are lauded by the American public for supporting the Christmas message of goodwill toward all people—they express and embody the national character of "neighbor helping neighbor."

CHAPTER 6

CHRISMUKKAH AND FESTIVUS

HOLIDAYS FOR THE REST OF US

When Elise and Phil Okrend began their line of interfaith greeting cards in 1989, they were responding to a significant increase in interfaith relationships between Americans from Jewish and Christian backgrounds. Based upon census reports, the interfaith marriage rate had dramatically increased.[1] Realizing that intermarried couples, families, and friends were looking for an ecumenical way to greet each other beyond the generic "Happy Holidays," the Okrends created a line of cards that juxtaposed images of Christmas and Hanukkah. In response to critics who immediately accused them of undermining Jewish identity, they cited an increasing demand for greeting cards that combined the two religious holidays in a positive way.[2] The Okrends designed cards with each of the following images: Santa and a Jewish counterpart playing dreidel together; a menorah growing out of a reindeer's antler; and a Star of David atop a Christmas tree. These novel images anticipated a new age in Jewish-Christian relationships in the United States by envisioning the two religions coming together in a joint celebration of the holiday season. The designers presented a hope and vision that underlay this new way of thinking: Christmas and Hanukkah could cross the threshold of interfaith homes with the same ease that juxtaposed the two holidays in shopping malls and civic venues. Within the American interfaith home, Christmas and Hanukkah would be complementary holidays; their symbols could carry an overlapping message of joy, peace, and goodwill. The juxtaposition of images in the American home formed a hybrid celebration, one that was neither solely Christmas nor only Hanukkah, but a measure of both. In the popular parlance of the 1990s, this hybrid form of celebration was cleverly dubbed *Chrismukkah.*

Secular Americans, however, who eschewed celebration of any religious holiday, even in symbolic gesture, yearned for alternative seasonal rites and ceremonies that could be shared by others who might be disenfranchised from both Christmas and Hanukkah. *Festivus* appeared in the 1990s as a whimsical seasonal secular celebration that garnered a following as a result of the popular television series *Seinfeld,* which introduced the concept. Both the hybrid Chrismukkah and the secular Festivus, new responses to the December dilemma, provide alternative meaningful involvement for new generations of Americans, including American Jews.

HANUKKAH AND CHRISTMAS: COMPLEMENTARY HOLIDAYS FOR INTERFAITH FAMILIES

Until the 1960s, it was commonplace for some Jewish households to display Christmas decorations as reflections of civic pride and assimilation. Signs of Christmas were everywhere, and some American Jews viewed them as emblematic of the December holiday spirit. Many Jewish parents did not want to deprive their children of the opportunity to join in expressions of holiday joy. Others refused any Christmas concession in the home and instead favored the menorah. After the 1970s, when intermarriage rates slowly began to rise, the question was rephrased: not whether to display a Christmas tree or a Hanukkah menorah, but how to integrate the two in a joint interfaith celebration. Once in the home, the Christmas tree and the menorah took center stage and served as centerpieces for giving gifts, singing songs, and feasting on holiday foods.[3]

Deciding how to correlate two religions with conflicting belief systems created challenges for interfaith couples, their children, and their parents. In considering the entire yearly holiday calendar, the December celebrations of Christmas and Hanukkah generated the most emotion, given childhood holiday attachments. Christmas and Hanukkah evoked positive feelings about home, food, rituals, holiday displays, and gift-giving. Arguments to retain familiar December holiday customs in the presence of a spouse from another religion also served to express loyalty to one's faith and family. The feelings of parents and grandparents had to be respected, and interfaith couples needed to negotiate how they would practice Christmas and Hanukkah at home as well as in the homes of parents and grandparents. Children needed explanations for why each parent was celebrating different holidays. Compromise was often reached that allowed interfaith couples to be more selective and creative about the symbols that were to be displayed at home, while joining more freely in the traditional religious home ceremonies of parents and grandparents. The children of interfaith couples learned how to vacillate between the two holidays and why holiday practices sometimes differed between parents and grandparents. The advantage of labeling a home Christmas-Hanukkah celebration as hybrid was that couples could skirt issues of religious conflict and concentrate on the underlying commonalities of Christmas and Hanukkah, such as family gatherings and dinners, gift-giving, and display of holiday lights. In time, the union between Christmas and Hanukkah seemed natural for both parents and children of interfaith households.

The title of Elise and Phil Okrend's line of holiday greeting cards, "Mixed Blessings," identified the ideal metaphor for addressing both the phenomenon of interfaith marriage and the challenges facing interfaith couples.[4] For those who have joined in interfaith marriages, (approximately 51 percent by 2010), successfully bridging Judaism and Christianity depends upon coming to terms with deep religious contradictions and conflicting familial ties. In 1989, the Okrends initiated their line of cards that appealed to a growing interfaith population. These interfaith couples had been facing real and potential conflicts to navigate in their personal lives. One particularly pressing conflict is the issue of raising children in a dual religion household. Many strategies have been developed by couples to bridge this divide. In one solution to this conflict both spouses simply eschew matters of religion by focusing on acceptable universal cultural teachings and images; in other cases, spouses agree to honor each other's religion by allowing each partner to continue to worship or celebrate as he or she wishes. These two strategies do not necessarily succeed when children are born. Certain parents teach universal messages and images that gloss over religious contradictions while others, less often, immerse children in both religions. Other couples have adopted an approach whereby the children follow the religion of either one parent or the other and, in certain instances the children are divided up in two religions and then allowed to choose which path they will ultimately follow when they reach a certain age, for example, the age of thirteen.[5]

Church and synagogue representatives typically counsel parents to raise children in one religion so as to lessen confusion about religious identity. Indeed, it is rare to find parents taking their children to worship in or be educated at both church and synagogue simultaneously. It is more common for parents to offer opportunities for children to sample the celebratory aspects of each religion that involve cuisine, music, charity, and displays of holiday images. The December dilemma, the term most often used to describe confusion in Jewish circles over whether Jews should engage in recognizing Christmas, began to dissolve as increasing numbers of interfaith couples integrated both Christmas and Hanukkah in their personal seasonal celebrations. A new spirit of mutual cooperation and understanding emerged between faiths in the United States as Christmas and Hanukkah were viewed as mutually supportive.[6]

The gauge of whether this integration of the two religious traditions has succeeded is reflected in attempts by parents to explain to their children the benefits of fusing the celebrations of Hanukkah and Christmas. Parents often turned to books written on a child's level to help explain difficult issues, thereby enabling families to better adapt to their parents' different religious backgrounds, needs, and practices. Unlike earlier publications, which suggested that children might be harmed if raised in two distinct religions, more recent children's books tout the benefits of sharing inter-faith religious customs and ceremonies. Authors have tried to relate the advantages of drawing customs and rituals from both Hanukkah and Christmas as a means to draw from the backgrounds of, and ameliorate the concerns of, both parents and grandparents. These authors have painted an optimistic, if untested, picture of the effect such exposure would have on children's identification with their parent's religion. They have also assumed that children would happily follow whatever degree of religious identification their parents suggested.

EXPLAINING INTERFAITH DECEMBER HOLIDAY CELEBRATIONS TO CHILDREN

In 1983, when Susan Sussman wrote her book *There's No Such Thing as a Christmas Bush, Sandy Goldstein,* it was hard for many within the Jewish community to sanction the presence of a Christmas tree in a Jewish home.[7] In this particular story, Sandy Goldstein's mother refuses her daughter's request to have a tree in the house. Sandy points out that one of her Jewish friends has a Christmas tree, and her friends refer to it as a Hanukkah bush. Further, Sandy argues that her mother has nothing to fear by having a tree in her home because the tree is not a religious symbol. Sandy's mother, unconvinced, explains to her daughter that no matter what you call the tree, it is in reality a major symbol associated with Christmas. And she states emphatically: "Jewish families do not have Christmas trees." Grandpa comes to the rescue by offering to take Sandy to a Christmas party spon- sored by his union where she can indulge in popular Christmas traditions. After having a marvelous time, she asks her grandfather what the difference is between hosting a Christmas party and attending somebody else's

Christmas party. Grandpa explains to Sandy that it is nice to help others celebrate what they believe, but that it would not be proper to borrow and use a symbol from another religion, a symbol of which Jews do not approve.

By 1991, certain authors of children's books openly addressed the possibility of Jewish families being involved in Christmas celebrations. Susan Enid Gertz's popular book *Hanukkah and Christmas at My House* presumed that intermarried parents were emotionally tied to their birth religions through positive associations with family holiday celebrations.[8] The young narrator in this book tells the story of how her mother loves everything about Hanukkah and her father reveres everything about Christmas. Moreover, each parent wishes to share his or her holiday joy with the children by celebrating Hanukkah and Christmas traditions on their respective dates. After telling how Mommy and Daddy celebrated their holidays before she was born, she tells the reader: "Now my mommy and daddy are grown up and I'm their little girl. My brother and I wait all year for Hanukkah and Christmas. We always tell them, 'We love every-thing about Hanukkah *and* Christmas.'" And, as if to strengthen the point, the daughter adds at the end of the story: "In my family, we wouldn't want it any other way!"[9] The book's message is that seasonal family celebrations drawn from two religions can be successfully transmitted to children as long as they are introduced in an atmosphere of mutual respect.

Upon surveying children's books concerning interfaith households published since 1990, a primary focus concerns the benefits of trying to understand and experience two differing religions. Margaret Moorman in *Light the Lights! A Story about Celebrating Hanukkah and Christmas* tells of a daughter from an interfaith marriage that is regarded as blessed because she has an opportunity to celebrate both holidays in succession.[10] And Elise and Philip Okrend, in their 1996 book *Blintzes for Blitzen*, portray a reindeer named Blitzen inadvertently stumbling upon the home of a Jewish baker where he is introduced to the beauty of blintzes (a Jewish delicacy—thin, rolled crepes, usually filled with sweetened cottage cheese). The image and its attendant wordplay illustrates that there is something very natural about Christians and Jews in the United States sharing each other's traditions.[11] Matthew Black, in his 2004 book *What's a Jew to Do on Christmas Eve*, relates the story of neighboring families of differing religions whose children, a Jewish son and a non-Jewish daughter, each wish to experience the other family's holiday celebration.[12] The son of the Jewish family secretly desires to celebrate Christmas, and the daughter of the non-Jewish household pines to celebrate Hanukkah. Their wishes come true when their parents decide to extend invitations to each other to join in celebrating their respective holidays. Although seeming to endorse Sussman's conclusion, that Jews and Christians during December should celebrate their respective holidays in their own homes and religious institutions, Black's characters treat Christmas and Hanukkah as interchangeable, each appropriate for children from either religion. Accordingly, Hanukkah and Christmas belong mutually to Jews and Christians. On learning the good news that he will be able to celebrate Christmas at the home of his friend's family, the Jewish boy declares: "You can imagine my surprise as I heard the great, big news. We were all celebrating Christmas, the Christians and the Jews."[13] Unlike Sussman, whose message is that Jews should not display Christmas symbols because they do not reflect Jewish religious beliefs, Black implies that holiday symbols transcend particularities of belief and refer to a common goodwill and seasonal joy. At the end of the book, the Jewish boy brings an African American friend to the Christmas festivities. The Jewish boy then expresses his hope that Kwanza might also be shared with Jews and Christians so as to produce an even greater inclusive universal holiday season. In Black's vision, Hanukkah, Christmas, and Kwanza belong to the civil religious affirmation of all Americans and should be regarded as unifying rather than dividing forces in American society.

INSTITUTIONAL SUPPORT FOR INTERFAITH COUPLES AND DECEMBER CELEBRATIONS

After the 1990 National Jewish Population Survey, a census report that documents an intermarriage rate of 43 percent, the organized Jewish community in the United States responded with massive outreach efforts to welcome interfaith couples into formal Jewish institutions. The Reform movement of American Judaism did not require conversion of the Christian spouse but sought to involve the couple in a formal synagogue setting, hoping thereby that Judaism would be the preferred choice in the intermarried couple's home.[14] The Conservative denomination, however, required conversion as a means to accept the couple fully into the synagogue's membership. Both the Reform and the Conservative denominations devoted considerable resources toward interfaith outreach programming because statistics demonstrated that only a third of interfaith households raised their children in the Jewish faith. The underlying rationale of both denominations was to encourage and provide support for the Jewish choices made by the interfaith couple.

The problem with outreach methods used by Jewish religious institutions in the United States is that they neither recognized nor addressed the myriad of home practices that intermarried couples were more than willing to introduce from both religions. Christmas trees, for example, graced many an interfaith home, a practice that none of the formal Jewish religious institutions condoned. To help confront dilemmas experienced by interfaith family dynamics and choices, grass-roots organizations and websites produced materials to answer questions, offer suggestions, and guide couples and families to interfaith friendly resources. One of the earliest efforts was Interfaithfamily.com, a website developed by an interfaith couple, Ed and Wendy Case. In 1998, the Cases were asked to contribute to an emerging on-line magazine on intermarriage. Ed Case saw the potential value of such a magazine and eventually oversaw its growth and expansion. Together with Ronnie Freidland, the magazine's editor, the Cases published in 2001 their first handbook on intermarriage (culled from essays on the website) entitled *The Guide to Jewish Interfaith family Life: An Interfaithfamily.com Handbook* that includes entries from rabbis, Jewish agencies, educators, and intermarried couples. These resources provided discussions and articles on all aspects of intermarried life and even suggested where couples contemplating marriage could obtain rabbis willing to officiate.[15] The views expressed on Interfaithfamily.com did, however, slant toward raising children in one religion only, and the stated preference was the Jewish religion.

Realizing that many intermarried families did not wish to select a single religion in which to raise their children, Dovetail Institute's Joan Hawxhurst, an Episcopalian married to a Jew, introduced an alternative website using a more ecumenical approach. In a 1992 retrospective on the recent birth of the organization, Hawxhurst stated, "Our mission is not to decide right or wrong, not to steer couples toward any particular direction but to provide couples with the tools and information they need to make their own best choice."[16] The institute, organized in 1994, continues to offer a journal, forums, conferences, and resources for intermarried couples searching for ways to help families bring their religious practices in closer harmony.

Interfaith families began to demand that classes be organized to teach aspects of both religions. Interfaithcommunity.org was instituted in 1987 by parents who envisioned a religious after-school curriculum that could introduce both religions to children in an unthreatening environment. In 1987, Sheila Gordon, cofounder (along with Lee F. Gruzen) and dean of a community college, helped parents establish an interfaith class geared for the sixth grade. The inaugural class consisted of twelve children and was team-taught by a rabbi and a minister. The class was successful, and the school expanded to include grades three through eight. The class met at the Trinity School in Manhattan, an independent day school with an Episcopalian tradition. The organization, which came to be known as "Interfaith Community," grew to sponsor five chapters across the country, organizing adult, family, and children's programs offering resources, holding workshops, and counseling parents and their children.[17]

Throughout this period, an increasing number of American rabbis from the Reform movement were willing to officiate at interfaith weddings, along with a priest from the Catholic Church, if requested. It, therefore, became possible to have the mixed marriage sanctioned by representatives of each religion.[18] Jewish marriage certificate (*ketubah*) manufacturers began to create innovative ketubahs that often used the traditional Jewish religious forma, while substituting universal words and imagery drawn from the traditions of both Judaism and Christianity.

TELEVISION SHOWS ON INTERFAITH CELEBRATIONS IN DECEMBER

Responding to the growing phenomenon of interfaith marriages in the Jewish community in the United States, the popular media in the 1970s began to explore their viability by highlighting the difficulties interfaith marriages had to overcome. Episodes of popular television series and sitcoms featured interfaith couples broaching their differences in an atmosphere that combined concern and conviviality. The comedy was based in the incongruity of two religious cultures. These television series portrayed couples maturing in such relationships and coming to understand and respect each other's differences with the help of family and friends. An early instance of the portrayal of a successful intermarriage occurred in the 1972 prime-time television series *Bridget Loves Bernie*. Bernie, played by actor David Birney, and Bridget, portrayed by actress and Birney's real-life wife, Meredith Baxter, overcame their religious differences mainly because of their relative lack of religious identification. The conflict in the series arose from their respective families' resistance to the relationship. Each family objected to the marriage based primarily on class difference. Bridget's wealthy family was in sharp contrast to Bernie's working-class background in the deli business. Over time, the families warmed to each other, finding themselves willing to participate in the first made-for-television interfaith marriage officiated by both a rabbi and a priest. After expressing differences in how the December holidays should be spent, Bridget's brother, a priest, joins with a rabbi in educating Bernie's father and uncle in the beauty of appreciating Christmas. Bernie's family thus becomes more accepting of Bridget and her family. Bernie's Uncle Moe is seen donning a Santa costume to appear as Santa. Despite the popularity and seeming realism of the series, organizations in the Jewish community protested vociferously because the series was seemingly condoning intermarriage. Viewed as too controversial, the show was cancelled despite its ranking as the fifth most popular series on television.[19]

By the 1980s, the increased frequency of intermarriages in the American Jewish community meant that they could no longer be treated as atypical. The thought-provoking 1980s television drama, *thirtysomething*, explored for the first time the full complexity of interfaith relationships. It took several episodes for the seminal characters, Michael and Hope Steadman (he being Jewish, she not), to decide whether to have a *bris* (a Jewish ritual circumcision) for their son. The entire extended family was involved in the often agonizing discussion as the couple struggled to make a decision. Ironically, the Jewish father, Michael, doubted the necessity for having a *bris*. Michael's mother's new boyfriend, Ben (played by Alan King), reminded Michael that the purpose of a bris is to continue the chain of Jewish tradition. Michael's non-Jewish wife Hope encouraged her husband to search for what she characterized as a sincere Jewish identity that would include following Jewish traditions. In another interfaith-themed episode, the Steadmans broach the subject of whether to display a Christmas tree or a menorah or both, with Michael confused once again about his own feelings about the issue.[20] As in the case of the bris, Hope decides for Michael that their children should experience lighting a menorah on Hanukkah. Hope, in fact, has the menorah ready to light as Michael walks into the house bearing (ironically) a Christmas tree to appease his non-Jewish wife.[21] The two episodes reflected the prevailing popular belief that love conquers all differences, including those based on religious preference. The television series *thirtysomething*, now considered a 1980s period piece, reflected the growing debate among intermarried couples about Christmas. The show raised issues about how connected each partner should be to the religion of birth and how much each partner's respective religious beliefs, customs, and ceremonies should be transmitted to future children.

CHRISMUKKAH IS BORN: COMBINING HANUKKAH AND CHRISTMAS

By the beginning of the twenty-first century, both the Christmas tree and the menorah found acceptance in the home of intermarried couples across the United States. The once prevalent conflict between Christmas and Hanukkah, dubbed the December dilemma, was resolved in favor of blending holiday symbols. The twenty-first century signaled a new period of experimenting with hybrid celebrations incorporating symbols from both religions, each complementing the other while drawing from the same holiday fervor and cheer.

As interfaith couples began to introduce symbols from both Hanukkah and Christmas in a single household, serious attention was given to how these symbols might be combined into one festival format. This concept of creating a Christmas and Hanukkah hybrid was first envisioned by Michael Nathanson, a resident of and teacher in New Haven, Connecticut, who wrote a spoof that he posted on the Internet in December 1997. Written tongue-in-cheek as an announcement of a corporate merger, Nathanson satirically publicized that Christmas and Hanukkah had finally merged. The monetary overhead occasioned by the celebration of two separate holidays, one for twelve days, the other for eight, would be reduced by this merger. "By combining forces," we're told, "the world will be able to enjoy consistently high-quality service during the fifteen days of Chrismukkah, as the new holiday is being called."[22] The combination of terms is purposeful; the letter *t* in Christmas is deliberately omitted.

This enhanced and streamlined celebration provided both the underlying rationale and the impetus for the 2003 Fox television network teen soap opera *The O.C.* The television character Seth (his father is Jewish, and his mother is Protestant) proclaims that he is searching for a substitute for the bland, routine, and half-hearted attempt that his intermarried parents make to recognize both Christmas and Hanukkah. He finds the solution in organizing "the best Chrismukkah ever." Seth envisioned this hybrid holiday to include presents for eight days and many more presents for the one additional day of Christmas.

Fictional and not descriptive of any one family's specific holiday celebration, *The O.C.* website merchandized the Chrismukkah logo and promoted Chrismukkah as a viable celebration. One could order a "yarmu-claus," a cap that fuses the Jewish religious head covering known as the *yarmulke* and Santa's hat.[23] The amalgam represented by Chrismukkah appealed to intermarried couples because it freed them from having to choose between one religion and symbol or another. It mattered little that the name Chrismukkah was an invention of popular culture and, therefore, rarely used by intermarried families. Reporters, who from year to year interviewed intermarried couples about their successes blending elements from both religions, popularized the concept of Chrismukkah. Kimberly

Duran of *DallasNews.com*, for example, referenced restaurants that served Chrismukkah foods in 2005 when Hanukkah and Christmas coincided. A spokeswoman for the Loews Hotel chain is quoted as having said that in their New York City, Miami, and Santa Monica locations a multifaith menu enabled patrons to order fare like "apple-cranberry latkes with eggnog ice cream and shalom sangria and Star of David cookies made of gingerbread."[24]

Capitalizing on the perceived need for intermarried couples to find common ground upon which to celebrate the holiday season and recognizing the commercial benefits arising from creating a line of Chrismukkah products, Ron Gompertz inaugurated the website "Chrismukkah.org. Married to a Christian, Gompertz sought to create a mechanism by which to avoid the anxiety he experienced when being introduced to the Christmas celebration of his in-laws. In the hybrid form of celebration, interfaith spouses would more readily accept the alternative religious holiday symbols because they had become transformed into secular and novel holiday items. Gompertz referred to Chrismukkah as a "merry mishmash," a "celebration of diversity, a global gumbo of cherished secular traditions."[25] On his website and in subsequent publications, Gompertz demonstrated the applicability of Chrismukkah to a range of cultural forms, practices, and material arts. The Chrismukkah line of products included examples from greeting cards, recipes, songs, and decorations. Gompertz provided a full treatment of the Chrismukkah convention in a book with the same name and examined the definitional myths for developing the hybrid holiday; the merger of Christmas and Hanukkah was a natural outgrowth of their annual interaction in a commercialized holiday season. If Hanukkah menorahs and dreidels could exist side by side with Christmas trees and Santas in shopping malls across the country, then they could easily coexist and reinforce the holiday spirit by a process of deliberate blending in individual households.

Gompertz's imagination allowed for a fluid combination of clever Christmas and Hanukkah props by helping to legitimatize the establishment of this new hybrid holiday. One could purchase or make a "bagel menorahment" decoration, a "'kris kringle' yarmulke (head covering or skullcap)," and "Chrismukkah pareve (neutral, neither meat nor milk) egg nog." One could participate in such activities as "spinning the dreidel under the mistletoe," playing with "Bible belt *gelt* melt," eating a "noel nosh" for a snack, and displaying a "matso bread house." These alliteratively named comic fusions are just a few examples of Gompertz's imagination and creativity.

Gompertz's witty Chrismukkah amalgams of holiday objects and practices are meant to keep the holiday mood lighthearted, bypassing the more
serious issues of holiday compatibility. As Gompertz puts it, "Chrismukkah
combines the dual messages of Christmas and Hanukkah and wraps
them in a one-size-fits all, super-sized secular spree. With Chrismukkah,
you can have your fruitcake and eat your latkes, too, without guilt."[26]
Thus Chrismukkah, describing more a process of hybridization than a
fixed body of items and rituals, allows for additional creative holiday
combinations in the future.

Both anecdotal evidence and the results of formal research on interfaith
holiday customs gleaned since the onset of the twenty-first century reveal
that interfaith couples view joint religious celebration as mutually enrich-
ing and rewarding. In a 2006 web-based report from the *Detroit Free Press*
(www.freep.com), the author introduces Arnie, who is Jewish, and his wife
Andrea, who is Christian, living together in Birmingham, Alabama, and
finding great merit in combining Jewish and Christian holiday practices.[27]
During the holiday season, the couple lights the menorah for Hanukkah and
decorates a Christmas tree. Although they are formally affiliated with a
synagogue, they believe that it is important to honor each other's holiday
traditions. Echoing the sentiments of many interfaith couples, the reporter
explains that Arnie and Andrea's motives for displaying symbols of two
religious traditions, the menorah and the Christmas tree, side-by-side are
based on respecting the traditions of each spouse in a manner that guaran-
tees "having fun." As the author states, "Like other interfaith couples,
[Arnie and Andrea] have found that respecting and sharing in each
other's faiths and traditions keeps the spirit of the season alive in their
households." Rather than diminishing one religion or the other, observing
both holidays allows family members to learn about and experience the joy
of combining traditions from both religions. "It doubles the fun," the
author says. Having fun, in the form of playfulness and inventiveness, is the
key to understanding how couples can blend powerful holiday symbols
from two different religions, where a Christmas tree and a menorah can be
intertwined.

INTERFAITH HOLIDAY GREETING CARDS

The foundation for combining Hanukkah and Christmas is a belief that
they refer to a common set of secular referents that convey wishes for peace
and goodwill among all people on earth. The lights of the menorah and
the lights of the Christmas tree are regarded as equivalent symbols, to be

interpreted as communicating states of freedom, joy, and peace. In this sense, light as a universal symbol overrides any religious context and ideology. Focusing on light does not require any association with either Jesus or the religious zealotry of the Maccabees. Christmas is reinterpreted to refer vaguely to the dawning of a new era of universal peace and Hanukkah, the festival of lights, as a rekindling of the struggle for religious freedom. According to this reasoning, even when prayers are recited over the menorah they are not meant to make a theological statement; rather, the prayers represent a means of appreciating the religious liberties that Americans enjoy. Through this interpretation, many interfaith couples consider Hanukkah and Christmas to be functionally equivalent. Hanukkah is taken to be the Jewish Christmas, and Christmas is regarded as the Christian Hanukkah.

This new ecumenical perspective is supported by the presence of other common activities—serving festive meals, listening to songs and music, and giving gifts. What parallels can be found for the Christmas tree and the ornament, for Santa Claus, stockings, wreaths, and streamers? The answer is in the playfulness factor that was evident in Chrismukkah's efforts to blend holiday symbols in other art forms, such as greeting cards and cartoons that envision parallels that exist in every facet of Christmas and Hanukkah. A Christmas tree is transformed into a Hanukkah bush (so as not to draw attention). Christmas stockings are decorated in Hanukkah colors and themes. The Star of David, Hanukkah dreidels, and Hanukkah *gelt* are fashioned as ornaments to be hung on the Christmas tree-Hanukkah bush. Blue-and-white streamers are substituted for tinsel, and blue-and-white bulbs take the place of outdoor red, green, and white lighting. Because Santa Claus plays such an important role in Christmas gift-giving, Hanukkah invents a Jewish Santa who is given a Hebrew name (Hanukkah Harry and Moishe, in Hanukkah parody, are two such candidates).

The Hanukkah greeting card industry and the genius of Jewish comedians capitalize on this parity by designing cards and comic scenes that depict icons of both Christmas and Hanukkah as fluid and malleable. On paper, the two images are not just coincident. They are placed artfully in a playful albeit appositional stance, leading the reader to enjoy the incongruity Christmas Eve and to envision a transformation of one to the other. The best known example of this creativity is Art Spiegelman's "'Twas the Night Before Hanukkah" cover of the December 18, 2000, issue of *The New Yorker* magazine (also on the cover of this book). The cartoon portrays two figures back-to-back with long white beards—one dressed in red, Santa Claus, and the other in black, a Hasidic Jew. The image implies it is only their mode of dress that separates Santa from his Jewish equivalent. Similarly, the image on an interfaith greeting card depicts Santa and his Jewish counterpart (who is dressed in Orthodox garb and looks like a rabbi) toasting the holiday season together next to a menorah and Christmas tree. On another card, Santa is even shown kissing his Jewish counterpart under the mistletoe.[28] Other cards visualize the holiday transformation by showing that beneath the Christmas symbol lurks a Jewish one. The generic snowman on one interfaith card wears a top hat under which we find a *yarmulke*, a Jewish head covering, and another shows Santa's hat under which is discovered a Hasidic Jew with the accompanying caption "Happy Hanukkah to an Unorthodox Kind of Guy." Another, even more direct greeting card shows one of Santa's elves reading a book next to a lit menorah. Upon being seen, the elf remarks, "What, just because an elf works for Santa, he can't have a private life?" Yet another card shows Santa riding his sleigh being pulled by reindeer. One of the reindeer turns around to look at the reader and comments, "What the heck am I doing here? I'm Jewish." Underneath the sleigh the caption reads: "Blitzen has a revelation." The point of transformation is further strengthened when visualizing one symbol morphing into the other. Elise Okrend writes that her first card depicted the outline of a Christmas tree, which is drawn in the shape of sticks forming multiple triangles that when looked at closely resembles the interlocking triangles of a Star of David.

For interfaith couples seeking a compromise to differing religious and cultural orientations, the holiday form and function need to blend, thereby ensuring that Christmas and Hanukkah are one and the same holiday. The emphasis for these couples is not on differences but on similarity and connection. Each representative symbol therefore not only functions equivalently but is also viewed, in the interfaith world, as arising from the same blended holiday viewed from slightly varying perspectives.

Although interfaith greeting cards and cartoons are earmarked primarily for an interfaith audience, they are produced by Jews in the United States and typically transform Christmas symbols into Jewish symbols or juxtapose them side-by-side. Christmas symbols, of course, outnumber Jewish ones and are found in abundance on every street and town in America during the Christmas season. It is incumbent upon the Jewish artist who wishes to point out the equivalency of holiday symbols to show that there are Jewish counterpoints to Christian holiday icons. Captions that often accompany greeting cards also help to lessen Jewish stress associated with Christmas by turning the interfaith scene into an object of Jewish wit and humor. In one greeting card, a rabbi is asked if it were possible to make latkes without using flour (another version prefaces the question by setting the context of a village in fear of not having any latkes because they had run out of flour). He replies, "Yes, simply substitute matzo meal for the flour and no one will taste the difference." The punch line is: "Rudolph, the reb (short for rabbi), knows grain, dear," a play on "Rudolph the Red-Nosed Reindeer." In one card, Frosty the Snowman, dubbed Frosty the "Snowmench," is wilting in the sun and complains: "Oy, that sun! Look at me. I'm *shvitzing* [sweating] like a *shmendric* [idiot]. God forbid anyone should help me out here. Noooo . . . they'll all just let me melt till I'm nothing but a pile of *shmootz* [dirt]. But that's okay . . . that's okay." The greeting continues, "Season's Freezings!" In another card, Joseph and Mary are depicted under a tent looking admiringly on their baby Jesus. The card describes the scene: "The most powerful image of the season is the manger scene with Joseph, Mary, and Baby Jesus. What isn't shown is Mary's mother in the background screaming, 'What do you mean the caterer can't do the *bris* [circumcision ceremony]? I'll sue his *tuchis* [rear end) off, the lousy *goniff* [thief]!'" In one greeting card, Santa has a revelation that he is Jewish when he is riding his sleigh and one of the reindeer's antlers becomes a menorah holding candles. If Santa were Jewish, this is what he would say, explains another card: "On *kugel*, on *rugal*, on matzo, on *shmatte*, on lentil, on *yenta*, on Hanukkah."

The cards allude to the fact that, from a Jewish perspective, there is humor in holiday observance. Holidays require certain banter and "*kvetching*" (complaining) to appreciate them. "Which would you rather have?" asks a card, "latkes for Hanukkah or fruitcake for Christmas?" The clear answer is latke, and the inside of the card says, "Lesson No. 21: Why it's a mitzvah to be Jewish." Again, this barb is from a Jewish perspective for which the oft-regifted dry, hard fruitcake directly competes with latkes, a food that everyone loves, regardless of ethnicity and religious tradition. The misunderstanding that comes from cultural miscue is lampooned in the following card: "Is this what you wanted?" A man brings back a lock which he is holding in his hand after fulfilling the questioner's request to bring him lox. On the inside of the card is the reminder: "Never send a gentile to get your lox."

Many greeting cards comically address the supposed advantage of celebrating Hanukkah in comparison to celebrating Christmas, thereby insinuating that perhaps all Americans would benefit from celebrating Hanukkah. Following David Letterman's famous top ten countdown on his late night television show, an assortment of holiday cards portray song titles numbered from ten to one, and these greeting cards come down to the number one reason for celebrating Hanukkah over Christmas. In one card, number one is "Silent night? I should be so lucky." Hanukkah is associated with raucousness and the banter characteristic of Jews, while Christmas seemingly is epitomized by seriousness and quiet. Printed lists of top ten Hanukkah songs reveal, in contrast to the seriousness of Christmas carols, how much fun Jews can have when Christmas is not taken seriously. In these cards, Yiddish expressions are used to describe Christmas and Hanukkah activities, as in the greeting card listing the following top Hanukkah tunes:

"Oy to the World."
"Schlepping through a Winter Wonderland."
"Come On, Baby, Light My Menorah."
"Deck the Halls with Balls of Challah."
"And the # 1 Hanukkah song that never quite caught on . . . 'No, It Was a Very Good *Shmear* (a cheese spread on bread or bagel).'"

Remarks made by the Jewish narrator, unseen in these greeting cards, demonstrate that Christmas is not threatening. Upon even closer inspection, Christmas symbols depicted in the cards appear as caricatures that are more humorous than pointed. In the manger scene illustrated in one card, perhaps the most revered of Christmas iconography, the characters are more concerned with extraneous matters, like the caterer, than with the religious implications of the event. For the creator and the purchaser of these cards, Christmas is almost interchangeable with Hanukkah. In the greeting card version, the Jewish holiday becomes replete with Hanukkah and Jewish references. Ultimately, in the wide variety of greeting cards, as well as in other mass media and popular cultural expressions, Hanukkah and Christmas are celebrated with examples of light-hearted humor, reciprocal goodwill, and societal coexistence that fill the holiday season with feelings of good wishes and cheer.

How Pervasive Is Chrismukkah?

The ease with which interfaith couples are willing to share in the respective December religious and cultural traditions of their spouses is documented by the results of recent Jewish institutional surveys. Since 2003 the website InterfaithFamily.com has annually surveyed the extent to which interfaith couples celebrate both Hanukkah and Christmas.[29] In each survey, the population studied is selected from interfaith households that have agreed to raise their children as Jewish (reflecting the organization's mission). In the 2005 survey, the topic of Chrismukkah was raised in order to determine how interested couples were in joining symbols from both religions. While a majority of those surveyed had heard of the term Chrismukkah, only slightly more than one-third of the 396 people interviewed were willing to characterize their holiday practices as blended. These couples believed that thinking about how to blend religious symbols helped families openly discuss issues of compatibility in a spirit of compromise, thereby opening the door for both Christmas and Hanukkah to be included in the holiday mix. The majority of respondents, however, found the term Chrismukkah to be inappropriate, believing that the label Chrismukkah overlooks differences between religions and contributes to children's confusion about the underpinnings of the two religious celebrations.

In a 2008 survey, 58 percent of respondents preferred to keep Hanukkah and Christmas distinct, which was unproblematic to do when Hanukkah and Christmas did not coincide in a calendar year. However, more than 42 percent felt that Christmas and Hanukkah symbols do overlap and convey similar messages of peace and goodwill, thereby creating a meaningful and natural blend. This percentage might even be higher if the authors of the survey were to describe what they meant by blending. For example, 36 percent of households put up stockings at home, but it is not clear whether these are strictly Christmas stockings or ones dressed up with Hanukkah colors—blue-and-white trim—and symbols, like the Star of David. Interfaith homes in which blue-and-white stockings hang serve as instances of holiday blending, reflecting the aim, if not the name, of Chrismukkah.

Whether couples actually use the term Chrismukkah, there is strong support among interfaith families for bringing Hanukkah and Christmas symbols into interfaith homes. Given the commitment of the sampling of surveyed parents to raise their children as Jewish, the 2005 survey indicates that 90 percent of respondents expect to observe Hanukkah. At the same time, a full 85 percent were expected to participate in Christmas celebrations. Of these, 71 percent said that they would decorate a Christmas tree in their own home (an increase of 53 percent from the year before) and 76 percent expected to have a Christmas dinner in the homes of relatives or friends (an increase of 64 percent from the year before).

In the 2008 survey, fewer households planned on celebrating Christmas in the home, yet 33 percent still sang or played Christmas music, 25 percent prepared Christmas foods, and 64 percent gave Christmas gifts at the home of relatives (versus 50 percent who gave gifts at their own homes).[30]

A major benefit of these surveys is to identify which customs and rituals accompany the celebration of Hanukkah and Christmas in interfaith homes, thereby creating a useful index to anecdotal reports of interfaith practices. Surveys report the following behaviors as statistically relevant: setting up and decorating Christmas trees, hanging stockings, giving gifts to family and friends, singing or playing Christmas music, eating or preparing Christmas foods, drinking eggnog, watching Christmas movies, and telling the Christmas story. Similar practices are indicated accompanying the celebration of Hanukkah: lighting the menorah, giving gifts, putting up Hanukkah decorations, singing or playing Hanukkah music and songs, eating or making Hanukkah foods, watching Hanukkah movies, telling the Hanukkah story, and playing dreidel. Most of these activities are practiced to some degree among the interfaith couples surveyed, indicating that within a single family, the celebration of both Hanukkah and Christmas is important, extensive, and emotionally satisfying.

The richness of Christmas displays in interfaith homes is occasioned by the remembrance of positive symbols associated with childhood and family ties. They are regarded as neutral in terms of evoking religious sentiment. One survey respondent exemplifies the compelling desire of one interfaith partner to bring Christmas symbols into her home: "I feel that even though we will be raising our children Jewish, I have known Christianity for the past twenty-eight years of my life. I love Christmas; it is a time of happiness and peace on earth. This is the feeling that I want my children to enjoy! They won't need to celebrate it as a religious holiday."[31]

These surveys clarify that when couples introduce symbols from Christmas and Hanukkah, they believe they are devoid of religious reference. In the 2008 survey, only 5 percent of respondents participating in Christmas viewed accompanying symbols as religious.[32] While a greater percentage (20 percent) viewed Hanukkah as "fairly" religious, no one (0 percent) considered his or her involvement as "deeply" religious; at best, Hanukkah is regarded as "half secular, half religious." The ambiguity of the religious nature of Hanukkah, coupled with the secular orientation of Christmas celebration, allow interfaith couples to avoid religious conflict that might potentially arise from introducing symbols characterized as representing two faiths. The secularization of holiday symbols is what leads a quarter of Jewish husbands to be comfortable introducing a Christmas tree into a Jewish home. "I do not have a problem with having a tree," one husband remarked. "I do not believe it is a religious symbol."[33] The Jewish husband, though, admitted that his parents might not be appreciative of the tree because to them it is a religious symbol connected to Christianity.[34] However, when the home features a Jewish wife and if she grants that a Christmas tree is not religious, then having her husband introduce a Christmas tree does not dilute the Jewishness of her home; rather the tree honors her husband's heritage and his emotional need to have a connection to his familial past. For many couples, the overriding factor remains: Christmas and Hanukkah bring warmth and joyfulness to both the holiday season and their homes.

According to the results of the 2008 survey, the primary reason for inviting the Christian spouse to engage in Christmas celebrations is to respect the traditions of the spouse and his or her extended families. There is also a desire on the part of interfaith couples to expose children to the differing faith traditions of each parent (28 percent) and, more generally, a desire to exhibit an atmosphere of tolerance and open-mindedness (51 percent).

Surprisingly, surveys have consistently reported that family Christmas involvement does not have a significant effect on the identification of the children who understand that they are being raised in a Jewish home. Indeed, the 2008 survey indicates that only 7 percent of parents desire to expose their children to differing religions so that they will one day make up their minds about which faith to follow.[35] Christmas involvement is viewed as a way to accommodate the non-Jewish parent and his or her side of the family without defining the family's actual religious identification.

The 2008 survey also suggests a greater willingness to celebrate Christmas at home when the female partner in an interfaith relationship is Christian. Fifty-one percent of households with a Christian female partner celebrate Christmas at home, whereas, when the wife is Jewish, Christmas is celebrated more at the home of relatives and friends (38 percent). As for displaying Hanukkah symbols, because parents in the survey have made commitments to raise their children as Jewish, there is little difference whether the Jewish or non-Jewish spouse is male or female. Whether the mother is Jewish or not, approximately 49 percent of families surveyed lit the Hanukkah menorah.

Even when the woman in an interfaith partnership converts to Judaism, she often retains an emotional attachment to the Christmas celebration of her youth. The 2008 survey finds that 66 percent of intermarried families in which the female partner converts to Judaism plans to participate in Christmas celebrations.[36]

Although these surveys do not necessarily support labeling the new holiday mix as Chrismukkah, they do suggest a coexistence between and mutual support for allowing symbols of both religions to be present in an interfaith home. Rather than referring to celebrating two separate holidays, each is seen as contributing to creating a globalized sense of seasonal joy, more secular than religious, and sharing more in common with each other than hitherto perceived.[37]

FESTIVUS: A SECULAR HOLIDAY ALTERNATIVE

The December holiday season registers as festive to most American citizens; however, a minority of people are annoyed by and frustrated with the holiday season. Newspaper reporters and bloggers from year to year discuss several groups within the population that are alienated from Christmas. These groups include those non-Christian Americans who are overwhelmed by the domination of Christmas motifs and symbols as well as those who are lonely or depressed during the season. Another segment of the population is secularly oriented and repulsed by either the overly religious nature or crass commercialism of the holiday period. How might these groups express joy during the holiday season?

Festivus, a made-for television ceremony that stemmed from a 1997 *Seinfeld* television episode called "The Strike," is a celebration touted as "the festival for the rest-of-us."[38] Festivus, an artificial holiday, had no historical reference, except to a purported family ritual initiated by the father of one of the *Seinfeld* TV series writers. During that episode, actor Jerry Stiller, who played the role of Frank, the father of George Costanza, explains to Kramer (played by Michael Richards) that when George was a boy, the family celebrated Festivus. Frank reminisces about his family's involvement with this fictional holiday, and Kramer encourages Frank to revive it. Frank explains to Kramer that he conceived of Festivus after an altercation with a fellow shopper with whom he jostled to grab the one remaining doll they both coveted. Believing that the entire holiday season was overly commercialized, Frank Costanza thought that there should be a less frenzied and formulaic way to celebrate the holidays. Frank, in the presence of his son George, informs Kramer that he would like to revive the holiday. George, however, responds negatively, presumably out of bad childhood memories of his involvement in Festivus.

Apparently, George had good reason for his misgivings about reviving the holiday. A primary feature of Festivus is the Airing of Grievances, a ritual that encourages participants to say what annoys them about others who are present, all the while recording these complaints on cassette tape. In the Festivus episode, while having dinner with his guests, who include

George's boss, Frank begins this ritual bickering by informing George's boss what George really thinks of him and the company that he heads. George is humiliated.

George also has frightening memories of having to participate in another main feature of the festival, which involves a family member pinning down the head of the household—in this case Frank—to the ground. George is mortified at having yet again to proceed with this embarrassing custom of besting his father.

In place of a uniform format for celebrating Christmas and Hanukkah, suggested by a common commercialized ethos, Festivus rejects conformity and the typical holiday fare—there is no Festivus dinner and no gift-giving—in favor of expressions of individuality and simplicity. Celebrants are encouraged to express their frustration of being left out of the generalized holiday cheer and to act out their feelings in competitive rituals. The Festivus scriptwriter, Daniel O'Keefe, modeled the *Seinfeld* episode on his family's invention and celebration of Festivus in the 1960s, believing that this thoroughly secular holiday more appropriately reflected the anti-holiday spirit of many Americans who seek opportunities to share their iconoclastic holiday views with one another.[39] In 2005, he authored a book, entitled *The Real Festivus: The True Story Behind America's Favorite Made-up Holiday*, detailing his family's creation and observance of this unique holiday from 1966 through 1991.[40]

The real simplicity of the Festivus ritual is its priority on eschewing excess. A pole is substituted for the ubiquitous Christmas tree. The pole is to be made out of aluminum, Frank explains, because of its "strength to weight" ratio, and it should not be decorated with tinsel because Frank consider such decoration as an example of cheapened traditions. The pole is likened to the centerpiece of ancient ceremonies that demonstrate a group's unity through dancing around it, although the aluminum pole in Festivus has no such attendant ritual.

Like Chrismukkah, Festivus has been adopted and adapted from year to year among those who have looked for alternative ways to acknowledge the holiday season.[41] It is a tongue-in-cheek, irony-laced celebration with no religious connotation. Colleges around the United States have even adopted Festivus. One example is the campuswide nondenominational celebration of the holidays, entitled Festivus, hosted by each dormitory at Connecticut College in New London, Connecticut. Celebration of the holiday, scheduled for December 23 on the *Seinfeld* episode, has been enlarged to include any time of the year, such as in the O'Keefe home where it could be celebrated anytime from May to December. Others have chosen February, for example, when the holiday season has ended and the frenzy of holiday shopping ceased.

Latitude is also given to the Festivus pole because no mention is made of its dimensions, foundation, or positioning. Wagner Companies, for example, have created a six-foot pole as well as a mini table that is sold on their website. People have used "cardboard tubes painted silver, aluminum foil, and heating pipes" and have placed them in flowerpots, inside and outside the home.[42] Similar variations have been reported regarding the "Airing of Grievances," which, in addition to direct verbal attacks on character and behavior, include written comments placed on refrigerator doors or attached to Festivus poles; these statements are then read by family members.

Perhaps the greatest variation is in the category "Feats of Strength" that have celebrants choosing less physical competition. Allen Salkin, an American Jewish author, in his book *Festivus: The Holiday for the Rest of Us*, describes celebrants engaged in competitive thumb wrestling or television gaming as well as solo challenges, such as hula hooping, punching balls, and dipping one's head in ice water.[43] Due to Salkin's book, impromptu Festivus parties have occurred throughout the United States. *Heeb* magazine, an edgy cultural periodical for young Jewish hipsters, has hosted an annual storytelling event at Joe's Pub in New York City. On several occasions, Allen Salkin has organized a follow-up Festivus party to the *Heeb* event.

As if to recognize the durability and geographical spread of Festivus, many commercial products and events have been named after Festivus. These include a Festivus wine produced by Grape Ranch of Okemah, Oklahoma, and the name of a seasonal Ben & Jerry's Festivus ice cream made from brown sugar ice cream laced with gingery caramel and chewy chunks of gingerbread that was produced in 2000 and 2001.[44] Sporting activities have also taken on the name of the holiday. The Dupage County (Illinois) Football League has a winter schedule called "Festivus Football." During the 2000 season, the coach of the Baltimore Ravens referred to the playoffs as "Festivus" and the Super Bowl as "Festivus Maximus."[45] A concert series taking place in 2007 at Jobbin.com stadium in Glendale, Arizona, is called the "Peak's Festivus," and a 2011 film festival in Denver, Colorado, was called the "Festivus Film Festival."[46]

Given the popularity of the Festivus holiday, it was inevitable that attempts would be made to elevate Festivus to the level of Christmas or Hanukkah. In 2007, a Green Bay, Wisconsin, man asked permission from administrators of Green Bay City Hall to place a Festivus pole next to a nativity scene. In 2008 and 2009, an eighteen-year-old student erected a handle of a pool cleaner in the rotunda of the Illinois Capitol where Governor Rod Blagojevich aired grievances on behalf of the people of Illinois. The 2009 display was an unadorned aluminum pole.[47] At the capitol in Olympia, Washington, state officials approved a Festivus display to be placed next to both the twenty-five-foot noble fir tree and a nativity scene. The Festivus display, sponsored by a private citizen, protested the presence of religious displays on public property.[48] Following the trend of commercial establishments that capitalize on Christmas, AirTran Airways recently created a "Festivus for the Rest of Us" sale, beginning on December 1, 2010, and continuing for eleven days thereafter. In this clever advertising campaign, the fares rose, and the airline offered a final surprise to be revealed on the last day.[49]

In the December 21, 2004, section of the *Chicago Tribune* internet site entitled "Article Collections," an anonymous author compared Chrismukkah and Festivus for their respective levels of popularity and referred to each as a hybrid holiday, given the fact that each holiday's customs are drawn from different cultural elements that have coalesced. Festivus was declared the overall winner because it is devoid of any religious meaning and is "ACLU—bulletproof." "Finally," the author concluded, Festivus is a "holiday party where you can invite atheists and agnostics."[50]

In 2004, the Virgin Mobile USA, LLC, a cellular telephone company launched in 2002, introduced a popular and provocative advertising campaign centered on Chrismahanukwanzakah, a completely blended holiday. Based upon the popularity of this advertising campaign, in 2005, Virgin Mobile declared December 13 the official celebration day for the holiday. The campaign featured a cast of characters, including Hasidic Jewish twins, a Hindu sitar-playing Santa, a gay elf, a Latino angel, an Afro-sporting angel, a pagan caveman, and a Scientologist, all poking fun at the holiday season while proclaiming cheerily "Happy Chrismahanukwanzakah" and singing the anthem, "We're All Snowflakes." A "truly blended holiday," the festival officially begins upon lighting the ceremonial Chrismahanukwanza-kah tree. The Virgin Mobile parody of the progressively more blended nature of households in America was popularized on television, YouTube, and radio. The goal of Chrismahanukwanzakah, selling Virgin Mobile cellular phones, belies the sincerity underlying this tongue-in-cheek melding of icons of Christmas, Hanukkah, Kwanzaa, Islam, paganism, Eastern religions, and even agnosticism and Scientology into one big festival: "We figured we would acknowledge everything and celebrate the diversity of it in our own way," said Howard Handler, chief marketing officer, adding, "We didn't really try to zero in on religion in and of itself."[51] Handler said of Chrismahanukwanzakah: "For so many people, this really is a very, very upbeat time of year, and without being goofy, it's a time of hope, too. We just wanted to be festive and bring everyone in—pagans and elves and cavemen. It's a little bit of, can we all get along? Can everybody just relax and lighten up? It doesn't have to be about red or blue or north or south," he said. "Let's just have fun and celebrate the things that are good."

IN VOGUE: DECEMBER HYBRID CELEBRATIONS

Until recently, Jews have had few choices for celebrating during the December season. They could celebrate Christmas or Hanukkah. Now they can celebrate both. The decision to participate in one holiday or the other creates a dilemma for Jews who related to Hanukkah and Christmas as antithetical. Those who enjoy Christmas, even if only in its secular aspects, are accused of abandoning their Jewish faith. Those who participate exclusively in Hanukkah, turn a blind eye to the power that Christmas festivities hold on the American public. Those who incorporate elements of both are attempting to synthesize the symbols and values of each holiday.

The surge in interfaith marriages has brought a new appreciation for the relationship between Christmas and Hanukkah and the symbols representing them. Interfaith couples build on the overlapping themes inherent in the holidays to form a new hybrid celebration, one that regards the two holidays as complementary. Their children are taught that juxtaposing holiday displays is natural and does not necessary create religious conflict. In the imaginative pairing of Chrismukkah, holiday symbols from each religion are wedded so that each is referenced by both Christmas and Hanukkah names and concepts.

The new holiday hybrid Chrismukkah is often mentioned by the American media as a descriptive term for blending Christmas and Hanukkah symbols, even though as interfaith surveys indicate, some families still believe their presence stems from two differing religious viewpoints. The emphasis among parents and grandparents of interfaith couples on traditional beliefs and practices requires interfaith parents to explain to their children why grandparents regard holiday traditions as separate when parents find them compatible. For adult children of inter-married families, doubts about the differences between Christmas and

Hanukkah will likely fade, and in time their differences in the home will be considered even more perfunctory. As more classes for interfaith families focus on the commonalities between the two religions, fewer questions will be asked about the differences, and, when such questions arise, the differences will be explained away as relics of historical disagreements. Segments of the Jewish population in the United States condemn the artificial blending of two religious traditions and argue that creating hybrid symbols seems unnatural, glosses over serious differences, and remains an affront to Jewish identity. Nevertheless, intermarriage today is considered pervasive, and the resulting trend to blend symbols from the two religions will continue unabated. Such hybrid celebration represents a new response to Christmas, one that welcomes Christmas as an equal partner with Hanukkah, by bringing both holidays into the home as honored traditions to be cherished, admired, and applauded.

Some Jews, however, like other Americans, wish to participate in neither Christmas nor Hanukkah. Staunchly secular, they are dismissive of any association to religion, even when Christmas and Hanukkah symbols are divested of any overt religious references. Certain Jews and others in America complain about the commercial hype and frenzy that propels so many to reduce Christmas and Hanukkah into an economic enterprise. While they would prefer that neither holiday be used for commercial gain, they are still receptive to the wonder of the holiday season and seek a secular outlet for their holiday needs. Eating at Chinese restaurants on Christmas Eve, attending movies, or visiting Jewish museums is not satisfying enough because there is an absence of any opportunity for home celebration. Festivus offers a new home-based celebration that provides enough social activity, albeit one whose symbols mock the pretentiousness of the traditional holiday season. Based as it is on an episode of the very popular *Seinfeld* television series that is now in syndicated reruns, there is evidence that this mock festival shows no signs of slowing down.

Although Christmas and Hanukkah have drawn closer together in the home of interfaith couples, a parallel process occurs in the public arena, where displays of the Christmas tree, crèche, and menorah are debated in local government and in the court system, leading to landmark decisions from the Supreme Court and a national debate about the role of religion in public life. A predominant question revolves around whether December holiday symbols placed separately or together in the public square are consonant with or in violation of the country's insistence on separating religion and state. In a final assault on Christmas, Jewish organizations from differing perspectives offer two suggestions: either abolish Christmas symbols from the public arena altogether so as not to favor one religion over the other or display them openly along with symbols from other faiths to give equal representation to all religious groups in the America. Jews throughout the United States have been instrumental in raising these questions publicly and in helping American citizens realize that focusing only on one holiday in December is counterproductive to a multiethnic and multireligious country that takes pride in recognizing the contributions of all its citizens.

MENORAHS NEXT
TO MADONNAS

SHAPING THE FUTURE OF
CHRISTMAS IN AMERICA

In 1993, Myrna Holzman, a retired public school teacher in New York and an avid stamp collector, started a crusade to convince the U.S. Postal Service, a quasi-federal agency, to produce a Hanukkah stamp. Initially rebuffed by the Citizen's Stamp Committee of the Postal Service on grounds that the U.S. Postal Service does not consider religious themes, Myrna reacted with skepticism. She counted many stamps that featured Christian icons, such as the Madonna and Child. Myrna then suggested that the postal service consider selecting a secular symbol such as the dreidel to commemorate Hanukkah.[1] In the ensuing years, Myrna waged a national write-in campaign to prove to the postal service committee that there was great public demand for the stamp and that it was warranted because of Hanukkah's contribution to the religious diversity of American society.

Myrna's campaign was, in essence, the culmination of a battle against the postal service's annual issuance of Christmas-themed stamps. In 1966, the postal service issued a Christmas stamp depicting the "Madonna and Child with Angels." Rabbi Arthur J. Lelyveld, the president of the American Jewish Congress, protested in a letter to John A. Gronouski, the postmaster-general, whose Jewish deputy, Ira Kapenstein, defended the post office's action. In 1968, the U.S. Postal Service issued a Christmas stamp depicting Jan Van Eyck's painting *The Annunciation* in which the winged archangel Gabriel tells the Virgin Mary (who is standing in the doorway of a church) that she is pregnant with Jesus, the Son of God. Once again, the American

Jewish Congress complained, objecting on the grounds that the postal stamp portrayed Christian belief in the virgin birth and was thus in violation of the First Amendment to the Constitution's provision of separation of religion and state. The American Jewish Congress found willing allies in the American Civil Liberties Union (the ACLU), the Society of Separationists, and other social and religious groups who opposed the government's display of religious symbols. In 1971 the post office printed a new Christian-themed stamp, Lorenzo Lotto's "The Nativity." A coalition of Jewish organizations, including the Joint Advisory Committee of the Synagogue Council of America and the National Jewish Community Relations Advisory Council, protested the issuance of the stamp. These organizations argued, without success, that the issuance of such stamps violated the First Amendment of the Constitution.

Ironically, Myrna Holzman's Hanukkah stamp campaign, not the assorted legal battles that were being waged in the court system, finally resulted in the U.S. Postal Service's release of a Hanukkah stamp in 1996. The postal service invited Holzman to the launching ceremony for the new Hanukkah stamp, the first stamp to be a joint-issue between the United States and Israel. To Myrna's surprise, the symbol chosen to represent Hanukkah was a modern rendition of the menorah, consisting of playful, colorful shapes; the choice was ironic because the post office committee had previously rejected the menorah as a religious symbol.[2] In 2004, the postal service released another Hanukkah stamp, this time featuring a dreidel, as Myrna had originally suggested. And in 2009, the postal service issued a stamp bearing a more traditional menorah design. A far-reaching outcome followed from Holzman's Hanukkah stamp campaign: the introduction of both a Kwanza stamp (1997) and another depicting the Muslim holiday Eid (2001). Through the issuance of these stamps, the U.S. Postal Service acknowledges the various religious and cultural celebrations that occur during the December holiday season and recognizes the diversity of religious and social groups in American society today.[3]

Regardless of which strategies Jews in America have employed to face Christmas, most Americans remained largely unaware of the internal December debates taking place within Jewish communities throughout the United States. The cumulative effect of more than one hundred years of Jews questioning the role of Christmas in America increasingly helped the population at large to understand that not every citizen celebrates Christmas. As minority groups immigrated in increasingly large numbers to the United States and brought with them various religious traditions, Americans in leadership positions within local municipalities, school districts, and public schools became more sensitive to those who felt excluded from Christmas festivities. Municipalities and public schools, reflecting their growing awareness of diversity, neutralized the holiday celebration so as not to offend Americans with differing religious traditions. By the early twenty-first century, instead of wishing one another a "Merry Christmas," for example, Americans began to wish each other "Happy Holidays." School programs and concerts began to be referred to as winter celebrations rather than Christmas festivals. Moreover, office celebrations during December became known as holiday parties rather than Christmas parties.

From the 1980s onward, Hanukkah assumed a role of public prominence, and the American media regularly featured stories of citizens responding either positively or negatively to the presence of Hanukkah displays proximal to those of Christmas. What historically had been internally based December dilemmas, once faced exclusively by Jews, expanded to become Christmas wars, pitting Americans of different political orientations against each other over whether Christmas and Hanukkah symbols should be displayed in public places. In response, fundamentalist Christian religious organizations and conservative political and social groups waged a fierce media campaign to complain that certain Americans, particularly Jews, were trying to take the "Christ" out of Christmas.[4] In these thinly veiled attacks and very pointed media campaigns, anti-Semitic comments often ensued.[5]

Two significant historical events facilitated the growing awareness for Americans that Hanukkah was a major holiday for Jewish people and that it was fast becoming attendant to Christmas festivities. The first was the formal recognition of Hanukkah by the White House that was accompanied by a menorah lighting ceremony. On December 17, 1979, President Jimmy Carter became the first sitting American president to participate in the lighting of a public menorah, located across the street from the White House in Lafayette Park. Chabad-Lubavitch Rabbi Abraham Shemtov attended the presidential lighting ceremony and presented President Carter with a small menorah as a keepsake.

It is interesting to note that controversy surrounds whether President Carter actually lit a candle on the menorah or lit a candle that then was used to light the *shamash* (the servant candle that is used to light the other candles on the menorah). Two pieces of evidence support the fact that President Carter did light a candle on the menorah. The entry for December 17, 1979, at 6:53 until 7:05 P.M. in the official daily diary for President Jimmy Carter records that "The President illuminated the

Figure C.1. President Jimmy Carter illuminates the middle candle (*shamash*) of the National Hanukkah Menorah on 17 December 1979, in Lafayette Park with Rabbi Abraham Shemtov by his side. Courtesy Jimmy Carter Library.

Figure C.2. President Bill Clinton participates in a Hanukkah menorah lighting ceremony in the Oval Office of the White House with students from the Jewish primary day school of the Adas Israel Synagogue of Washington, D.C. Danny Lew lights the menorah. 23 December 1997. Courtesy William J. Clinton Presidential Library, photo: Barbara Kinney.

Middle Menorah Candle."[6] Furthermore, official photographs archived in the Carter Presidential Library depict the president actually lighting the middle candle on the menorah (presumably the *shamash*). However, representatives of the Hasidic movement, Chabad-Lubavitch, question this occurrence.

In 1982, the menorah lit in Lafayette Park was publicly referred to as the National Menorah by President Ronald Reagan, thereby equating its lighting with the National Christmas tree lighting. The first display of a menorah in the White House is ascribed to President George H. W. Bush in 1989, upon receiving it as gift from Synagogue Council of America. By 1993, the menorah lighting rite had officially moved into the White House when President Bill Clinton hosted a small ceremony for school children in the Oval Office. In 2001 George W. Bush became the first president to hold a White House Hanukkah party at which he actually lit a menorah.

The second historical factor that contributed to the presence of Hanukkah in the public domain was the campaign waged by Chabad-Lubavitch to place menorahs in as many public venues throughout the

United States, from malls to city halls and parks. The drive was initiated by the late Chabad-Lubavitch Rabbi Menachem Mendel Schneerson in the 1970s. In 1980, Rabbi Schneerson issued a directive encouraging menorah lightings in public places and initiated a movement by sending rabbinic emissaries to cities throughout the United States with the express mission of publicizing the miracle of Hanukkah to inspire pride in Jewish onlookers.

At first, public displays of menorahs began appearing in cities with large Jewish populations, such as Philadelphia, San Francisco, Los Angeles, and New York.[7] Media coverage of the menorah lighting ceremonies in these cities often showed the local mayor and prominent government officials helping Chabad-Lubavitch rabbis to light menorahs.[8] The first such lighting, in 1974, occurred in front of the Liberty Bell in Philadelphia and involved a small group of Jews holding a small menorah. The following year, in San Francisco, the local Chabad-Lubavitch rabbi, Chaim Drizin, and public radio station KQED program director Zev Putterman arranged for concert promoter Bill Graham to sponsor the creation of a twenty-two-foot-high mahogany menorah to be erected in Union Square.[9] The menorah, affectionately called Mama Menorah, was erected next to Macy's ornate Christmas tree, the largest public tree in the city. Bill Graham also underwrote an attendant festival—now called the Bill Graham Menorah Day Festival, which includes musical performances, arts and crafts, food— that is capped by the Chabad-Lubavitch-sponsored menorah lighting. Perhaps the largest menorah lighting to take place in this early period was at Dolphins Stadium in Miami in 1987, when Florida Chabad-Lubavitch Rabbi Tennenhaus lit a menorah in front of seventy thousand people.[10] In this same year, Rabbi Schneerson launched a global Hanukkah menorah lighting campaign.

As the Chabad-Lubavitch mission to light menorahs extended to more and more cities, certain American citizens, including those of the Jewish faith, began to question whether erecting a Hanukkah menorah in a public space was constitutionally protected. This same question arose about Christmas displays in the public domain, particularly those featuring a crèche, a religious Christmas symbol of the nativity scene that is regularly featured in Christmas celebrations. Passions flared when Christmas wars broke out between those who wanted a complete separation of religion and state and those who desired increased religious displays; as a result, citizens pressured their elected representatives to decide in favor of their, often conflicting, points of view.

Complaints ultimately led to the court house where lawsuits were filed by proponents and antagonists. Ultimately, these cases reached the U.S.

Supreme Court. The high court's decisions were anxiously awaited because much was at stake for municipalities and schools throughout the country; they wanted a final resolution to the question of whether the menorah and the crèche could legally be displayed in the public domain. The toll of these lawsuits and countersuits was the creation of a divisive atmosphere at the local level where communities remained uncertain from year to year whether their Christmas and Hanukkah plans could proceed.

The task of bringing such cases to court was often left to American attorneys of the Jewish faith who were hired to represent Jewish agencies on both sides of the issue at hand. Typically the American Civil Liberties Union (ACLU), an agency with a long history of defending civil liberties and a staunch advocate for strict separation of religion and state, initiated legal actions. The ACLU brought lawsuits against the Chabad-Lubavitch movement for erecting menorahs in public venues.[11] The same agency (often joined by the American Jewish Congress and American Jewish Committee and church groups with similar political leanings) brought legal suits to stop crèches from being displayed in the public domain. In other instances, lawyers representing the Chabad-Lubavitch movement went to court to force a municipality to allow the erection of a menorah in a public setting under government jurisdiction.[12] Those observing the spectacle of two Jewish lawyers arguing major Establishment Clause cases before the Supreme Court could not help but conclude that Jews are passionately invested in shaping the future of holiday displays in America.

One such lawsuit, *Allegheny County v. ACLU* (1989), became the landmark case regarding whether a religious display in the public domain violated the Establishment Clause because the case involved both the menorah and the crèche. *Allegheny County* set the standard for future cases in which city agencies wished to plan December holiday events according to the law.[13] The facts of the case concerned the placement of a crèche portraying the Christian nativity scene on the Grand Staircase of the Allegheny County Courthouse in Pittsburgh, Pennsylvania, for several years. The crèche was donated by the Holy Name Society, a Roman Catholic group, and bore a sign to that effect. A banner declaring "Gloria in Excelsis Deo," meaning "Glory to God in the Highest" was incorporated into the nativity scene. The second of the holiday displays, an eighteen-foot Hanukkah menorah was placed just outside the city-county building next to the city's forty-five-foot decorated Christmas tree. At the foot of the tree was a sign bearing the mayor's name and containing text declaring the city's "salute to liberty." The menorah, owned by Chabad-Lubavitch, was stored, erected, and removed each year by the city. In 1986, the ACLU argued that the crèche and the menorah were in violation of the Establishment Clause of the First Amendment. The District Court, upholding the constitutionality of both the manger scene and the menorah, decided that neither demonstrated government endorsement. In 1988, the Third Court of Appeals reversed the District Court's ruling and held that both symbols violated the Establishment Clause. The case reached the Supreme Court in 1989. The final decision was based on reviewing the context within which each symbol was displayed and deciding if either of them was glaringly religious, which would therefore render the display unconstitutional. The crèche, the Supreme Court ruled, was proximal to the seat of government and could therefore be perceived as having government approval. Furthermore, the crèche appeared as an obvious religious symbol because it was accompanied by a sign that read "Glory to God in the Highest." The crèche was, therefore, ruled unconstitutional.

The menorah, however, was deemed not to be at the center of government activities and stood near a much taller Christmas tree, one that was forty-five feet high. Justice Blackman, writing for the Supreme Court majority, opined that the Christmas tree provided sufficient secular context for the menorah and that, although the justices agreed upon the menorah's religious symbolism, the menorah should be allowed because it was part of a secular winter holiday celebration. This decision followed the precedent established by the Supreme Court in *Lynch v. Donnelly* (1984), wherein the Supreme Court considered the narrow question of whether there is a secular purpose for the public display of a crèche included in a city's holiday display, which also involved secular Christmas symbols. The secular symbols included Santa Claus's house, reindeer pulling Santa's sleigh, candy-striped poles, a Christmas tree, carolers, cut-out figures representing such characters as a clown, an elephant, and a teddy bear, hundreds of colored lights, and a large banner that read "SEASONS GREETINGS." The public display of the crèche was not deemed to be a violation of the First Amendment's Establishment Clause because the city had not "impermissibly advanced religion" and by including the crèche did not create "excessive entanglement between religion and government."[14]

The Supreme Court's decisions of 1984 and 1989 prompted municipalities to organize Christmas festivities because it was understood that the menorah and the crèche could be displayed if they were adjacent to secular holiday symbols and if the funding for the displays derived from private sources. The decisions, however, also sparked controversy because certain Americans, both Jewish and Christian, believed the court appeared to be minimizing the importance of religious symbols during the holiday season by rendering them secular.[15] Those supporting the ACLU were equally upset that once again religious displays would be allowed in public, making it appear as if government favored one religion over another.[16]

The Supreme Court is partly responsible for the confusion over the legitimacy of religious displays because the justices were split in their vote regarding the question of whether the menorah and the crèche were religious symbols. The *Allegheny County* case was settled in a five-to-four decision. The Supreme Court majority decided that a Christmas display including a nativity scene constituted a presentation of symbols of a secular, not a religious, national holiday. The more conservative justices, such as Justice Anthony Kennedy, who wrote the dissenting opinion, believed that no one viewing a religious display in and around government facilities would feel coerced into following a particular religion. In his opinion, no citizen is forced to look upon religious displays, whether Christian or Jewish. Justices Brennan, Marshall, and Stevens, however, felt that both the menorah and the crèche should be prohibited because their religious character could not be contextualized away. Certainly, the "plastic reindeer" requirement of the *Lynch* case subjected the court to ridicule and made it more difficult for people to gauge in advance just how secular the context had to be to transform a religious object into a secular one.[17]

The purported winner in these and other court cases appeared to be the Chabad-Lubavitch group, which now possessed the legal foundation to seek enforcement of its right to place menorahs in public places of its own choosing.[18] The public display of the crèche, which had a long venerated history, also received the Supreme Court's imprimatur. Outside observers to these Supreme Court decisions, particularly those supporting the ACLU, continued to view the federal government as endorsing religious public displays and to believe that non-Christians viewing these displays would feel excluded.

This conclusion was borne out, in part, in cases involving public schools where students are considered to be more vulnerable to the control of school teachers and administrators and where historically Christmas concerts and pageants are regarded as important parts of a school's holiday programming. As early as 1906, Jewish parents in Brownsville, New York, rebelled against the principal of Public School 144 who admonished students to be more "Christ-like."[19] Parents were outraged. With a rallying cry of a "battle for civil rights," the *Tageblatt* newspaper called for a boycott of Brownsville's public schools by Jewish students to be held on December 24, the day marked by closing exercises before the Christmas holiday school vacation. According to a *New York Times* report, between 20,000 and

25,000 students, one-third of the Brownsville public schools' enrollment, stayed away from classes. The *Tageblatt*'s newspaper headline victoriously proclaimed, "Empty Schools: Tens of Thousands of Jewish Children Shun the Christmas Tree." The boycott succeeded. Many parents had been worried that their children would be embarrassed to voluntarily opt out of participating in Christmas activities, including singing Christmas carols that referred specifically to the divinity of Jesus.[20] Two weeks after the boycott, the Elementary School Committee endorsed a ban by the public schools upon the singing of hymns and the writing of essays concerning religious themes during Christmas. The School Committee continued to allow for Christmas trees and Santa images in the schools. The public battle over Christmas had begun.

The Supreme Court finally ruled on the permissibility of religious symbols in *Florey v. Sioux Falls School District* (1980). Foreshadowing the logic to be used in later court cases involving displays in the public square, the court found that religious symbols displayed or performed in schools were constitutional as long as they were organized as part of general cultural festivities and their purpose was educational rather than religious. This decision did not satisfy Jewish parents who were left with the challenge of discussing with their children how to behave when overt references to Christianity surfaced.

In the aftermath of decisions such as *Lynch v. Donnelley* and *Allegheny County v. ACLU*, school districts across the country developed a heightened sensitivity to the needs of minority groups. Administrators began to neutralize religious references in school systems by referring to December programs in secular terms and by encouraging representations of Hanukkah and Kwanza.[21] In the late 1990s, public opinion in America increasingly favored religious expression in the public domain in order to counter a perceived decline in religious and social values. Accordingly, the ACLU's views on strict separation of religion and state grew out of favor, and the Chabad-Lubavitch's promotion of religious display in the public domain gained wider support.[22]

By the second decade of the twenty-first century, despite vocal assertions by certain conservative religious and political groups that America should be considered a Christian nation, most American citizens had come to accept the reality that Christmas was not the only December holiday that should be accorded national recognition.[23] With this realization came an acknowledgment that certain accommodations had to be made to allow other religious symbols to join those of Christmas in the public domain, particularly when those symbols also reinforced American values.

Seventy-five years ago, songwriter Irving Berlin taught the American people, through the ever popular song "White Christmas," that the country's goal in celebrating Christmas was not to practice religion but to employ its symbols to promote American ideals of home, family, freedom, and patriotism. Certainly, both Christmas and Hanukah now accomplish this goal for many Americans.

Given their extensive history of responding to Christmas and debating the merits of erecting religious displays in America, Jews in the United States have contributed to the way in which the December holiday season is currently observed.[24] In responding to Christmas in a myriad of ways, Jews across the country have not only satisfied their respective holiday needs but have also opened the way for other minority groups to bring to national attention the importance of their own December holidays festivities. How Jews respond to Christmas is thus a uniquely American story. It illustrates how one constituent minority group has helped the country as a whole to fashion a larger vision of inclusivity for people of differing religious, cultural, racial, and ethnic persuasions throughout the year and particularly during the Christmas season.

Redefining and transforming Christmas for American society is an important achievement for a Jewish community that had in prior centuries known only fear at the onset of Christmas. While December dilemmas and Christmas wars continue to vex American citizens, Jews in America have succeeded in lessening the anxiety over the December holiday season not only for fellow Jews but also for other American citizens.[25]

Today in America Jews freely invoke any number of strategies, both private and public, to respond to Christmas. They enhance and enrich the celebration of Christmas in the United States by joining a wide spectrum of America's religious and social groups in helping to fashion a universally shared message of hope for the holiday period. The cumulative effect of Jews developing a myriad of strategies to face Christmas is that Jews no longer feel excluded by the holiday. To the contrary, most Jews enjoy the American holiday season. In the second decade of the new millennium, Jews now consider themselves active participants in shaping an inclusive, rich, and varied tapestry of holiday entertainment, customs, and traditions. Today, for many Jews in the United States, Christmas is a time to assert their pride in being both Jewish and American.

NOTES

FOREWORD

1. *Public Papers of the Presidents of the United States: John F. Kennedy . . . 1962* (Washington, D.C.: Office of the Federal Register, 1962), 888.

2. Harvey G. Cox, *The Seduction of the Spirit: The Use and Misuse of the People's Religion* (New York: Simon & Schuster, 1973), 121.

INTRODUCTION — COPING WITH CHRISTMAS

1. Jonathan D. Sarna, "Is Judaism Compatible with American Civil Religion? The Problem of Christmas and the 'National Faith,'" in *Religion and the Life of the Nation: American Recoveries*, ed. Rowland A. Sherrill (Urbana: University of Illinois Press, 1990), 163.

2. Ibid.

CHAPTER 1 — COMING TO THE NEW WORLD

1. John Rothmann, E-mail correspondence with author, 30 December 2010.

2. Frances Bransten Rothmann, *The Haas Sisters of Franklin Street: A Look Back with Love* (Berkeley: Judah L. Magnes Memorial Museum, 1979), 8.

3. Few photographs of these Christmas celebrations exist in family archives. However, the Haas family descendants assembled Christmas party photo albums from their family celebrations. Another rare example is a photograph of Virginia and Ellis Gimbel, part of the prominent Gimbel retail family, in front of a Christmas tree party in Philadelphia at a 1928 Christmas that the family hosted. From the private archives of John Langeloth Loeb and Frances Lehman Loeb, with Kenneth Libo, *All in a Lifetime: A Personal Memoir* (New York: John L. Loeb, 1996). See also Elizabeth Lilienthal Gerstley, "Christmas Parties" album (1954–1971), 2008, www.magnes.org/memorylab; Francesco Spagnolo and Lara Michels, "Jewish Digital Narratives," www.magnes.org/narratives.htm.

4. Elizabeth Lilienthal Gerstley, "Christmas Parties" album (1954–1971), 2008, www.magnes.org/memorylab, Francesco Spagnolo and Lara Michels, "Jewish Digital Narratives," www.magnes.org/narratives.htm.

5. Frances Dinkelspiel, "San Francisco's Christmas Jews," www.Jewcy.com.

6. John Rothmann, E-mail correspondence with author, 30 December 2010.

7. Eric Hobsbawm and Terrance Ranger, eds., *The Invention of Tradition* (Cambridge: Cambridge University Press, 1983).

8. Penne L. Restad, *Christmas in America* (New York and Oxford: Oxford University Press, 1995), viii.

9. Richard Michael Kelly, ed., *A Christmas Carol* (New York: Broadview Press, 2003), 9, 12.

10. Philip B. Meggs and Alston W. Purvis, *Meggs' History of Graphic Design*, 4th ed. (Hoboken: John Wiley & Sons, 2006), 155.

11. Elizabeth H. Pleck, *Celebrating the Family: Ethnicity, Consumer Culture, and Family Rituals* (Cambridge, Mass.: Harvard University Press, 2000), 46–47.

12. James H. Barnetts, *The American Christmas* (New York: Macmillan, 1954), 59.

13. Michael Steinberg, E-mail correspondence with author, 1 January 2002.

14. Michael A. Meyer, ed., *German Jewish History in Modern Times*, vol. 3: *Integration in Dispute, 1871–1918* (New York: Columbia University Press, 1998), 82. See also e-mail correspondence from Herbert Anker to author, 12 December 2010.

15. Professor Michael A. Meyer, E-mail correspondence with author, 28 January 2002.

16. "Arnstein," in *Enyclopedia Judaica* (Jerusalem: Keter Publishing, 1972), 3: 490. See Leo Baeck Institute (www.lbi.org) and The Jewish Women's Archives (www.jwa.org).

17. *The Complete Diaries of Theodor Herzl*, trans. Harry Zohn, ed. Raphael Patai (New York: Herzl Press and Thomas Yoseloff Press, 1960), 1: 285.

18. Gershon Scholem, *From Berlin to Jerusalem: Memories of My Youth*, trans. Harry Zohn (New York: Schocken Books, 1988), 28. (The original text, *Von Berlin nach Jerusalem*, was published in 1977 by Suhrkamp Verlag.)

19. The first historical mention of the Christmas tree as a fir tree decorated with roses cut from paper, apples, and wafers was in Strasburg in 1605.

20. Alexander Tille, "German Christmas and the Christmas-Tree," *Folklore* 3, 2 (July 1892): 170.

21. Scholem, *From Berlin to Jerusalem*, 28.

22. *The Jerusalem Report*, 28 January 2002, 11.

23. Rothmann, *The Haas Sisters of Franklin Street*, 70.

24. Rabbi Abraham Karp, E-mail correspondence with author, 19 June 2002.

25. *American Israelite* 35 (7 December 1888), 3, and *American Israelite* 35 (14 December 1888), 7.

26. *Occident and American Jewish Advocate* 24 (February 1867), 510.

27. *American Israelite* 37 (8 January 1891), 1.

28. *American Israelite* 30 (18 January 1884), 2.

29. *American Israelite* 35 (7 December 1888), 3; *American Israelite* 35 (3 January 1889), 5; *American Israelite* 36 (9 January 1890), 2; *American Israelite* 38 (7 January 1892), 1; *Jewish Advance* 2 (20 December 1878), 4; and *American Israelite* 38 (31 December 1891), 2.

30. Henrietta Szold [Sulamith], "Our Baltimore Letter," *Jewish Messenger* 45 (10 January 1879), 5. This reference seems to be the first recorded mention of a Christmas tree as a Hanukkah bush.

31. *Sabbath Visitor 7* (12 November 1880), 364.

32. *American Israelite* 35 (7 December 1888), 3, and *American Israelite* 35 (14 December 1888), 7; 27 (8 December 1876), 7 (New York); *American Israelite* 31 (2 January 1885), 3 (Minneapolis); "In Honor of Christmas," *American Hebrew* 5 (31 December 1881), 77 (West Chicago); and *American Israelite* 34 (6 January 1888), 9 (Pittsburgh).

33. *American Israelite* 32 (11 December 1885), 7; *American Israelite* 32 (11 December 1885), 7, *American Israelite* 32 (18 December 1885), 8; *American Israelite* 32 (25 December 1885), 1.

34. *American Israelite* 32 (3 January 1879), 5.

35. Jonathan D. Sarna, *Jacksonian Jew: The Two Worlds of Mordecai Noah* (New York: Holmes & Meier, 1981), 142.

36. Ibid.; *American Hebrew* 3 (10 December 1880), 44.

37. "On Last Christmas," *Saturday Visitor 7* (9 January 1880), 14.

38. Crape Myrtle, "A Christmas at the Cedars," *Sabbath Visitor* 18 (December 1888), 477.

39. *American Israelite* 30 (11 December 1883), 6. The topic of the lecture was reported in the 11 December 1883 issue of the *American Israelite*; however, an extended synopsis of the lecture was published in the 14 December 1883 issue of the *Jewish Tribune*, of which Sonneschein was the editor.

40. *Jewish Tribune New Series* 1 (14 December 1883), 498.

41. *American Israelite* 43 (7 January 1897), 5.

42. Restad, *Christmas in America*, 157–158.

43. "Rabbi's Diverse Views: Sermons on Christmas. Dr. Magnes Doesn't Object to Celebration; Dr. Schulman Does," *New York Tribune*, 24 December 1906, 24.

44. Louis Witt, "The Jew Celebrates Christmas," *Christian Century*, 6 December 1939, 1497.

45. Editorial, "Jews and Christmas," *Christian Century*, 20 December 1939, 1566–1567.

46. Rabbi Edward L. Israel, "A Communication: A Jewish Answer to Dr. Witt," *Christian Century*, 20 December 1939, 1580–1581.

47. Naomi Shephard, *A Price Below Rubies: Jewish Women as Rebels and Radicals* (Cambridge, Mass.: Harvard University Press, 1993), 115.

48. Jeffrey Shandler, ed., *Awakening Lives: Autobiographies of Jewish Youth in Poland before the Holocaust* (New York: YIVO Institute for Jewish Research, 2002), 264–265.

49. Mrs. Hadassah Yanich Plaut, interview with the author, Laguna Hills, Calif., 25 December 2001; they discussed Mrs. Plaut's mother, specifically Nechama Yanich's experience as a young girl in the early 1900s in Novogrudok, Minsk province, White Russia.

50. Jeffrey Shandler, "Responses to Christmas, Old World and New: The Yiddish Evidence" (paper, presented at the Association for Jewish Studies Conference, Boston, December 1990), referencing a questionnaire for the *Language and Cultural Atlas of Ashkenazic Jewry*, a dialectological and folkloristic study of European Yiddish conducted at Columbia University in the 1960s, 4.

51. Ruth Gay, *Unfinished People: Eastern European Jews Encounter America* (New York: W. W. Norton, 1996), 28–29.

52. Figee Heinmfield, Interview with the author, Rancho Bernardo, Calif., 17 December 1997.

53. Marc Shapiro, "Torah Study on Christmas Eve," *Journal of Jewish Thought and Philosophy* 8 (Overseas Publishers Association, 1999), 337, citing Hans-Martin Kirn, *Das Bild vom Juden in Deutschland des frühen* 16. Jahrhunderts (Tübingen: Mohr Seibeck, 1989), 319, citing R. Eliezer of Metz, *Sefer Yereim* (Vilna: 1881), no. 245.

54. Shandler, "Responses to Christmas," 4.

55. See Philologos, "Putting the X Back in Xmas," *Forward*, 27 December 2002, 11. The origin of the word "Nittel" remains controversial. The earliest Jewish contextual connection of *Nittel* is ascribed by Jews to the Babylonian Talmudic tractate *Avodah Zarah 8a* in which *Nittel* begins on the date that marks the winter solstice and the lengthening of the day in terms of increased daylight. "Philologos" (a weekly column written for the *Forward* newspaper by an anonymous author) notes that Christmas was not widely celebrated by Christians prior to the fourth century C.E., thus rendering unlikely any Jewish usage prior to that date.

56. Shapiro, "Torah Study on Christmas Eve," 320–321. See also Yom Tov Lewinsky, *Encyclopedia of Folklore, Customs and Traditions in Judaism*, vol. 1 (Tel Aviv: Dvir Co., 1975), 446.

57. See Yisroel Messinger, *Nittel u'Maorotav* (Union City, N.J.: Gross Brothers, 2000) for a definitive compilation of Ma'ashe Talui legends.

58. It is interesting to note that the dates mentioned in the legends do not correspond with those of the historical Jesus of Nazareth.

59. Shapiro, "Torah Study on Christmas Eve," 337, citing Hans-Martin Kirn, *Das Bild vom Juden in Deutschland des frühen* 16. Jahrhunderts (Tübingen: 1989).

60. Jeffrey Shandler, *Jews, God, and Videotape: Religion and Media in America* (New York: New York University Press, 2009), 192.

61. I. Rivkind, *Der Kampf Kegen Azart Schpielen bei* Yiden, 29ff. cited in "Jewish Attitude toward Gambling," in *American Reform Responsa, Jewish Questions, Rabbinic Answers* (New York: CCAR Press, 1990), 529, refers to the game as *Kvitlach*, meaning cards, but played to special rules. There are no face cards, and cards are numbered one through twelve. There are two wild cards, and a twelve can also count as a nine or ten. The game is still played by Hasidic Jews, and decks of *kvitlach* can be purchased in Boro Park, New York. The game was also played during Hanukkah. For those not attracted to card playing, chess was also sanctioned as an activity that would stop Hasidim from thinking about Jesus. Professor Marc Shapiro, in his seminal article "Torah Study on Christmas Eve," dates cessation of studying Torah to the 1600s.

62. Shapiro, referencing card playing as a popular diversion, cites Gotthard Deutsch: "It was also customary among the Jews to play cards on Nittel night, which was explained as being done in opposition to the solemn attention of that evening by Christians, while really it was merely a survival of the old German custom of merrymaking at this festival." Shapiro, "Torah Study on Christmas Eve," 332, citing Gotthard Deutsch, *Jewish Encyclopedia*, 9: 318. Shapiro also refers to card playing in the writings of R. Moses Sofer, who worked to abolish the practice in his community. Ibid., citing R. Moses Sofer, *Iggerot Soferim*, sec. 2, no. 3, in which Sofer admits that by prohibiting card playing, the general population, out of ennui,

would transgress in any number of ways. Shapiro also mentions that card playing on Christmas Eve was not favored by other scholars, including the Sabbatian Wolf Eybescheutz. Ibid., citing R. Jacob Emden's report in *Hit'avkut* (Altona: 1762), 72a. Interestingly, the apostate Paul Christian Kirchner, in *Judisches Ceremoniel* (Lauban: 1717), 43, claimed that Jews continued to play games of cards and dice for fourteen days after Christmas (and four days according to the 1726 Nuremberg edition, 135) and attributed the origin of this custom to the fact that Jesus also played such games. In the 1726 edition of Kirchner's book, Sebastian Jacob Jungendres commented with respect to Jews playing cards on Christmas Eve: "If they show this lack of consideration it is evident that they only wish to abuse our esteemed Savior, and the Christian authorities would have great cause to prevent these insults, especially by forbidding them from playing during this time." Ibid., citing Paul Christian Kirchner, *Judisches Ceremonial* (Nuremberg ed., 1726), 135. Ibid., 396, citing Masson, *Life and Times of Milton* (2d ed.), vol. 1, 136.

63. Abraham Chill, *The Minhagim: The Customs and Ceremonies of Judaism, Their Origins and Rationales* (New York: Sepher Hermon Press, 1979), 244; Israel Abrahams, *Jewish Life in the Middle Ages* (New York: Meridian Books and The Jewish Publication Society of America, 1958), 396. See also *Hawwot Ya'ir*, 126.

64. According to Israel Abrahams, the game of chess was firmly rooted as a Jewish pastime by the twelfth century. Voices against the playing of this game were not raised until the seventeenth century and only then on grounds of excessive playing or playing with money at risk. Abrahams, *Jewish Life in the Middle Ages*, 389–390; Herman Pollack, *Jewish Folkways in Germanic Lands (1648–1806): Studies in Aspects of Daily Life* (Cambridge, Mass.: MIT Press, 1971), 181; *The Jewish Encyclopedia*, vol. 5, s.v. "Gambling," 563.

65. Jerome R. Mintz, *Legends of the Hasidim* (Chicago: University of Chicago Press, 1968), 140.

66. www.Chabad.org.

67. Response to Author's Internet Survey Questionnaire, 20 December 2001. Beginning in December 1997, the author distributed questionnaires at various locations throughout the United States. Additionally, the author created a website that includes this questionnaire and the author's e-mail designation, ChristmasJew@ Hotmail.com.

68. Gay, *Unfinished People, Encounter America*, 246–247.

69. Andrew L. Heinze, *Adapting to Abundance: Jewish Immigrants, Mass Consumption, and the Search for American Identity* (New York: Columbia University Press, 1990), 76, citing the *New York Tribune*, 25 December 1904.

70. According to Heinze, the *Forward* stipulated that many of these gifts were expensive and bought subject to an installment plan. Ibid., 76, citing "They are Pious, But They Observe Christmas, Too," *Forward*, 25 December 1904. Heinze cites anecdotal evidence to support his theory: "Acknowledging the importance of liberal spending to the urban American, an official of a large East Side synagogue reported that many local leaders encouraged the practice of holiday gift-giving on the premise that 'it will do no one harm to open up his purse once a year and give generously where friendship dictates.'" Ibid., citing *New York Tribune*, 24 December 1904. 77. Ibid., citing Stern, Interview, *New York Tribune*, 25 December

1906 and *The Jewish Daily News* (*Yiddishes Tageblatt*), 24 December 1903, which noted the celebration of Christmas in the social settlements of the Lower East Side.

71. Jenna Weissman Joselit, *The Wonders of America: Reinventing Jewish Culture, 1880–1950* (New York: Hill and Wang, 1994), 232, 237–238.

72. Heinze, *Adapting to Abundance*, 204.

73. Dr. Nina Warnke, E-mail correspondence with author, 27 February 2002 and 11 March 2002.

74. Judith Thissen, "Film and Vaudeville on New York's Lower East Side," in *The Art of Being Jewish in Modern Times*, ed. Barbara Kirshenblatt-Gimblett and Jonathan Karp (Philadelphia: University of Pennsylvania Press, 2008), 54.

75. Heinze, *Adapting to Abundance*, 204.

76. Kenneth Libo pinpoints an earlier date for the inception of the nickelodeon. Libo cites 1903 as the turning point year when Carl Laemmle, Adolf Zukor, William Fox, and the Warner brothers happened upon this invention. See Kenneth Libo and Michael Skakun, "All That Glitters Is Not Goldwyn: Early Hollywood Moguls," from Treasures from the Archives, *Forward* 106, 31 (15 August 2003), 458.

77. William Uriccio and Roberta E. Pearson, *Reframing Culture* (Princeton: Princeton University Press, 1993), 32–34. See also Daniel Czitrom, "The Politics of Performance: Theater Licensing and the Origins of Movie Censorship in New York," in *Movie Censorship and American Culture*, ed. Francis G. Couvares (Washington, D.C.: Smithsonian Institution Press, 1996), 33, citing *New York Times*, 25 December 1908.

78. For a complete discussion regarding ascent of the Catskills resorts, see Herbert C. Tobin, "A Social History of Jewish Life in the Catskill Mountains: 1865–1975" (B.A. thesis, Brandeis University, 24 December 1974).

79. Elaine Grossinger Estes, owner of Grossinger's Resort from 1968 to 1985, E-mail correspondence with author, 28 January 2002 and 29 January 2002.

80. Jack Landman, E-mail correspondence with author, 27 January 2002.

81. Tobin, "A Social History of Jewish Life in the Catskill Mountains," 82.

82. Ben Kaplan, director of the Catskills Hotel Association until 1968, E-mail correspondence with author, 27 January 2002.

CHAPTER 2 — HANUKKAH COMES OF AGE

1. "President's Park—White House" with an article written by C. L. Arbelbide, "Introducing a Presidential Tradition," 6 January 2001, nps.gov.

2. The Daily Diary of President Jimmy Carter, Monday, 17 December 1979, from 6:53 to 7:05, 3 (Carter Presidential Archives, Atlanta, Georgia).

3. Jacob R. Marcus, *The Colonial Jew, 1492–1776*. 3 vols. (Detroit: Wayne State University Press, 1970), 2: 982–983.

4. *Jewish Messenger* 2 (18 December 1857), 100; *Jewish Messenger* 4 (26 November 1858), 113; *Jewish Messenger* 8 (7 December 1860), 172; *Jewish Messenger* 14 (4 December 1863), 21; *Jewish Messenger* 26 (31 December 1869), 4; and *American Israelite* 4, (18 December 1857), 188.

5. *Occident and American Jewish Advocate*, February 1867.

6. See "Chanukah and Christmas A Hundred Years Ago," *News from the Press Bureau*, Hebrew Union College—Jewish Institute of Religion, December 1969.

Contrast provides an even more interesting perspective. Dr. Eckman was the rabbi of Temple Emanu-El in San Francisco for a brief period during the mid-1850s. His successor was Dr. Elkan Cohn, a German intellectual who immigrated to America in 1854. According to a report in the *Occident and American Jewish Advocate*, Dr. Cohn decried the importance of Hanukkah shortly after arriving in San Francisco: "On Sabbath before Hanukkah, Dr. Cohn explained the meaning of the festival, and why our ancestors lit lamps in order to celebrate it; but that now we required only the light of religion in our hearts. In consequence of this edict *ex cathedra* no lamps were lighted as usual in the Synagogue."

7. *American Israelite* 11 November 1859 and continuing for thirty-nine issues.

8. *American Israelite* 35 (7 December 1888), 4.

9. *American Israelite* 27 (17 December 1880), 194.

10. "The Jewish Feast of Chanucka," *New York Times*, 17 December 1879.

11. Kenneth White, "American Jewish Responses to Christmas," 197.

12. Howard M. Sachar, *A History of the Jews in America* (New York: Vintage Books, 1992), 418–420.

13. Jenna Weismann Joselit, *The Wonders of America: Reinventing Jewish Culture, 1880–1950* (New York: Hill and Wang, 1994), 230.

14. Ibid., citing *Jewish Daily News*, 24 December 1902.

15. Jenna Weissman Joselit, "'Merry Chanukah': The Changing Holiday Practices of American Jews, 1880–1950," in *The Uses of Tradition: Jewish Continuity in the Modern Era*, ed. Jack Wertheimer (New York: The Jewish Theological Seminary of America, 1999), 312–313.

16. Andrew R. Heinze, *Adapting to Abundance: Jewish Immigrants, Mass Consumption, and the Search for American Identity* (New York: Columbia University Press, 1990), 170.

17. "Forward Looking Back, 100 Years Ago in the *Forward*," *Forward*, 24 December 2010, 18.

18. Joselit, *The Wonders of America*, 233.

19. Joselit, "'Merry Chanukkah,'" 318.

20. Gustav Gottheil, "What Christians Owe the Maccabees," *Jewish Messenger* (4 January 1884), 6.

21. Joselit, "'Merry Chanukah,'" 314.

22. Rabbi Emil Hirsch, "How the Jew Regarded Christmas," *Ladies' Home Journal* 24, 1 (December 1906), 10.

23. Mordecai Kaplan, *Judaism as a Civilization: Toward a Reconstruction of American-Jewish Life* (New York: Macmillan, 1934; enlarged ed., New York: Reconstructionist Press, 1957), 451.

24. Joselit, "'Merry Chanukah,'" 324.

25. Dianne Ashton, "Hanukkah Songs of the 1950s," in *Religion of the United States in Practice*, vol. 2, *Princeton Readings in Religion*, ed. Colleen McDannell (Princeton: Princeton University Press), 75–89.

26. Israel Goldfarb and Samuel E. Goldfarb, *The Jewish Songster. Part I* (Brooklyn, N.Y.: Goldfarb, 1927).

27. Israel Goldfarb and Samuel E. Goldfarb, *The Jewish Songster. Part II* (Brooklyn, N.Y.: Goldfarb, 1928).

28. Emily Solis-Cohen, ed., *Hanukkah: The Feast of Lights* (Philadelphia: Jewish Publication Society of America, 1937).

29. Ashton, "Hanukkah Songs of the 1950s," 89.

30. Harry Coopersmith, *The Songs We Sing* (New York: United Synagogue Commission on Jewish Education, 1950).

31. Ashton, "Hanukkah Songs of the 1950s," 81.

32. *Union Songster: Songs and Prayers for Jewish Youth* (New York: Central Conference of American Rabbis and Lili Cassel, 1960).

33. "I Have a Little Little Dreidel." The Yiddish lyrics are as follows:

> Ikh bin a kleyner dreydl, gemakht bin ikh fun blay
> Kumt (or to) lomir aleh shpiln, in dreydl eyns tsvey dray.
> Oy, dreydl, dreydl, dreydl, Oy, drey zikh, dreydl, drey
> To lomir aleh shpiln, in dreydl eyns un tsvey.
> Un ikh hob lib tsu tantsn, zikh dreyen in a rod
> To lomir ale tantsn, a dreydl-karahod.
> Oy, dreydl, dreydl, dreydl, oy, drey zikh, dreydl, drey
> To lomir ale shpiln, in dreydl eyns un tsvey.

34. Menorah Records, LP-206.

35. Shirley R. Cohen, narrated by Eli Gamliel (Kinor 1231) and Jesse Silverstein (KTAV R 318).

36. Jane Bearman, *Happy Chanuko* (New York: Union of American Hebrew Congregations, 1943).

37. Sara G. Levy, *Mother Goose Rhymes for Jewish Children* (New York: Bloch Publishing, 1945).

38. *Union Songster*, viii.

39. Will Herberg, *Protestant—Catholic—Jew* (Chicago: University of Chicago Press, 1983).

40. Marshall Sklare and Joseph Greenbaum, *Jewish Identity on the Suburban Frontier: A Study of Group Survival in the Open Society*, 2d ed. (Chicago: Chicago University Press, 1979), 53.

41. Jakob J. Petuchowski, "The Magnification of Chanukah," *Commentary Magazine*, January 1960, 38–43.

42. Solomon Bernardo and David Greenberg, *The Living Heritage of Hanukkah* (New York: New York Anti Defamation League of B'nai B'rith, 1964/1965), 35.

43. Clarence Mathews, "Jewish Group Fears Hanukkah Becoming a Substitute Christmas," *Louisville Times*, 24 December 1979, A1.

44. Philip Goodman, *The Hanukkah Anthology* (Philadelphia: Jewish Publication Society of America, 1976).

45. "V Mail" or "Victory Mail" correspondence was based on the British "Airgraph" system for delivering mail troops serving abroad during World War II and families in the United States. Censored mail was photographed and reduced onto reels of microfilm, which were then transported, enlarged, and printed out for the recipient.

46. Goodman, *The Hanukkah Anthology*, 365, 367.

47. Anne Roiphe, "Christmas Comes to a Jewish Home," *New York Times*, 21 December 1978.

48. Gamsin, "Letters: Readers Respond on Jews Celebrating Christmas," *New York Times*, 28 December 1978.

49. "Boycott Urged of New York Times," *Jewish Post & Opinion*, 5 January 1979.

50. Mark Blech, "Chanukah in America: History and Meaning," a *Dvar Torah* delivered at Tifereth Israel congregation, Washington, D.C., on 3 January 1998. Found in www.tifereth-israel.org/DvarTfila/berchch2.html.

51. Amy Sara Clark, "New Gifts Include Dowdy Barbie and 'December Dilemma' Chess," *Jweekly.Com*, 7 December 2001.

52. Bruce L. Berg, "The Chanukah Bush: Chanukah and Christmas Celebration among Jews," *Free Inquiry in Creative Sociology* 16, 2 (November 1988): 143–148.

53. Elizabeth A. Pleck, *Celebrating the Family: Ethnicity, Consumer Culture, and Family Rituals* (Cambridge, Mass.: Harvard University Press, 2000), 25.

54. See www. holidays.net/Chanukah/stamp.htm.

55. See "NYC Girl's Chanukah Wish Works," *Jewish Bulletin*, 19 December 1997.

56. Jeff Hoffman, "Astronaut Jeff Hoffman Spins Dreidel in SPACE," posted 3 December 2006, www.bangitout.com.

57. Julie D'Aprile, *National Post* online, 30 November 2010.

58. Robert Smith, "No Gelt, No Glory: A Dreidel Championship Is Crowned," *All Things Considered*, National Public Radio, 22 December 2008.

59. Nora Guthrie, Telephone interview with author, 17 August 2011.

60. www.maccabeats.com

61. See http://gov.idaho,gov/mediacenter/proc/proc04/procdec/Proc_Menorah Day.htm.

62. "The Christian Menorah: How Billings, Montana, Defended Hanukkah," in *A Different Light: The Hanukkah Book Celebration*, ed. Noam Zion and Barbara Specter (Englewood, N.J.: Devora Publishing, 2000), 169–171.

63. Mark Leibovitch, "A Senator's Gift to the Jews: Nonreturnable," *New York Times*, 9 December 2009.

CHAPTER 3 — WE EAT CHINESE FOOD ON CHRISTMAS

1. Jessica Carew Kraft, "Don't Ask, Just Eat," *New Voices*, November/December 2001, 11.

2. Gaye Tuchman and Harry Gene Levine, "'Safe Treyf': New York Jews and Chinese Food: The Social Construction of an Ethnic Pattern," in *The Taste of American Place*, ed. Barbara G. Shortridge and James Shortridge (Lanham, Md.: Rowman & Littlefield, 1999), 163–184, discuss the ethnographic and historical evolution of the Jewish passion for Chinese food in New York.

3. *American Hebrew* 65, 5 (2 June 1899/24 Sivan 5659): 156.

4. Irving Howe, *The World of Our Fathers: The Journey of the East European Jews to American and the Life They Found and Made* (New York: Harcourt, Brace, Jovanovich, 1976), 127.

5. Hannah Miller, "Identity Takeout: How American Jews Made Chinese Food Their Ethnic Cuisine," *Journal of Popular Culture* 39, 3 (2006): 439.

6. Joan Nathan, *Jewish Cooking in America* (New York: Alfred A. Knopf, 1994), 32.

7. Hasia Diner's historical account of this new social pattern and the ensuing "food fights" is discussed in *Hungering for America: Italian, Irish, and Jewish Foodways in the Age of Migration* (Cambridge, Mass.: Harvard University Press, 2001), 201, 204.

8. Jenna Weissman Joselit, *The Wonders of America: Reinventing Jewish Culture, 1880–1950* (New York: Hill and Wang, 1994), 214.

9. Miller, "Identity Takeout," 434.

10. Jewish humor, in fact, has the Chinese learning Yiddish, thinking that this is the language of America. "Bernstein goes to a kosher Chinese restaurant. To his surprise, he discovers that while he is ordering, the Chinese waiter is answering him in fluent Yiddish. Bernstein is very pleased and when he goes over to the owner to pay his bill, he says: 'That's really something. How did you manage it that even the Chinese waiter speaks Yiddish?' The owner replies in a whisper: 'Shh . . . not so loud. He thinks we're teaching him English.'" Avner Ziv, "Psycho-social Aspects of Jewish Humor in Israel and the Diaspora," in *Jewish Humor*, ed. Avner Ziv (New Brunswick, N.J.: Transaction Publishers, 1998), 59.

11. Philip Roth, *Portnoy's Complaint* (New York: Vintage Books, 1994), 90.

12. See Dr. Carol Nemeroff and Dr. Paul Rozin, "Sympathetic Magic in Kosher Practice and Belief at the Limits of the Laws of Kashrut," *Jewish Folklore and Ethnology Review* 9, 1 (1987): 31–32. Nemeroff and Rozin cite an observation made by Barbara Kirshenblatt-Gimblett: "There are some Jews who, in their practice of kashrut, are very sensitive to contamination (law of contagion), but don't mind appearance cues (the law of similarity), while others are sensitive to appearance while able to ignore the essential nature of substances." Nemeroff and Rozin conclude that the first type would not be bothered by eating "bacon bits," which are essentially vegetarian in nature and contain no ingredients that are nonkosher, but would not eat disguised pork in Chinese food. The second type would reject "bacon bits" because of their similarity to bacon, a nonkosher food, in name and appearance, but would eat the disguised pork in Chinese food because it had been so minced as to have disappeared.

13. Tuchman and Levine cite the late British critic Raymond Williams who pointed out that culture spawns the terms of its own rejection. Rebellion against the strictures of a food-oriented culture can be accomplished by eating forbidden foods. However, this form of rebellion is delimited by the revulsion factor: the food of rebellion cannot be so like the prohibited food in appearance that automatically triggers revulsion. Tuchman and Levine, "'Safe Treyf,'" 168.

14. Felix Mayrowitz, "Golden Jubilee: The Story of Brownsville," *The Menorah Journal* 14, 6 (June 1928): 589.

15. Joselit, *The Wonders of America*, 214, citing *Der Tog*, 20 August 1928. See also Tuchman and Levine, "New York Jews and Chinese Food."

16. Myrna Katz Frommer and Harvey Frommer, *Growing Up Jewish in America: An Oral History* (New York: Harcourt Brace & Company, 1995), 83, 88.

17. Molly Katz, *Jewish Is a Second Language: How to Worry, How to Interrupt, How to Say the Opposite of What You Mean* (New York: Workman Publishing Company, 1997), 67.

18. Nathan, *Jewish Cooking in America*, 156.

19. Kraft, "Don't Ask, Just Eat," 11.

20. Eastern European culture places emphasis on family meals, an abundance of food, dinners punctuated with intense conversation, and an appreciation for monetary value. Anecdotal evidence indicates that people savored the debate surrounding the ordering of food in a Chinese restaurant as much as the food itself. Additionally, the food was served in abundance and in a communal manner. "In Chinese restaurants, Jews ate off their own plates, they ate off the serving plates, and they ate off their friends' plates. They shared special tidbits. . . . A good meal, many said, required companions." Tuchman and Levine, "'Safe Treyf,'" 173.

21. Katz, *Jewish Is a Second Language*, 66.

22. Nathan, *Jewish Cooking in America*, 156.

23. Henry D. Spaulding, *The Best of American Jewish Humor* (New York: Bookthrift Co., 1987), 73.

24. Miller, "Identity Takeout," 449.

25. Ibid.

26. Ibid.

27. Ibid., 35.

28. Steven A. Shaw, "Temple of Taste," *Saveur*, December 2001, 16.

29. www.newyorkseriouseats.com.

30. Alan Teperow, executive director of Synagogue Council of Massachusetts, Interview with author, Newton, Mass., December 1999.

31. Shaw, "Temple of Taste," 16.

32. Chinese kosher restaurants have opened in all cities with substantial Jewish populations and are quite often the first kosher restaurants to appear in these communities. The *Jewish Telegraphic Agency Print News*, 25 August 1997, reported in "Around the Jewish World: the Far East meets the Deep South" of a thriving kosher Chinese restaurant in Atlanta, Georgia, that serves more than 700 pounds of chicken each week and more than 300 pounds of rice. Mariashi Groner, director of The Jewish Day School in Charlotte, North Carolina, hired a driver to make the four-hour trip from Atlanta through three states to pick up and deliver foil pans of moo goo gai pan, egg rolls, and fortune cookies to the school. The success of Chinese restaurants catering to Jewish clientele is subject to changing neighborhoods and economic crises, which can force some restaurants to close. Such was the fate of the only kosher Chinese restaurant in San Francisco; it closed on 1 July 1999, when its lease expired. About 60 percent of the restaurant's patrons were Jews who kept kosher. See Zevi Gutfreund, "San Francisco's Only Kosher Chinese Restaurant Closes," *Jewish Bulletin of Northern California*, 9 July 1999.

33. *Moment Magazine*, December 1990, 20.

34. The southern side of Harvard Street is lined with kosher supermarkets and bakeries, Jewish bookstores, and Judaica gift shops.

35. Details are derived from interviews conducted by the author, and questionnaires distributed on, Christmas Eve, 24 December 1997. Informants included restaurant patrons waiting in line outside of Shalom Hunan restaurant and its manager. At least nine of the thirteen questionnaires collected were from modern Orthodox Jews. Interestingly enough, the majority of modern Orthodox respondents chose to remain anonymous by not filing in their names on the questionnaire. The majority admitted feeling indifferent to Christmas Eve and Christmas Day in America. Many wrote in the questionnaire that they went to the movies and

Chinese restaurants on Christmas. They also indicated it was a day that they did nothing as most commercial establishments were closed for business. Some wrote they volunteered to help the needy on Christmas Day. Note sample questionnaire responses: A 26-year-old: "Going to Chinese restaurant with my husband and parents, as limited options, most places shut down." Ari Schochet, 25: "[We are] supposed to eat Chinese on Yontiff. Everything is closed—take advantage of vacation time. They light their candles, we light ours. Tradition." The people questioned on line at Shalom Hunan at first did not think they recognized Christmas in any formal way, but, after filling out the survey, several of them walked away humming Christmas carols or talking about Christmas lights.

36. Bruce Marcus and Lori Factor, "Erev Christmas," *Boston Globe*, 24 December 1993. The version of the poem as it appears was revised slightly by its authors in September 2011.

37. Bruce Marcus and Lori Factor-Marcus, E-mail correspondence between Marcus and Factor-Marcus and author, 2 October 2011.

38. Brandon Walker, "Chinese Food on Christmas," YouTube, December 2006.

39. Knight, "Kung Pao Kosher Comedy Offers Comedic Relief."

40. Examiner Staff Report, "Jewish Stand-Up in a Chinese Restaurant. It Must Be Christmas-Time," *San Francisco Examiner*, 24 December 1998.

41. Peter Stack, "One-Liners for Christmas," *San Francisco Chronicle*, 20 December 2001.

42. Kraft, "Don't Ask, Just Eat," *New Voices*, November/December 2001.

43. Author's Notes, Kung Pao Kosher Comedy, San Francisco, 24 December 1997.

44. *San Francisco Chronicle*, 1 December 1998.

45. Kung Pao has also acted as an inspiration to and springboard of sorts for younger aspiring comedians. In 2010, Nathan Habib was one of several stand-up comedians appearing at Kung Pao. In 2003, at the age of fourteen, Habib attended Kung Pao. He was so taken with the performances that after the show he approached Lisa and told her he wanted to perform comedy. Habib then started performing stand-up comedy routines at his Palo Alto high school. Today, in college, he continues to perform and had his official public debut as one of the three headliners at the Kung Pao show.

46. *San Francisco Chronicle*, 1 December 1998.

47. "'Kosher' Comedy with Hunan Spice," *San Francisco Chronicle Datebook*, 23 December 1995.

48. www.veoh.com Kung Pao Kosher Comedy, Scott Blakeman, 30 December 2001.

49. "Kung Pao Comedy," *Washington Jewish Week*, December 1997.

50. Marc Fisher, "God Jest Ye Merry Gentlemen; At Jewish Comedy Show, Having a Little Fun with Christmas," *Washington Post*, 26 December 1996, B01.

51. Ibid.

52. Ibid.

53. Ibid.

54. www.mooshujewshow.com.

55. www.theworldnyc.com.

56. www.carolines.com.

57. www.comicstriplive.com.

58. Interview with Sean Altman, 20 September 2011.

59. Sy Kleinman, "Jewish Humor Is No Laughing Matter," in *The 1986 Jewish Directory & Almanac.*

60. Jan Luxenberg, E-mail correspondence with author, 2 January 2002.

CHAPTER 4 — "'TWAS THE NIGHT BEFORE HANUKKAH"

1. Philip Roth, *Operation Shylock: A Confession* (New York: First Vintage, 1994), 157.

2. Jody Rosen, *White Christmas: the Story of an American Song* (New York: Scribner, 2002), 29.

3. Ibid., 23.

4. Ibid., 121.

5. Nate Bloom, "The Jews Who Wrote Christmas Songs" (2008), on www .Interfaithfamily.com.

6. Ace Collins, *Stories Behind the Best Loved Songs of Christmas* (Grand Rapids, Mich.: Zondervan, 2001), 147.

7. Ibid., 146–151.

8. See essays in Horsley and Tracy, *Christmas Unwrapped: Consumerism, Christ, and Culture* (Harrisburg, Pa.: Trinity Press, 2001).

9. See DVD, *Radio City Christmas Spectacular*, Time Life Entertainment, 4 November 2008, featuring the Rockettes.

10. Karal Ann Marling, *Merry Christmas: Celebrating America's Greatest Holiday* (Cambridge, Mass.: Harvard University Press, 2000), 197–242.

11. Ibid., 212.

12. S. J. Perelman, "Waiting for Santy: A Christmas Playlet," *The New Yorker* (26 December 1936), 17.

13. S. J. Perelman, "Waiting for Santy," in *The Most of S. J. Perelman* (New York: Simon and Schuster, 1958), 3.

14. Several websites catalog the scope and variety of these parodies. See David Emery, "Parodies of 'The Night Before Christmas and Twas the Spoof Before Christmas,'" in www.About.com and "Canonical List of 849 parodies of ''Twas the Night Before Christmas' Variations," Version 2007.1, part 9 (7 January 2007), compiled by Matthew Monroe. See www.alchemist.matt.com.

15. See Marie B. Jaffe, "Erev Krismes," in *Gut Yuntif, Gut Yohr: A Collection in Yiddish of Original Holiday Verses and Popular English Classics in Translation* (New York: Citadel, 1991), 12, 15.

16. Daniel Halevi Bloom, *Bubbie and Zadie Come to My House* (New York: Donald I. Fine, 1985).

17. Amazon.com, Shalom Yitz, posted comment, 3 December 2007; and Daniel Halevi Bloom, posted comment, 5 December 2008.

18. Amazon.com, Daniel M. Klein, posted comment, 6 December 2006.

19. "Chanukah Carols" (original recording 1962); re-recorded 2006 by Jewish Music Group.

20. Ibid.

21. Included on the website www.PlanckConstant.org, "'Twas the Night Before Hanukkah," by Bernie, 5 December 2007.

22. Canonical List of "'Twas the Night Before Christmas," part 9.

23. Jerome Coopersmith, illustrated by Syd Hoff, *A Chanukah Fable for Christmas* (New York: G. P. Putnam's Sons, 1969).

24. Lawrence Epstein, *The Haunted Smile: The Story The of Jewish Comedians in America* (New York: Public Affairs, 2001), 31.

25. Ibid.

26. Ibid., 171.

27. Ibid., 171–172.

28. Ibid., 178.

29. Ed Cray, "The Rabbi Trickster," *Journal of American Folklore* 77, 306 (October–December 1964): 331–345

30. Epstein, *The Haunted Smile*, 155–191.

31. Peter Stack, "King of One-Liners: Youngman Reigns at Kosher Comedy," *San Francisco Chronicle* (26 December 1997).

32. Ibid.

33. "Borscht Belt Comic Takes 'Kung Pao' Route to S. F. (Freddie Roman)," *Jewish Bulletin of Northern California* (11 December 1998).

34. Epstein, *The Haunted Smile*, 242.

35. Author's notes, Kung Pao Kosher Comedy, San Francisco, 24 December 1997.

36. Chris Knight, "Kung Pao Kosher Comedy Offers Comedic Relief for Just About Anyone Who's Not Into Celebrating Christmas," *San Francisco Metropolitan*, 21 December 1998.

37. Author's notes, Kung Pao Kosher Comedy, San Francisco, 24 December 1998.

38. "'Kosher' Comedy with Hunan Spice," *San Francisco Chronicle Datebook* (23 December 1995).

39. Arie Kaplan, "How Jews Revolutionized Comedy in America" (Part II: 1979–1981), *Reform Judaism* 9, 4 (Spring 2002). www.reformjudaismmag.org

40. *What the Hell Happened to Me?* (Warner Brothers, 1996).

41. "A Lonely Jew on Christmas," *South Park*, Episode 46, 1 December 1999, and included in *Mr. Hankey's Christmas Classics* (Sony Music Entertainment, 1999).

42. "Mr. Hankey, the Hanukkah Poo," *Mr. Hankey's Christmas Classics* (Sony Music Entertainment, 1999).

43. "The Night Hanukkah Harry Saved Christmas," *Saturday Night Live*, Season 15, Episode 9, 16 December 1989.

44. Hal Singer and Georgane Berry-Singer, "I Saw Hanukkah Harry Beat Up Santa," Hal L. Singer A.K.A. Sy Hymowitz, Sps Records (1 January 2002).

45. www.urbanDictionary.com. s.v. "Hanukkah Harry" 1 and "Hanukkah Harry" 2.

46. Eric Schwartz, aka Smooth E, "Hanukkah Bird," Youtube, SmoothEtv.

47. Introduction by Josh Kun, *Papa Play for Me: the Autobiography of Mickey Katz* (Middletown, Conn.: Wesleyan University Press, 1971), xiii.

48. Josh Kun, "The Yiddish Are Coming," *American Jewish History* 87, 4 (December 1999): 343–374.

49. Mark Cohen, "My Fair Sadie: Allan Sherman and a Paradox of American Jewish Culture," *American Jewish History* 93, 1 (March 2007): 51–71.

50. "Sir Greenbaum's Madrigal (Greensleeves)," on *My Son, the Folksinger* (Warner Brothers Records, 1962).

51. First recorded live on a 1963 TV special and released as a 45 rpm by Warner Brothers Records in the same year with the title "The Twelve Gifts of Christmas." Later versions identified the song as "The Twelve Days of Christmas."

52. Ken Kalfus, "Shine On, Harvey Bloom: Why Allan Sherman Made Us Laugh," *Commonweal* 22 (April 1994): 15–18.

53. Stanley Adams and Sid Wayne, *Stanley Adams and the Chicken Flickers Singing? Chanukah Carols* (Jewish Music Group, LLC. 2006).

54. What I Like About Jew, Sean Altman and Rob Tannenbaum, "Hanukah with Monica," *Unorthodox* (WILAJ Records, 11 April 2006).

55. Ibid.

56. What I Like About Jew, Sean Altman and Rob Tannenbaum, "Reuben the Hooked-Nose Reindeer," *Unorthodox* (WILAJ Records, 11 April 2006).

57. Barbara Barnett, B.C. Music Review of 'Jewmongous'—Taller than Jesus, www.Blogcritics.org, 13 April 2008.

58. Sean Altman, Interview with author, 21 September 2011.

59. Ibid.

60. *Philadelphia Daily News*, www.jewmongous.com.

61. Thomas Connor, music critic, "OY! Sean Altman's 'Jewmongous' Not Exactly Kosher," *Chicago Sun Times*, TConnor@SunTimes, 23 December 2010.

62. "Merry Christmas," *American Heritage* 5, 8 (December 2000) at American Heritage.com.

CHAPTER 5 — ɪ ʜᴇ CHRISTMAS MITZVAH

1. Leslie Berger, "On Christmas Jews Give of Themselves," *Los Angeles Times*, 26 December 1995, B, 1.

2. William B. Waits, *The Modern Christmas in America: A Cultural History of Gift Giving* (New York: New York University Press, 1993), 12.

3. www.RedCross.org.

4. *New York Times*, 17 December 1997, A27.

5. *New York Times* "Neediest Cases." Adjacent to the article entitled "Neediest Cases," which appears daily from Thanksgiving through New Year's Day, is a box titled "How to Help." Listed are contact addresses for private charitable giving agencies in metropolitan New York City.

6. "Home Holiday Pursuits—Volunteering," Sign on San Diego.com, December 2001.

7. "Starbucks Holiday Angels Toy Drive," *New York Times*, 9 December 2001, A30.

8. "Making a Difference at Christmas: Santa's Sleigh Filled with Food for the Hungry," *PRNewswire*, 21 December 1998, 1.

9. MIT Public Service Center, E-mail communication to Massachusetts Institute of Technology community, 26 November 2001.

10. Penne L. Restad, *Christmas in America* (New York and Oxford: Oxford University Press, 1995), 132.

11. Stephen Nissenbaum, *The Battle for Christmas: A Social and Cultural History of Christmas* (New York: Alfred A Knopf, 1997), 226.

12. *New York Times*, 25 December 1876.

13. Restad, *Christmas in America*, 135.

14. Nissenbaum, *The Battle for Christmas*, 215–217.

15. "Our Washington Letter," *American Israelite*, 8 January 1885, 6. This article, under the heading "Christmas Festivals," describes how Jews adopted the Christmas custom of helping needy children.

16. Nissenbaum, *The Battle for Christmas*, 215–217, citing *New York Tribune*, 28 December 1844.

17. The Salvation Army was founded by William Booth in 1865 in the slums of London for the purpose of helping "the underprivileged, hopeless and Godless masses" as described in Dickens's Christmas stories. In 1880, seven of Booth's uniformed "Hallelujah Lassies" arrived in New York City and took up proselytizing in front of Harry Hill's Variety Saloon on the corner of Crosby and Houston Streets. See Karal Ann Marling, *Merry Christmas!*, 144, citing "Soup, Soap, Salvation," *Newsweek* (21 March 1955), 64; and Edith Townsend Kaufmann, "Salvation Army Santa Claus," *Leslie's Weekly*, 5 December 1912, 590–591.

18. Nissenbaum, *The Battle for Christmas*, 151.

19. Ibid., 151, citing *New York Times*, 26 December 1899.

20. The Salvation Army's bell-ringing corps members were originally dressed in Dickensian costumes. See Marling, *Merry Christmas!*, 145, citing Minnesota Historical Society archival photographs.

21. Ibid., citing "Notable Events of the Holiday Season in New York," *Leslie's Weekly*, 9 January 1908, 41.

22. Ibid., 147–148, citing "Sullivan Dines the Bowery," *New York Times*, 26 December 1911.

23. Ibid., 148, citing "Santa Claus, Please Take a Look," *New York Times*, 15 December 1912.

24. "Our Washington Letter," *American Israelite 32 (8 January 1885)*, 6.

25. *Mishneh Torah*, 7:7.

26. *Mishneh Torah*, 8:3.

27. Israel Abrahams, *Jewish Life in the Middle Ages* (Philadelphia: Jewish Publication Society, 1993), 313.

28. Daily Jewish morning prayers said upon rising from sleep, versions of which are contained in the morning service of the Jewish prayer book.

29. Anonymous Jewish Sage as quoted in Carol Kort, "Helping the Needy Is Also Part of the Holiday," *Boston Sunday Herald*, 20 December 1992.

30. Boris D. Bogen, *Jewish Philanthropy: An Exposition of Principles and Methods of Jewish Social Services in the United States* (New York: Macmillan, 1917), 364–365.

31. Hyman B. Grinstein, *The Rise of the Jewish Community of New York, 1654–1860* (Philadelphia: The Jewish Publication Society, 1945), 155.

32. "Rebecca Gratz's 'Unsubdued Spirit,'" *Forward*, 26 October 2001, 13.

33. Barbara Kirshenblatt-Gimblett, "The Moral Sublime: Jewish Women and Philanthropy," in *Writing a Modern Jewish History: Essays in Honor of Salo W. Baron*,

ed. Barbara Kirshenblatt-Gimblett (New York: The Jewish Museum; New Haven, Conn.: Yale University Press, 2006), 36–54.

34. Bertram W. Korn, *American Jewry and the Civil War* (Philadelphia: The Jewish Publication Society, 1951), 98.

35. "Our Washington Letter," 6.

36. *American Israelite* 75 (4 January 1929), 4.

37. *American Israelite* 37 (8 January 1891), 3.

38. *American Israelite* 74 (29 December 1927), 4.

39. David Cedarbaum, "Beware of Hellenism in the Ranks," *A Set of Holiday Sermons, 5705–1944* (Cincinnati: Commission on Information about Judaism UAHC & CCAR, 1944), 37.

40. Rabbi Hank Skirball, Interview with author, New York, 23 May 2002.

41. *Boston Globe,* 25 December 1987, 36.

42. *Weekly Bulletin,* The Congregation Beth Israel, Hartford, Conn., 17 December 1964, series 40, no. 1, 18.17 December 1964.

43. Ibid.

44. Ibid., 14 January 1965, 4, series 40, no. 22.

45. *Miami Jewish Tribune,* 2 January 1987.

46. Laurena Pringle, "Of cabbages . . . and kings," *The Eccentric Newspaper,* 28 December 1972, 4-B.

47. In fact, Detroit's Temple Beth El volunteers also worked at the hospital on the last day of Passover, which encouraged the temple bulletin to call Easter Sunday volunteerism "Providential Haroset": "Instead of apples, we took 35 hardy individuals with thick skins and hearty souls, minced them delicately with sweetness and added a little spice of life and some joyful, holiday spirit. Then, on Sunday, April 14, we served this Haroset for 12 consecutive hours to Providence Hospital patients. . . . It was a soul-satisfying delight to all who partook." "Providential Haroset," *Temple Beth El Bulletin,* Detroit, Mich., 3 May 1974.

48. "Jews Volunteer for Hospital Work," *Cincinnati Enquirer,* 20 December 1974, 1.

49. Dan Phelps, "Community Council Has Christmas Spirit," *Needham Times,* 20 December 1990.

50. Carol Gerwin, "A Day of Giving for All, Jewish Families Spread Holiday Cheer," *The Patriot Ledger,* 26 December 1996.

51. Julia Lieblich, "'Jewish Elf' Let Others Be Home on Christmas," *Topeka Capital-Journal,* 24 December 1998.

52. A closer formulation of Rabbi Hillel's quote is "Where there is no one to be a mensch [a person], you should be one."

53. John Auerbach and Jon Milne, "Methuen's Unstoppable Hero," *Boston Globe,* 15 December 1995, Metro, 1. "The Mensch Who Saved Christmas: Aaron Feuerstein" (Methuen, Mass., 1995), in *A Different Light: the Hanukkah Book of Celebration,* ed. Noam Zion and Barbara Spectre (New York: Devora Publishing, 2000), 172–173.

54. Some blame Reform Jews for their overly enthusiastic willingness to play the role of Santa Claus, an accusation countered by Al Vorspan, in "Stop Bashing Reform Judaism," *Reform Judaism* (Spring 1998): 96. He referred to the example

reported in an article in *The New Yorker* depicting three Jewish men, an Orthodox Jew with *peyes* (side curls) carrying a Torah, a Conservative Jew with a short beard carrying a briefcase, and the Reform Jew dressed as Santa Claus as unfairly stereotyping Reform Jews.

55. Dorothy Brickman, Interview with author, Vineyard Haven, Mass., 21 December 2001.

56. Harvey Katz, E-mail correspondence with author, 31 January 2002.

57. *Forward*, 29 December 2000.

58. Harriet Stix, "Memoires of a Jewish Santa," *Los Angeles Times*, 24 December 1978.

59. Jay Frankston, "Dear Santa," in *Chicken Soup for the Soul Christmas Treasury: Holiday Stories to Warm the Heart*, ed. Jack Canfield and Mark Victor Hansen (Deerfield Beach, Fla.: Health Communications, Inc., 2001), 233.

60. *Boston Sunday Globe*, 22 December 1996, 2.

61. *Jewish Advocate*, 11 December 1986.

62. *The Patriot Ledger*, 28 December 1991, 19, 40.

63. *Jewish Advocate*, 1 January 1993, 1.

64. *Sun Chronicle*, 26 December 1992, 2.

65. *Congregational Newsletter*, Temple Emanuel of Newton, Mass., December 1986.

66. Elyse H. Cohen, Response to author's questionnaire, 16 December 1997.

67. Sydney Schwartz, *The Patriot Ledger*, 26 December 2008.

68. *Wayland / Weston Town Crier*, January 2, 1992.

69. Irene Cullen, "Temples Deliver Meals for Christmas," *Lexington Minuteman* (weekly), Bedford, Mass., 26 December 1996.

70. *North Shore Press*, Salem, Mass., vol. 12, no. 18.

71. *Boston Globe*, 26 December 1990.

72. Laini Blum-Cogan, "Communities Find Jewish Ways to 'Celebrate' Christmas," *Jewish Advocate*, Boston, Massachusetts, 25–31 December 1992, 4–5.

73. Ibid.

74. Jeff Karoub, Boston.com, 24 December 2009.

75. See washingtondcjcc.org/volunteer.

76. *Belmont Citizen Herald*, 23 December 1992.

77. *The Grapevine*, Kerem Shalom monthly newsletter, Concord, Mass., January 1997.

78. Letter to Project Ezra/Synagogue Council of Massachusetts from Michael J. Park, 7 January 1987.

79. Carol Gerwin, "A Day of Giving for All, Jewish Families Spread Holiday Cheer," *Patriot Ledger*, 26 December 1996.

80. Ibid.

81. Heidi B. Perlman, "Project Ezra: Sharing Hope for the Holiday," *Jewish Advocate*, Boston, Mass., 1 January 1993, 1, 19.

82. *The Patriot Ledger*, 24 December 1991, 41.

83. Harold Kushner, *To Life, A Celebration of Jewish Being and Thinking* (Boston: Little, Brown, 1993), 289–291. See also *The Universal Jewish Encyclopedia* (New York: Universal Jewish Encyclopedia Press, Inc., 1943), 225–226. Franz Rosenzweig (b. Cassel, German, 1886, d. Frankfort, Germany, 1929) was a

German-Jewish scholar who, owing to his affinity for Hegelianism and having been a product of a highly assimilated upbringing, came close to conversion to Christianity. Due to his intellectual honesty, Rosenzweig decided to ferret out the basis of Jewish belief before forsaking it. Although he decided to remain Jewish, his urbanity afforded him a high regard for both the "spiritual depth and beautify" of the tenets of Christianity. Accordingly, Rosenzweig rejected the concept of the unqualified truth of one religion over another. He proposed a "two-covenant theory" that affirmed the legitimacy of both Judaism and Christianity.

84. Bill Bilodeau, "Jewish 'Mitzvah,' a Gift on Christmas," *Foxboro Reporter*, 19 December 1996, 1.

85. See "Community Council, Temple Beth Shalom Offers Christmas Dinner Delivery," www.wickedlocal.com with news from *The Needham Times*, 6 December 2010, posted 11:00 A.M.; see also www.templeisaiah.org, "Project Ezra 2010 Volunteer for Project Ezra: A Mitzvah Program for All Ages, A Joint Program of Temple Isaiah and Temple Shir Tikvah," December posting.

86. Ronald Reagan: Radio Address to the Nation on Voluntarism, 28 December 1987, www.presidency.ucsb.edu.

CHAPTER 6 — CHRISMUKKAH AND FESTIVUS

1. *The National Jewish Population Survey* (NJPS), Mandell L. Berman Institute, North American Jewish Data Bank, 1990. Intermarriage rates climbed even higher after 1989. In the 1990 census report the intermarriage rate was reported to be 52 percent. The Jewish community was stunned, faced with the reality that half of new Jewish marriages were outside the faith. The figure was later revised downward to 43 percent, but the alarm had already been sounded.

2. See interview with Okrun on www.mixedblessing.com/testimon2.php. Just as initial reaction to the news of high intermarriage rates was condemning their existence, Jewish community leaders criticized juxtaposing Hanukkah and Christmas symbols. They reasoned that the copresence of symbols from different religions dilutes the integrity of each—even when done tongue-in-cheek. Rabbi Meir, however, says that these cards are "a travesty to both families." See Stanley N. and Mary Helene Rosenbaum, *Celebrating our Differences: Living Two Faiths in One Marriage* (Shippensburg, Pa.: Ragged Edge Press, 1994), 163.

3. Of all symbols associated with Christmas, the Christmas tree served as a flashpoint for discussions about the extent of assimilation and intermarriages. Until intermarriage became the norm, the formal Jewish community did not sanction bringing Christmas trees into the home. In some extreme cases, in-laws of the opposite faith would not accept the marriage as valid and would not sanction organizing religious weddings for their children.

4. The name of the Okrend's combined faith greeting cards—"mixed blessings"— was taken from Rachel and Paul Cowan's book with the same title that was published in 1988, a year before the Okrends went to press. See Rachel and Paul Cowan, *Mixed Blessings: Overcoming the Stumbling Blocks in an Interfaith Marriage* (New York: Penguin Books, 1988). The Cowans' pioneering treatment offered interviews with couples from a range of experiences, family, situations, and degrees of religious involvement as well as advice on how to negotiate religious differences and relationships with in-laws.

5. Anecdotal evidence reveals the following examples: in some families the boys were raised in the religion of one parent and the girls in the religion of the other; and in other families every other child was raised in the religion of one parent and the rest in the religion of the other.

6. The evolution of this change in perspective can be seen by following the progression of books guiding intermarried couples beginning with Rachel and Paul Cowan's pioneering study, *Mixed Blessings*. The Cowans treated intermarriage issues as problems to be overcome, while the Rosenbaums in *Celebrating our Differences* advise avoiding introducing practices with "heavy religious overtones" so as to built trust, increase understanding, and avoid conflict. Joan C. Hawxhurt suggested that families follow four key elements: "fun, food, festive decorations, and family togetherness." Joan C. Hawxhurst, *The Interfaith Family Guidebook: Practical Advice for Jewish and Christian Partners* (Kalamazoo, Mich.: Dovetail Publishing, 1998), 53.

7. Susan Sussman, *There's No Such Thing as a Chaukah Bush, Sandy Goldstein* (Morton Grove Ill.: Albert Whiteman & Company, 1983).

8. Susan Enid Gertz, *Hanukkah and Christmas at My House* (Middletown, Ohio: Willow & Laurel Press, 1992).

9. Ibid.

10. Margaret Moorman, *Light the Lights! A Story about Celebrating Hanukkah and Christmas* (New York: Scholastic, 1994).

11. Elise and Philip Okrend, *Blintzes for Blitzen* (Raleigh, N.C.: Mixed Blessings, 1996).

12. Matthew Black, *What's a Jew to Do on Christmas Eve* (Victoria, B.C.: Trafford Publishing, 2004).

13. Ibid.

14. The Reform movement introduced the concept of "patrilineal descent" whereby a child of a Jewish father is considered Jewish even when the mother is not. Conversion of the non-Jewish spouse was not considered mandatory.

15. The Internet site and Case's management of it proved its appeal and value to intermarrieds when it responded to the Reform movement's decision to cut back on the number of regional outreach interfaith directors. Interfaithfamily.com organized a petition that was circulated to the Reform movement, and several of these positions were reinstated. This overwhelming response demonstrated that interfaith couples and families were a force to be reckoned with and that the organized Jewish community must pay heed.

16. Joan C. Hawxhurst, "Looking Back, Moving Forward: Dovetail's First Ten Years." Dovetailinstitute.org/articles-lookingback.html, 2010.

17. See Interfaithcommunity.org, "About us" and "Chronology."

18. Interfaith weddings are recorded as far back at the late 1970s, as reported in "The Rabbi and the Priest: Interfaith Weddings No Longer Revolutionary, but Co-officiating Still Raises Eyebrows," *J-Weekly.com*, Friday, 13 August 2004. The rabbi of note was Rabbi Yeshaia Charles Familant from the San Francisco Bay area. Officially, the Reform movement discouraged rabbis from performing intermarriages, in a resolution passed by participants of a 1973 CCAR conference. The resolution was not, however, binding. Currently, there are designated rabbis

who specialize in conducting interfaith weddings because only half of Reform rabbis agree to do so.

19. See David Zurawik, *The Jews of Prime Time* (Lebanon, N.H.: University Press of New England, 2003), 93–96.

20. *Thirtysomething*, episode 109, pts. 1–5, entitled "I'll Be Home for Christmas."

21. Steven Bayme points out that television series such as *thirtysomething*, *Northern Exposure*, and *L.A. Law* reflect the viewer's desire to be exposed to open and honest dialogue between intermarried spouses. See Steven Bayme, *Jewish Arguments and Counterarguments: Essays and Addresses* (Hoboken, N.J.: KTAV Publishing House, 2002), 198. See also Zurawik, *The Jews of Prime Time*, 109–113.

22. Cited in Ron Gumpertz, *Chrismukkah* (New York: Stuart, Tabor, and Chang, 2006), 17.

23. As mentioned in Jeffrey Shandler and Aviva Weintraub, "'Santa, Shmanta': Greeting Cards for the December Dilemma," *Material Religion: The Journal Objects, Art, and Belief* 3, 3 (November 2007): 396. 24. Durnan, "Could 'Chrismukkah' Appeal to All?" *DallasNews.com* (the *Dallas Morning News*), 23 December 2005.

25. Ron Gompertz, *Chrismukkah*, 10.

26. Ibid., 67.

27. Cassandra Spratling, "Chrismukkah: How Interfaith Families Celebrate," *Detroit Free Press*, 10 December 2006, J1.

28. This card, as well as others described in chapter 6, is drawn from the extensive greeting card collection that I have amassed during the past thirty years. Most cards sited are published by American Greetings under the series "L'Chayim" and "Recyled Paper Greetings" (formerly published independently); Hallmark Cards under the series "Tree of Life"; Marcel Schurman Collection; and Mixed Blessings. Each card lists the designer and/or the text writer, and none is dated.

29. Edmund Case, "What We Learned from the Second Annual December Dilemma Survey," as reported in InterfaithFamily.com.

30. Micah Sachs, Amy O'Donnell, and Edmund Case, "What We Learned from the Fifth Annual December Holidays Survey," 4–6.

31. Ibid., 6.

32. Ibid.

33. Ibid., 8.

34. Case, "Second Annual December Dilemma Survey," 7–8.

35. Sachs, O'Donnell, and Case, "Fifth Annual December Holidays Survey," 6–10. This statistic is similar to the results in the "Second Annual December Dilemma Survey," 7–8.

36. Sachs, O'Donnell, and Case, "Fifth Annual December Holidays Survey," 11.

37. In the 2009 survey by Ed Case, "What We Learned from the Sixth Annual December Holiday Survey," the findings present a set of contradictory evidence: on the one hand, Christmas displays and activities are more prevalent this year (the survey evidenced an increase from 45 percent to 48 percent between 2008 and 2009 in Christmas participation, with greater percentages of couples giving Christmas gifts at home and serving Christmas foods), but couples tend in greater numbers to separate their celebrations of Christmas from those of Hanukkah (89 percent in

2009 compared to 83 percent in 2008). The reason for this anomalous finding requires further exploration.

38. The episode aired on December 18, 1997, as the tenth episode during *Seinfeld*'s ninth season.

39. In the *Real Festivus: The True Story According to O'Keefe*, Daniel O'Keefe tells the family origins of the holiday and how it is modeled after ancient mythical themes and rites. Dan O'Keefe, *The Real Festivus: the True Story Behind American's Favorite Made-up Holiday* (New York: Penguin Group, 2005).

40. Ibid.

41. The flexibility and personalization of the holiday is noted in Allen Salkin, *Festivus: The Holiday for the Rest of Us* (New York: Time Warner Book Group,, 2005).

42. Ibid., 18.

43. Ibid.

44. *Wikipedia*, s.v. "Festivus."

45. Dupage County Football League" Facebook entry, abbreviated "DCFL" and *Wikipedia*, s.v. "Festivus."

46. Heather Larson, "The Peak's Festivus," *suite101.com*, 12 August 2007, and www.festivusfilmfeslival.com/festivalinfo.html.

47. Ibid.

48. KOMO staff, "Coming to Capitol: 'Festivus' Display," *KOMOnews.com*, 5 December 2008.

49. Peter E. Toma, "Festivus: Seinfeld, Culture, and Society," in *The History Role*, 2 December 2010.

50. Articles.ChicagoTribune.com, 21 December 2004.

51. Adrienne Mand Lewin, "Happy Chrismahanukwanzakah to You," ABCNews.com, 10 December 2004.

CONCLUSION — MENORAHS NEXT TO MADONNAS

1. Matt Schuman, "The Saga of 'Mrs. Hanukkah Stamp' and Family," *Attitudes: A Journal of Jewish Life* (Winter/Fall 2005): 22, 60.

2. This newsworthy item was reported in *The Parent Trader*, 27 November 1996, 1.

3. The 1999 *USA Philatelic* catalogue presents a full page array of holiday stamps, including a new Madonna and Child stamp based upon Bartolomeo Vivarini's 1475 masterpiece (labeled Holiday Traditional), a new stamp featuring an antique-gold deer design (labeled Holiday Contemporary), the reissued Hanukkah stamp (labeled Holiday celebration: Hanukkah) and the reissued Kwanzaa stamp (labeled Holiday Celebration: Kwanzaa). The language describing holiday stamps is devoid of religious terminology. *USA Philatelic* catalogue 4, no. 1 (Holiday 1999): 8.

4. See, for example, John Gibson, *The War on Christmas: How the Liberal Plot to Ban the Sacred Christian Holiday Is Worse Than You Thought* (New York: Sentinel Trade, 2005), and Stephen M. Feldman, *Please Don't Wish Me a Merry Christmas: A Critical History of the Separation of Church and State* (New York: New York University Press, 1997).

5. For an example of a case resulting in anti-Semitism, see Gerald Houseman, "Anti-Semitism in City Politics: The Separation Clause and the Indianapolis

Nativity Scene Controversy, 1976–1977," *Jewish Social Studies* 42, 1 (Winter 1980): 21–36.

6. The Daily Diary of President Jimmy Carter, Monday, 17 December 1979, from 6:53 to 7:05, 3 (Carter Presidential Archives: Atlanta, Georgia).

7. City Councilwoman Joan Milke Flores accepted the fate of menorahs in Los Angeles because she believed that the City Hall menorah is not a religious symbol but a cultural artifact. In her words, "Courts have previously ruled that Christmas trees are not religious symbols and the unlit rotunda menorah is the same." Quoted in Bob Pool, "Hanukkah Dispute: Menorah in City Hall Shines Light on Controversy," *Los Angeles Times*, 13 December 1989.

8. The first Lubavitch lighting took place in San Francisco in 1975 when a twenty-two-foot-high menorah was raised in Union Square ("Victory Sign," *San Francisco Chronicle*, 27 November 1975). Actually, there is reference to pre-Lubavitch public lighting ceremonies in New York City when, for example, Hanukkah candles were lit in the office of Mayor Robert Wagner in 1964 ("Chanukkah Candles Aglow," *New York World-Telegram and Sun*, 24 November 1964).

9. www.Chabad.org.

10. See *The Hallandale Digest*, 24 December 1987, 11B.

11. The ACLU's reputation followed them for being lawsuit-happy, ready to attack any city that has religious symbols in obvious display. Expecting this fate has reached the level of caricature: one cartoon depicts a teacher declaring that a Christmas program will take place as long as the ACLU attorney is not in sight, and another cartoon shows a Christian pageant in which actors are dressed in period pieces followed in the rear by an ACLU lawyer holding a briefcase. As shown in Samuel Rabinove, "The Crèche Mess," *Reform Judaism* (Winter 1989): 12–13.

12. For a debate between these two groups, see the Op-Ed piece, "Menorahs on Public Land Stir Controversy," *Jewish Exponent*, 6 December 1991.

13. This case falls under the general category of First Amendment rights and refers to the issue of separation of religion and state. The First Amendment reads: "Congress shall make no law respecting the establishment of religion, or prohibiting the free exercise thereof." The criteria for what came to be known as the "Establishment Clause" was developed in *Lemon v. Kurtzman* (1971) and included: (1) whether government action has a religious purpose; (2) whether the primary effect of the government's action is to advance or endorse religion; and (3) whether the government's action fosters excessive government entanglement with religion.

14. The high court followed the lead of Justice Sandra Day O'Connor who interpreted the Establishment Clause in her concurring opinion to allow religious displays so long as there was no obvious government endorsement and that bystanders viewing the displays would come to that same conclusion. O'Connor's reasoning has been criticized for using a highly subjective experience, one that, in particular, led Jews to believe that they were excluded from Christmas festivities precisely because they were surrounded by so many Christmas symbols. See B. Jessie Hill, "Putting Religious Symbolism in Context: Linguistic Critique of the Endorsement Test," *Michigan Law Review* 104, 3 (December 2005): 491. Justice Brennan, speaking for the minority in *Lynch v. Donnelly* felt that claiming the crèche a secular symbol is an insult because the "essential message of the nativity is that God became incarnate in the person of Christ." Quoted in Leonard W. Levy,

The Establishment Clause, Religion, and the First Amendment, 2d ed. (Chapel Hill: University of North Carolina Press, 1994).

15. Justice Brennan, speaking for the minority in *Lynch v. Donnelly* said as much when he felt that people would be insulted when told that the crèche is a secular symbol because the crèche demonstrates that the "essential message of the nativity is that God became incarnate in the person of Christ." Quoted in Levy, *The Establishment Clause, Religion, and the First Amendment.*

16. For the rationale against placing religious displays in public, see Carol Plotkin, "Why We Fight Public Menorahs," *Jewish Journal of Greater Los Angeles,* 4–10 January 1991.

17. See Michael McGough, "Menorah Wars," *The New Republic,* 5 February 1990.

18. Exceptions to this tendency to support requests by Chabad to place menorahs in public places occur from time to time when judges in courts, particularly at the lower and appellate levels, deem the menorah to be a strictly religious symbol that cannot have any secular purpose. See "Menorah Display in Vermont Park Is Held to Violate the Constitution," *New York Times,* 13 December 1989.

19. "The Brownsville Public School Boycott: Christmas, 1906," *Heritage Magazine* (Fall 2004/Winter 2005), 29.

20. For a discussion of the passions arising in the public schools, see Bea Firestone, "Christmas and Hanukkah in the Public School—One Community's Dilemma," *Journal of Jewish Education* 37, 4 (1967): 180–187.

21. In an ironic twist of judicial fate, one pastor's lawsuit to add Christian iconography to a school program where only symbols from Hanukkah and Kwanza were on display was denied by a U.S. District Court on grounds that religious Christian symbols would be inappropriate and that the presence of symbols from two other religions does not constitute endorsement thereof. *Sechler v. State College Area School District* (2000).

22. Chief Justice Burger in *Lynch v. Donnelly* (1984) observed that the religious divisiveness that gave rise to the First Amendment's religious clauses "are of far less concern today . . . Any notion that these symbols pose a real danger of establishment of a state church is farfetched indeed." See McGough, "Menorah Wars," *The New Republic,* 5 February 1990.

23. The 17 December 2010 edition of the *New York Times* showcased a new wrinkle in the Christmas wars: a battle was shaping up between Democratic and Republicans in Washington. Responding to accusations by Republican senators that Democrats were disrespectful of Christmas, Vice President Joseph Biden accused Republican senators of using Christmas as an excuse to avoid voting in Congress. Senator Harry Reid of Nevada, the majority leader, had warned that amount of work left would require Congress's reconvening the week between Christmas and New Year's Day. Republicans reacted by accusing Senator Reid of not respecting Christmas. Reid responded by saying: "It is deeply offensive to me and millions of working Americans across this country for any senator to suggest that working through the Christmas holiday is somehow 'sacrilegious' or 'disrespectful.'" Reid then added, "If they [the Republicans] decide to work with us [the Democrats], we can all have a happy holiday." Michael D. Shear, "At This Holiday Time, the Spirit of Rancor," *New York Times,* 17 December 2010, A25.

24. The same can be said of the rising influence of the African American Kwanza celebration every December and the emerging recognition of Eid for Muslims.

25. Even though these attacks have persisted, they have also taken on a more current political spin. For example, social conservative Gary Bauer, a former Republican presidential candidate, focused upon city officials in Portland, Oregon, who had renamed the annual tree-lighting ceremony "Tree Lighting." Bauer called the city officials "Radical Islam's secular enablers" who had "been driving Christianity from the public square for decades." Gail Collins, "My Favorite War," Op-Ed, *New York Times*, 11 December 2010, A21.

INDEX

Abrahams, Israel, 33
Adams, Stanley, 95–96, 110
The Adventures of K'tonton (Weilerstein), 47
Al-Kaleem, Rahim, 130
Allegheny County v. ACLU (1989), 169–172, 197n13
Allen, Woody, 98
Altman, Sean, 85, 111–113
American Civil Liberties Union (ACLU), 5, 164, 169, 197n11
anti-Semitism, 44–45, 49–50, 55–56, 63
Ashton, Dianne, 48–49, 51
assimilation, 3, 43–45; Christmas and, 15, 42, 55–56, 138, 193n3; Jewish humor and, 97, 108, 113; resistance to, 43, 49
atheists, 3
At This Season (Pitlik), 50
Autry, Gene, 91
Azar, Rasheeda, 63

Bataitis, Gertrude, 132
Baxter, Meredith, 144–145
Bearman, Jane, 52–53
Begg, Victor, 130
Benny, Jack, 97
Berg, Bruce L., 57
Berle, Milton, 97
Berlin, Irving, 4, 88–91, 173
Berman, Shelley, 81
Bernardo, Solomon, 54
Bernheimer, S., 43
Bethesda North Hospital (Md.), 123
Billings, Mont., 63
Birney, David, 144–145

Black, Matthew, 141–142
Blagojevich, Rod, 159
Blakeman, Scott, 82
"Blame-a da Jews" (Jewmongous), 113
Bloom, Daniel Halevi, 94
B'nai B'rith, 43
Boisvert, Laurie, 133
Brandeis, Louis, 49–50
Brennan, William, 197n14, 198n15
Brenner, David, 81
Brice, Fannie, 97
Brickmann's Department Store (Vineyard Haven, Mass.), 124
Bridget Loves Bernie (television show), 144–145
Brooklyn Bridge (television show), 71
Bruce, Lenny, 97–98, 113
Bubbie and Zadie Come to My House (Bloom), 94
Buddhists, 3
Burger, Warren, 198n22
Burns, George, 97
Bush, George H. W., 167
Bush, George W., 41–42, 167
Buttons, Red, 39, 97

Caesar, Sid, 39
Cahn, Sammy, 90
"Candlelight" (YouTube music video), 62
Cantor, Eddie, 97
card playing, 33, 35, 178n61, 178n62
Carter, Jimmy, 41, 165–166
Case, Ed and Wendy, 143
Catskills hotels, 39, 97

Cedarbaum, David I., 121
Chabad-Lubavitch organization, 5, 34–35,
    167–169, 172
Chanukah. *See* Hanukkah
A Chanukah Fable for Christmas
    (Coopersmith), 96
Chanukkah Song Parade (album), 52
charitable giving, 115, 117–121
chess, 34–35, 56–57, 179n64
children's books, 47, 52–53, 140–142
Chinese food, 4, 7, 65–86, 161, 185n32,
    185n35; Jewish humor and, 69–71, 77–86;
    Jewish immigrants and, 65–69, 185n20;
    traditionally eaten on Christmas,
    71–77
"Chinese Food on Christmas" (Walker),
    76–77
Chrismahanukwanzakah, 159–160
Chrismukkah, 5, 137–138, 145–148, 152–156,
    159–160
"Christian Baby Blood" (Altman), 112
Christmas, 2–4, 3, 25–28, 40; associated
    with persecution, 35–36; author's
    experience of, 1; celebrated by Jewish
    families, 141; charitable giving and,
    117–121; Chrismukkah and, 145–148;
    contemporary meaning of, 173;
    co-opted by Jews, 4, 37; games played
    on, 33–35; German Jewish immigrants
    and, 12–13, 15–25, 28, 42–43; greeting
    cards and, 148–152; interfaith families
    and, 138–142, 152–156, 160–161, 195n37;
    Jewish comedy and, 100–101; marketing
    of, 91; musical satire and, 110–111, 114;
    music written by Jews for, 88–91;
    nickelodeons on, 37–39; in nineteenth
    century, 13–14; parody of, 87–88,
    92–97, 113; postage stamps and, 163–164,
    196n3; public celebration of, 8, 170–172,
    197n14; public schools and, 171–172;
    rejected by Eastern European
    immigrants, 29–36; secularization of, 14,
    22, 45; social balls and, 23–25;
    volunteerism and, 115–116, 122, 126–136;
    work substitution on, 121–123. *See also*
    Chrismukkah
Christmas cards. *See* greeting cards
A Christmas Carol (Dickens), 14, 117
Christmas songs, 4, 88–91
Christmas Spectacular (Radio City Music
    Hall show), 91
Christmas trees: greeting cards and, 149;
    in interfaith homes, 143, 145–146, 155;
    in Jewish homes, 2, 15–23, 35–37, 55,

140; origin of, 13–14, 176n19; public
    displays of, 169–170; at social balls,
    24–25
Christmas wars, 165, 169–173, 198n23
Christmas yid, 134
Clinton, Bill, 41, 167
Cohen, Jaffe, 101
Cohn, Eklan, 180n6
Collins, Ace, 91
Coolidge, Calvin, 41
Coopersmith, Harry, 51
Coopersmith, Jerome, 96
Cowan, Rachel and Paul, 193n4
Crosby, Bing, 88

Davis, Wesley, 124
Dayan, Moshe, 48, 96
Day of Service (Washington, D.C.),
    130–131
December dilemma, 3–4, 139–140, 173;
    Chrismukkah and, 146
"Deck the Halls with Matzoh Balls"
    (Adams and Wayne), 110
delicatessens, 65, 67, 69
Dershowitz, Alan, 2
Dickens, Charles, 13–14, 117
Dinkelspiel, Frances, 12
Doctoroff, Sheila, 130
dreidels, 56, 58–60; songs about, 51
"The Dreidel Song" (Grossman, Gelbart,
    and Goldfarb), 51–52, 182n33
Dreyfus, Alfred, 44
Drizin, Chaim, 168
Dukakis, Michael, 135
Duran, Kimberly, 146–147

Eckman, Julius, 22, 42, 180n6
Educational Alliance, 44
"The Eight Days of Chanukah" (Adams
    and Wayne), 110
"Eight Days of Hanukkah" (Hatch), 63
Eisenstein, Judith K., 51
Elf (movie), 3
Epstein, Lawrence, 97
"*Erev* Christmas" (Marcus and Factor),
    73–76
ethnic pride, 54
Evans, Ray, 90

Factor, Lori, 73–76
"The Feast of Lights" (Lazarus), 50
Festivus, 5–6, 138, 156–159, 161, 196n39
Feuerstein, Aaron, 124
Fletcher, Steve, 4

Florey v. Sioux Falls School District (1980), 172
Frankston, Jay, 125–126
Friedland, Ronnie, 143
Fuller, Margaret, 117

Gamsin, Sharon, 55
Garber, Roz, 127
Gay, Ruth, 35–36
Geduldig, Lisa, 77–81, 83, 100–101
Gelbart, Mikhl, 52
Gerstley, Elizabeth Lilienthal, 12
Gertz, Susan Enid, 141
Gewirtz, Gladys, 52
gift-giving, 36–37, 45–47, 54, 115, 179n70
Gods of Fire (musical group), 59
Goldberg, Jeff, 129
Golden Temple restaurant (Brookline, Mass.), 73
Goldfarb, Samuel, 52
Goldman, Pamela "Pamskee," 59
Gompertz, Ron, 147–148
Goodman, Philip, 54–55
Gordon, Sheila, 143
Gotheill, Gustav, 47, 48–49
Graham, Bill, 168
Graham, Ian Maxtone, 102
Graham, Lindsey, 65
Gratz, Rebecca, 120
Greenberg, David, 54
Greenblatt, Aliza, 60
greeting cards, 5, 7, 14, 56; for interfaith couples, 137, 139, 148–152
Greitzer, Mallory Blair, 58
Gronouski, John A., 163
Grossman, Samuel S., 52
Gudemann, Moritz, 17
Guthrie, Arlo, 61
Guthrie, Nora, 60–62
Guthrie, Woody, 60–62

Haas, Alice, 11–12, 21–22
Haas, Florine, 21–22
Haas-Lilienthal gathering, 10–13, 175n3
Habib, Nathan, 186n45
Hackett, Buddy, 70, 97
Handler, Howard, 160
"Haneros Halolu," 51
"Hanuka Tree" (Guthrie), 60–61
Hanukkah, 41–64; as alternative to Christmas, 3, 5, 23, 26, 53–55, 63–64; Americanization of, 62–64; author's experience of, 1; Chrismukkah and, 145–148; contemporary meaning of, 173; contemporary popularity of, 57, 60; gift giving and, 45–48; greeting cards and, 148–152; interfaith families and, 138–142, 152–156, 160–161, 195n37; Jewish immigrants and, 42–45; marketing of, 91; musical parody and, 111–112; music for, 48–53, 60–63; in nineteenth century, 180n6; novelties for, 56–60; postage stamps and, 58, 163–164, 196n3; public celebrations of, 165–170; secularization of, 45; and social balls, 23–25; as superior to Christmas, 114; U.S. presidents and, 41–42, 165–167; Zionism and, 19, 21, 47–48. *See also* Chrismukkah
Hanukkah and Christmas at My House (Gertz), 141
The Hanukkah Anthology (Goodman), 54–55
Hanukkah bird, 105–106, 108
Hanukkah bush, 20, 140, 149, 176n30
Hanukkah cards. *See* greeting cards
Hanukkah Harry, 20, 104–106
Hanukkah music, 7, 48–53, 60–62
Hanukkah pageants, 43, 51
"The Hanukkah Song" (Sandler), 98, 102–103
Hanukkah: The Feast of Lights (Solis-Cohen), 49–50
"Hanukkah with Monica" (Altman and Tannenbaum), 111–112
Happy Chanuko (Bearman), 52
Harding, F. F., 26–27
Hatch, Orrin, 63
Hawxhurst, Joan, 143
Hebrew Female Benevolent Association of Philadelphia, 120
Heimfield, Figee, 30–31
Heinze, Andrew R., 36–37, 38, 45–46
Helmsley, Leona, 58
Herberg, Will, 53
Herzl, Theodore, 17
Hindus, 3
Hirsch, Emile G., 26, 47
Hoffman, Jeffrey, 58
holiday cards. *See* greeting cards
Holiday Inn (movie), 88–89
Holzman, Myrna, 58, 163–164

"I Have a Little Dreidl." *See* "The Dreidl Song"
Interfaith Community, 144

interfaith couples, 2, 5, 137–156; children of, 139–142, 194n5; Chrismukkah and, 145–148, 152–156; greeting cards for, 148–152; institutional support for, 142–144; television shows about, 144–145, 195n21
Interfaithfamily.com, 143
intermarriage, 5, 138, 142–147, 161, 193n1, 193n2; performed by rabbis, 194n18
Irving, Washington, 13
Isaac M. Wise Temple (Cincinnati, Ohio), 123
Israel, Edward, 28
Israel, state of, 5, 48, 50
Issokson, Bernie, 124–125
It's a Wonderful Life (movie), 89
"(It's Good to Be) a Jew at Christmas" (Altman and Tannenbaum), 111
Itzig, Daniel, 17

Jaffe, Marie, 94
Jessel, George, 97
Jewish humor, 69–71, 77–86; Chinese food and, 184n10; musical satire and, 109–114; in poetry, 93–97; Santa and, 92–93; stand-up comedy and, 97–101; television and, 101–104
Jewish Songster (Goldfarb), 49
Jewmongous (comedy act), 85, 112–113
The Jew's Christmas (movie), 38
Joselit, Jenna Weissman, 37, 45–47
Judas Maccabees (Longfellow), 44

Kagan, Elena, 65
Kapenstein, Ira, 163
Kaplan, Ariel, 102
Kaplan, Cynthia, 85
Kaplan, Mordecai, 47
Katz, Harvey, 125
Katz, Jonathan, 81
Katz, Mickey, 108–109
Katz, Molly, 69
Kaye, Danny, 39, 97
Kazin, Alfred, 67
Kempthorne, Dirk, 62–63
Kennedy, Anthony, 171
"Kindle the Taper" (Lazarus), 50
King, Alan, 97, 125
King, Hy Jr., 120
Kipnis, L., 51
Kirschenblatt-Gimblett, Barbara, 120
Klezmatics (musical group), 60–62
Korn, Bertram, 3

kosher dietary restrictions, 66, 73, 184n12, 185n32
Kron, Lisa, 81
Krozennik, Bernard, 122
Kung Pao Kosher Comedy (comedy show), 7, 77–86, 99–101, 186n45; impact of, 83–86
Kushner, Harold, 134
Kutner, Rob, 84
Kwanza, 199n24

Ladman, Cathy, 81
Landman, Jack, 39
Lazarus, Emma, 49–50
Lehman Brothers, 43
Lelyveld, Arthur J., 163
Letterman, David, 151–152
Levine, Danny, 56
Levine, Ed, 72
Levine, Harry Gene, 68
Levinger, Elma Ehrlich, 50, 51
Levy, Sara G., 53
Lewis, Dan, 101
Lewis, Jerry, 39, 97
Light the Lights! A Story about Celebrating Hanukkah and Christmas (Moorman), 141
Lippman, Eve, 52
Livingston, Jay, 90
Longfellow, Henry Wadsworth, 44
Luxemburg, Rosa, 29
Lynch v. Donnelly (1984), 170–172, 197n14, 198n15, 198n22

Magnes, Judah Leon, 26
Maimonides, Moses, 119
Major League Dreidel championship, 59–60
"Ma'oz Tzur" (traditional), 48
Marcus, Bruce, 73–76
Marks, Johnny, 90–91
Marx Brothers, 97
Mason, Jackie, 97–98
May, Robert L., 90–91
Mayrovitz, Felix, 68
Mazie, Marjorie, 60
McClellan, George B. Jr., 39
Melnikoff, Alice, 130
Menorah Day, 62
menorahs, public displays of, 168–170, 197n7, 197n8, 198n18
Menorah Society, 45
Michaels, Lorne, 102
Mintz, Jerome, 35

Miracle on 34th Street (movie), 3, 89
Mission House (New York City), 117
"Mitzvah Day" Project, 130
Moore, Clement Clarke, 13, 92–94
Moorman, Margaret, 141
"Moo Shu Jew Show" (comedy show), 84
Morton, Lewis, 102
Mother Goose Rhymes for Jewish Children
   (Levy), 53
movie attendance, 4, 39, 154, 161, 185n35;
   comedy as alternative to, 84;
   volunteering as alternative to, 128
Mozart, Wolfgang Amadeus, 17
musical parodies, 7, 62, 108–111, 187n14
musical satire, 108–114
Muslims, 3
Myers, Isidore, 49

Nast, Thomas, 92
nickelodeons, 38–39, 180n76
Nittel Nahkht, 31–32, 178n55
"No Limit Texas Dreidel" (NLTD), 58–59

Obama, Barack, 41
The O.C. (television show), 146
O'Connor, Sandra Day, 197n14
O'Keefe, Daniel, 157, 196n39
Okrend, Elise and Phil, 137, 139, 141, 150,
   193n4
Operation Shylock (Roth), 88
Oppenheim, Liz, 128
Oppenheim, Moritz, 33–34
oyessen [eating out], 66
Ozick, Cynthia, 2

Parish, Mitchell, 90
patrilineal descent, 194n14
Pavony, Eric, 59–60
Pavony, Howard, 60
Perelman, Sidney Joseph "S. J.," 92–93
Petuchowski, Jakob J., 54
Pfefferkorn, Johann, 32
Pitlik, Samuel, 50
Pleck, Elizabeth, 57
Pogebrin, Letty Cottin, 67
pogroms, 30–31
The Polar Express (movie), 3
postage stamps, 58, 163–164, 196n3
Postman, Neil, 69
Prang, Louis, 14
Priest, Lilian, 132
Project Ezra, 126–129, 132, 134–135
Providence Hospital (R.I.), 122–123,
   191n47

public schools, 8, 171–172
Purim, 43, 47
Putterman, Zev, 168

Raanan, Uzzi, 115
Randall's Island (New York City), 117–118
Ratner's restaurant (New York City), 67
Ravina, Menashe, 50
Reagan, Ronald, 135, 167
Restad, Penne L., 14, 26, 28
"Reuben the Hook-Nosed Reindeer"
   (Altman and Tannenbaum), 111
Richards, Michael, 156
Rivers, Joan, 97
Roberts, Jennie Rivlin, 58–59
Rockdale Temple (Cincinnati, Ohio), 123
"Rock of Ages" (Gottheil), 48–49
Roiphe, Anne, 2, 55–56
Rollins, Walter, 4
Roman, Freddie, 7, 81, 99–100
Rooks, Dan, 129
Rosen, Albert, 123–124
Rosen, Jody, 88
Rosenstock, Raymond, 129
Rosenwald, J., 43
Rosenzweig, Franz, 134
Roth, Philip, 68, 88
Rothman, Frances Bransten, 21
Rothmann family, 10–13
Rozenzweig, Franz, 192n83
"Rudolph the Red-Nosed Reindeer"
   (Marks), 90; parody of, 111

Sabra Grill restaurant (San Francisco), 80
Saint Elizabeth Hospital (Brighton,
   Mass.), 121–122
Salkin, Allen, 158
Salvation Army, 118, 190n17
Sandler, Adam, 98, 102–103
Sands, Gerald and Lucille, 121
San Francisco, 80. *See also* Kung Pao
   Kosher Comedy
Santa Claus, 92–94, 104–108; greeting
   cards and, 150; Jewish variations on,
   94–96, 104–106; origin of, 13–14; played
   by Jews, 123–126, 191n54
SantaCon, 107–108
Sarna, Jonathan D., 3–4, 6
Saturday Night Live (television show),
   101–104
Schiff, J. H., 43
Schneersohn, Menachem Mendel, 34–35,
   168
Schneersohn, Yosef Yitzchak, 34–35

Schnitzer, Isaac and Tami, 63
Scholem, Gershon, 17, 19
Schreiber, Mordecai, 54
Schulman, Samuel, 26
Schumer, Charles, 65
Schwartz, Eric, 105–106
Seinfeld, Jerry, 100
Seinfeld (television show), 6, 71, 138, 156–157, 161. *See also* Festivus
Seligman, Jesse, 43
Seligman, Joseph, 44
separation of religion and state, 5, 163–164, 168–172
Shabbes goy, 134
Shalom Hunan restaurant (Brookline, Mass.), 73
Shandler, Jeffrey, 31–32
Shemtov, Abraham, 165–166
Sherman, Allan, 108–110, 113
Silvers, Phil, 97
Simon, Paul, 4
Singer, Hal L., 105
Sklare, Marshall, 53
social balls, 23–25
Social Gospel, 116–117
Solis-Cohen, Emily, 49–50
Sonneschein, Solomon, 25
South Park (television show), 101, 103–104
Sovak, Tobi, 77
Speigelman, Art, 149–150
stand-up comedy, 77–86, 97–101
Stanley Adams and the Chicken Chokers, 110
State of Israel, 5
Stern, Abraham, 37
Stewart, Jon, 100
Stiller, Jerry, 156
Stone, Madeline, 63
Streisand, Barbra, 63, 91
Styne, Jule, 90
Sullivan, Timothy D., 118
Supreme Court, 169–172, 197n13, 197n14
Sussman, Susan, 140–142
Synagogue Council of Massachusetts, 126–127, 135. *See also* Project Ezra
Szold, Henrietta, 23

Tannenbaum, Rob, 111–112
television shows, 101–104, 144–146. *See also individual shows*
Temple Beth El (Belmont, Mass.), 130
Temple Beth El (Detroit, Mich.), 122, 191n47
Temple Beth El (Hartford, Conn.), 122

Temple Emanuel (Newton, Mass.), 128
Temple Isiah (Lexington, Mass.), 129
Temple Shalom (Cincinnati, Ohio), 123
Temple Shalom (Milton, Mass.), 128, 133
Teperow, Alan, 126–127
Thanksgiving, 22
There's No Such Thing as a Christmas Bush, Sandy Goldstein (Sussman), 140–141
thirtysomething (television show), 145
Thissen, Judith, 38
Three Stooges, 97
Tille, Alexander, 19
Tin Pan Alley, 88–89
Torah, 33, 35
Torme, Mel, 90
toy drives, 116, 123
Tuchman, Gaye, 68
"'Twas the Night Before Chanukah" (Adams and Wayne), 95–96
"'Twas the Night Before Christmas" (Moore), 13; parodies of, 92–97
"'Twas the Night Before Hanukkah" (Spiegelman), 149–150
tzedakah [charitable acts], 119, 133

Union Songster: Songs and Prayers for Jewish Youth (songbook), 51–53

volunteerism, 5, 115–116, 126–136, 191n47; function of, 133–135; interfaith, 130, 132–133; Project Ezra and, 126–129, 134–135; Santa Claus and, 123–126. *See also* charitable giving; work substitution
von Arnstein, Fanny, 17–19

"Waiting for Santy" (Perelman), 93
Walker, Brandon, 76
Wayne, Sid, 95–96, 110
Weisbeger, Ralph Moses, 55
What I Like About Jew (comedy duo), 111–112
What's a Jew to Do on Christmas Eve (Black), 141–142
White Christmas (movie), 3, 89
"White Christmas" (Berlin), 4, 88–90, 173
"Who Can Retell?" (Ravina), 50
Wise, Isaac Mayer, 32
Witkin, N., 55
Witt, Louis, 27
Woody Guthrie's Happy Joyous Hanuka (album), 60–62
work substitution, 121–123, 134

World War II, 55, 89, 182n45
Wyle, George, 90
Wynn, Ed, 97

Yiddish theater, 38
Youngman, Henny, 7, 39, 78, 81, 97,
   99–100

Young Men's Hebrew Association
   (YMHA), 43
YouTube, 62, 76, 105, 113–114

Zionism, 17, 47–48, 49–50; and Hanukkah,
   19, 21
Zukor, Adolph, 38

ABOUT THE AUTHOR

For more than twenty years Rabbi Joshua Eli Plaut, PhD, has documented the social history of Jews and Christmas in America through the combined lenses of a historian and folklorist, photo-ethnographer and rabbi. He is the author of *Greek Jewry in the Twentieth Century* (1996). A native New Yorker who grew up in Jerusalem and an avid world traveler, he resides with his wife and son in New York City and Martha's Vineyard. He is the executive director of a nonprofit organization in New York City.